Library of
Davidson College
VOID

# THE JUMPS
Contemporary Theory, Technique and Training

Edited by Fred Wilt

TAFNEWS PRESS
Book Division of
Track & Field News

First published in 1972 by Tafnews Press,
Book Division of Track & Field News,
Box 296, Los Altos, California 94022 U.S.A.

Copyright © 1972 by Tafnews Press
All rights reserved.

Library of Congress Catalog Card Number: 73-189447
Standard Book Number: 0-911520-35-X

Printed in the United States of America

# INTRODUCTION

The idea behind this collection is to offer in a single volume a cross-section of modern theory and progress in the technique and training of the four "jumping" events in track and field athletics. While there is a lot of published material extant on the four events (pole vault, high jump, long jump, triple jump), these writings are widely scattered throughout the track and field literature and many are not accessible to the average coach or athlete. Thus this book brings together some of the most important of the already published works, and in addition provides a number of articles translated into English for the first time, as well as contributions never before published in any language.

Within each event, an attempt was made to offer various types of articles, from general and even historical reviews of technique and training matters to contributions on a single specific, important aspect of a jumping event. Further, different shades of opinion and changes in theory are presented, illustrating the ongoing process of technical development. The book is not a comprehensive, exhaustive text, but it does furnish a good view of contemporary thinking in the events covered.

We, the publishers, wish to thank all contributors, translators, and those track and field journals which kindly permitted us to reprint pieces from their pages. And we'd particularly like to express our appreciation to the man whose efforts made this book possible. Not only is Fred Wilt a track author, coach and former athlete of the first rank, but in his capacity as editor of one of the sport's foremost technical publications, *Track Technique*, he keeps abreast of the current literature and has wide contacts throughout the world. No one else in the USA would have been more qualified to select and assemble these articles.

It is our sincere hope that this collection will abet the continuing technical advancement of our sport and hope that there will be sufficient favorable response to provide an impetus for further volumes of this nature.

The Publishers
Tafnews Press
(Book Division of
Track & Field News)

# ACKNOWLEDGMENTS

The editor and publisher wish to thank the following publications for their cooperation and permission to reprint articles which originally appeared in their pages:

*Athletics Arena*, Charles Elliott, editor, 325 Streatham High Road, London S.W. 16 3NS, England
*Athletics Weekly*, Melvyn Watman, editor, 344 High Street, Rochester, Kent, England
*Coaching Review*, Legion House, Ottawa, Canada
*Der Leichtathlet*, 1005 Berlin, Den Dimitroffstrasse 157, East Germany
*Der Leichtathletik-Trainer*, published as part of Der Leichtathlet, address above
*Der Lehre der Leichtathletik*, Toni Nett, editor, published as part of Leichathletik, see address below.
*Lehka Athletika*, Praha-8-Karlin, Sokolovska, 140 CSSR, Czechoslovakia
*Lehkaja Atletika*, Rojdeatvenskie Bulvar D, 10/7, Moskow K-45, USSR
*Leichtathletik*, c/o Bartels & Wernitz KG, 1 Berlin 65, Reinickendorferstrasse 113, West Germany
*Lekka Atletyka*, Warszawa, UL., Sienkiewicza, 12/14, Poland
*Modern Athlete and Coach*, Jess Jarver, editor, 70 South Terrace, Adelaide, South Australia, Australia
*Track & Field News*, Dick Drake, Managing editor, Box 296, Los Altos, California 94022 USA
*Track Technique*, Fred Wilt, editor, Box 296, Los Altos, California 94022 USA
*Yessis Review of Soviet Physical Education and Sport*, c/o Dr. Michael Yessis, Dept. of Physical Education, California State College, Fullerton, California USA

Also, thanks to:
*Amicale des Entraineurs Francaise d'Athletisme*, France
*Atletika*, Czechoslovakia

# CONTENTS

| | |
|---|---|
| Introduction | 3 |
| Acknowledgments | 4 |

### HIGH JUMP

| | |
|---|---|
| 1. Teaching the High Jump, by Kenneth O. Bosen | 9 |
| 2. High Jump Technique, by Klement Kerssenbrock | 13 |
| 3. The High Jump Take-Off, by Fletcher McEwen | 16 |
| 4. An Interpretation of Fosbury Technique, by Claude Labescat | 19 |
| 5. Teaching the Fosbury Flop, by Hans Steiner | 24 |
| 6. Latest Developments in the Flop | 28 |
| 7. Should High Jumpers Use the Straddle or the Fosbury Flop? by Carlo Vittori | 33 |
| 8. Improving Spring in the High Jump, by Adam Bezeg | 37 |
| 9. Perspectives in the Improvement of Speed-Strength Preparation of Jumpers, by Yuri Verhoshanski | 39 |
| 10. The Matzdorf Windmill, by K. Kerssenbrock | 43 |

### POLE VAULT

| | |
|---|---|
| 1. Developments in Pole Vaulting, by Richard V. Ganslen | 53 |
| 2. Comparison of Rigid and Flexible Pole Vaulting Technique | 55 |
| 3. Teaching Beginners to Vault in Ten Easy Steps, by Tom Olsen | 68 |
| 4. Some Basic Principles of Fiber Glass Pole Vaulting, by Denis Watts | 70 |
| 5. Pole Vault Technique, by Gerhard Jeitner | 72 |
| 6. The Keys to Successful Vaulting, by Walter R. Welsch | 79 |
| 7. Five Serious Misconceptions about the Attributes of Fiberglass Poles, by George Moore | 81 |
| 8. A Summary of Physical and Technical Characteristics of Outstanding Vaulters, by Pete Boudreaux | 83 |

### LONG JUMP

| | |
|---|---|
| 1. Teaching the Long Jump, by Kenneth O. Bosen | 89 |
| 2. The Long Jump Take-Off, by Jess Jarver | 93 |
| 3. The Long Jump | 96 |
| 4. The Most Important Phase in the Long Jump, by Jess Jarver | 107 |
| 5. The Dropping of the Legs in Long Jumping, by Bernard J. Hopper | 111 |
| 6. Importance of Swinging Movements at the Take-Off, by Yuri Verhoshanski | 115 |
| 7. The Long Jump and Triple Jump Approach, by Yuri Verhoshanski | 120 |
| 8. The Length of Long Jump Run-Up, by J. Vacula | 123 |
| 9. Optimum Speed in the Long Jump, by D.C. Chambers | 124 |
| 10. Landing in Beamon's Record Jump, by Toni Nett | 127 |

### TRIPLE JUMP

| | |
|---|---|
| 1. Coaching the High School Triple Jumper, by Robert Chappell | 131 |

2. Triple Jump Technique and Method of Teaching, by Gabor Simonyi — 134
3. Triple Jump Training, by Tadeusz Starzynski — 140
4. Training of Soviet Triple Jumpers, by Z. Chrominski — 145
5. Training a Modern Top-Class Triple Jumper, by C.M. Muthiah — 149
6. Practical Ratios for Triple Jumpers, by Toni Nett — 153
7. Distribution of Triple Jump Phases, by Vitold Kreer — 154
8. Shallow or Steep? by L. Prihoda — 156
9. Deviations in the Triple Jump, by Tadeusz Starzynski — 159

# High Jump

HIGH JUMP                          Credits

*Teaching the High Jump,* by Kenneth O. Bosen. Originally published in *Modern Athlete and Coach,* Vol. 6, No. 5A, October, 1968.

*High Jump Technique,* by Klement Kerssenbrock. Originally published in *Die Lehre der Leichtathletik,* Germany, No. 1, 1970. This English translation is by Glenn B. Hoidale.

*The High Jump Take-Off,* by Fletcher McEwen. Reprinted from *Modern Athlete and Coach,* Vol. 8, No. 6, November, 1970.

*An Interpretation of Fosbury Technique,* by Claude Labescat. Originally published in *Amicale des Entraineurs Francaise d'Athletisme.* This translation (and condensation) appeared in *Modern Athlete and Coach.*

*Teaching the Fosbury Flop,* by Hans Steiner. Originally published in *Die Lehre der Leichtathletik,* Germany, No. 29, July 28, 1970. Translated by Gabor Simonyi, North Battleford, Sask., Canada.

*Latest Developments in the Flop.* Reprinted from *Modern Athlete and Coach,* Vol. 9, No. 2, March, 1971.

*Should High Jumpers Use the Straddle or the Fosbury Flop?* by Carlo Vittori. First publication.

*Improving Spring in the High Jump,* by Adam Bezeg. Originally published in *Amicales des Entraineurs Francais d'Athletisme,* July, 1965. This translation by J.F. David appeared in *Modern Athlete and Coach,* Vol. 4, No. 1, and was reprinted in *Track Technique* No. 28, June, 1967.

*Perspectives in the Improvement of Speed-Strength Preparation of Jumpers,* by Yuri Verhoshanski. This translation appeared in *Yessis Review of Soviet Physical Education and Sport,* Vol. 4, No. 2, June, 1969.

*The Matzdorf Windmill,* by K. Kerssenbrock and Dr. K. Spilar. Reprinted from *Track Technique* No. 48, June, 1972.

# TEACHING THE HIGH JUMP

By Kenneth O. Bosen, Olympic Coach of India, 1964

We shall direct our efforts on two methods, the western roll and straddle. It is not always necessary to put every beginner through both forms, starting first with the western roll and then moving to the straddle. Coaches claim that the western roll makes for sounder take-off fundamentals than the straddle method. I personally feel it depends on the quality of the material one has to deal with and their general adaptability to a given form of bar clearance. This is easily determined by placing the cross bar at a reasonable height to have a preliminary jumping competition, which usually provides a lot of fun, and is always a good note to begin with. During the contest the coach keeps his eye on general ability, and also watches for the take-off leg. The latter is necessary when teaching begins. Always use an approach that keeps the squad busy doing the activity they came to learn instead of long lectures. Talks may be given at a later stage with the use of loop films to get your point across.

Stage 1—THE TAKE-OFF:— In jumping for height, the change of horizontal speed gained from the run-up to a vertical direction is possible through an efficient use of the take-off foot and leg. This is the most important single aspect of the high jump. Too many beginners lean into the take-off, anticipating the bar clearance. I believe this is due to the fact that far too much time is spent on jumping at very low heights which does not really force the boy to jump up first and then lay out. The form work should be done at a height that is not too difficult to clear, yet forces one to a real take-off.

(a) For the start in learning the take-off merely have the squad do stationary pop-ups to head a suspended ball while you stress the heel-ball roll foot action. Drive up to lift with the whole body, using the overhead object as an incentive.

(b) Place the cross bar about shoulder height and have the squad approach it from an angle of about 37-38 degrees. Those who take-off from the left leg come in from the left (facing the cross bar), those having a right leg take-off approach from the right. Make the squad perform the same pop-up exercise as previously, only this time they approach at an angle, first walking, then at a slow run. The task is to jump up and try to get the head, shoulders and free leg knee above the cross bar with the minimum amount of forward movement along the bar.

(c) Raise the bar slightly higher, forcing the person to look up and hence lean back at the

Stationary pop-ups for take-off drive

Walk-jog bent-knee take-offs.

Straight or semi-straight leg kicks. Back lean.

take-off. This time change the method of lead leg kick-up to a straight or semi-straight-legged movement, whichever comes more naturally to the jumper. Though the straight leg kick is more forceful, it is the semi-straight leg kick that is widely in use by most jumpers.

**Stage 2—THE BAR CLEARANCE:—** The choice of a particular method of bar clearance should take into consideration two aspects. Firstly, the over-all economy of the effort in work done in lifting the body's center of gravity over the bar; secondly, the suitability of the particular style to the individual needs. By this I mean, there is a vast variety in the execution of a particular method of bar clearance. Do not be rigid and enforce only the one you think is best. Instead try to adapt the good points of the technique to the natural talent and ability of your jumper. In other words, cut out cloth to suit the person who is going to wear it, but don't try to fit the person into what you think is a good fit.

**The Western Roll—** It is more economical than scissors and eastern cut-off due to the fact that the jumper is required to roll over the bar on his side rather than go over it in a sitting position.

(a) Place cross-bar at a low height over which one can hop easily. Approaching from the front at right angles, the athlete merely hops over the bar holding his free leg high and landing on the take-off leg. There is no turn or lay-out involved, just a simple hop with a high free leg knee.

(b) This time in mid-flight the jumper is required to turn and face to his left, if his take-off foot is left, and to the right, if his take-off foot is right. Land in the pit holding the free leg high. It is important to stress the need to turn after the take-off and not to start the turn at the take-off itself.

Hop over low bar with free leg knee high.

Hop and turn facing left.

Straight approach, layout, three point landing.

(c) Now place a handkerchief in the pit and have your jumper take off, turn in mid-flight, and extend his two hands with head and shoulders down towards the pit to pick up the handkerchief. He must make a three point landing, coming down on his two hands and take-off leg, with the free leg moved up and back.

(d) Finally, have the squad approaching from the angle they used for the high kick exercise (37-38 degrees). At this stage start stressing the proper use of the free leg kick. For this it is necessary to lift the bar slightly higher to force the use of the free leg and lean back at the take-off. Also stress the quick pick-up and tuck-in of the take-off leg. As in any style of high jumping it is the take-off leg that becomes a problem in bar clearance.

**The Straddle—** There are two variations of the straddle technique—the dive and the orthodox straddle. A third, a combination of the good points of both is used widely under different names. We shall merely concentrate on learning the straddle, whatever that may suggest.

Straddle roll on barrier with help of both hands.

Run-up and one-land roll with push-up and landing.

(a) Place a steeplechase hurdle on the edge of the pit and do repeated straddle rolls over it by placing both hands on the crosspiece for assistance. It is like vaulting over a fence and gives the beginner the feeling of rolling, taking off on one foot, and landing on the other in the pit.

(b) Try the same by placing only the left hand on the top of the bar. Kick up hard with the free leg and after the take-off is completed, push with the other hand to complete the roll, landing in the pit on the back in a semi-sitting position. When the left hand is removed from the bar, bring it up vigorously and away in a circular motion, co-ordinated with the outward rotary movement of the take-off leg. The take-off leg's knee and foot lift and spin out and up in a twisting-like motion, helped by the outward rotation of the left arm together with the lift and turn of the hips.

(c) Take the squad to a grassy strip where you mark a few circles about four feet in diameter. Ask them to imitate the free leg kick, arm lift, take-off and roll, landing within the circle on the opposite leg and two hands. Make sure the head and shoulders are not lifted up in doing this exercise.

(d) 1. Partner holds the lead leg while the jumper is face down, resting both hands and the take-off foot. The partner lifts the take-off leg up and at the same time twists the knee up and out in a twisting upward kick. This is an exercise to work on the back leg clearance over the cross bar.

2. Partner holds take-off leg while the jumper leans and kicks up hard with the free leg. He dives around and down with both arms, head and shoulders, while the free leg is swinging around and down for the landing made on both hands and the lead leg.

Partner exercise for leg rotation.   Partner exercise for rotation with take-off.

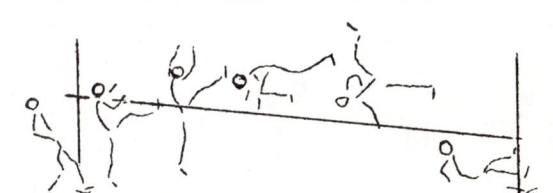

Head side bar lower to force correct take-off action.   Leg side of bar lower for easier rotation.

(e) 1. Put the cross bar at shoulder height at the head side of the approach and have it about a foot lower towards the leg side. Make the squad go through the straddle bar clearance. This method of bar placement makes it easy for the beginner to roll over on his stomach but, because the head side is at shoulder height, it forces him to lift first without being able to anticipate the lay out at the take-off.

2. Gradually raise the leg side of the bar so that it is brought level with the head end of the bar. By keeping the head end of the bar constantly at shoulder level or more, you are forcing the correct take-off fundamentals.

3. As learning progresses, it is possible to introduce a dive by merely keeping the head end of the cross bar constant and raising the leg end about 8 or 10 inches. The high leg end of the bar is a good method to overcome faults of the trailing leg. It may be used successfully also in the training of advanced jumpers, as by keeping the head end of the bar constant you are also avoiding any possibility of a premature lay-out.

**Stage 3—The RUN UP to the WHOLE JUMP:—** The number of strides in the run-up is usually seven, but more or less can be used with good success. As in every other event, the element of rhythm must be developed. The high jumper's rhythm is a comparatively simple 1,2,3,4—1,2,3 type approach pattern. The first four are used as a gradual build up of speed for a faster and longer stride pattern of the last three strides. On the second last stride before the take-off there is a positive settle over the right leg to enable a long drive out with the left leg at the take-off. This long last stride is important for the proper lift through the forward extended take-off leg. It also provides a long range for the free leg kick, made in coordination with the lift. Actually the jumper's spring comes from the forces of the two legs working in opposition to each other. The take-off leg drives down hard while the free leg swings up vigorously with the aid of the two arms.

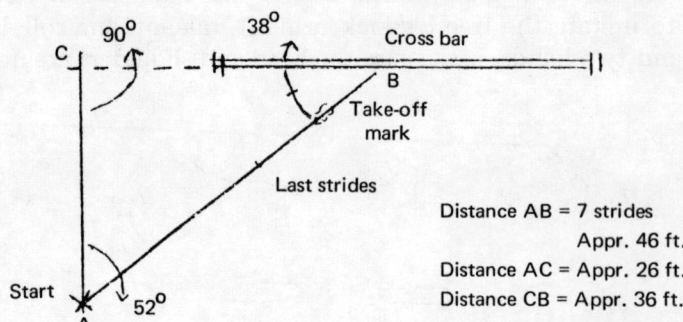

Distance AB = 7 strides
Appr. 46 ft.
Distance AC = Appr. 26 ft.
Distance CB = Appr. 36 ft.

For the beginner, use an angle of approach of about 37 or 38 degrees. The distance of the take-off is usually about 30 inches from the cross-bar. Both depend obviously on many factors. With experience, the approach angle may gradually be reduced to approximately 20 degrees.

A modified dive straddle

# HIGH JUMP TECHNIQUE

By Klement Kerssenbrock, Czechoslovakia

In the concept of the technique of a track and field discipline the development of the primary motion is commonly understood, i.e., the flight over the hurdles in hurdling, the stage of the throwing posture at the release in javelin throwing, the sequence from the take-off to the crossing of the bar in high jumping, etc. Preliminary phases are frequently not taken into consideration, although they are often quite important.

In the high jump the development of the approach steps has quite a special bearing on the total result of the jump. By working on this facet, an area is opened to many jumpers who "can't" improve.

More than 20 years ago Franz Schuppe, in his Physics of Physical Training, presented the mechanics of the take-off. He compared the path of the center of gravity of the body to a shot which moves along an arched path and translates horizontal speed into an inclined slope. For the human body, the shape of the path is established from the individual body movements.

From Schuppe's presentation we know the great importance of the approach speed, which affects the speed of flight of the jumper to a considerable degree by the addition of a distance component.

Now it is of value to use the approach to the best possible advantage by minimizing the waste developed in the transition to the inclined slope. The approach has two functions to fulfill:

1) to impart the greatest possible horizontal speed to the body's center of gravity,

2) to provide the best possible configuration of the path of the body's center of gravity from the horizontal to the inclined slope.

Point one is accomplished by a rapid approach and point two by a lowering of the jumper's pelvis so that there is a minimum change of direction of the body's center of gravity in the transition to an upward slope because the larger the angle to be surmounted (for constant or even shortened radius), the greater the loss of speed.

It is extremely difficult to accomplish both tasks in 7 to 9 approach steps since speed complicates the dipping; the dipping retards the speed. Only two possibilities remain for the jumper: (1) the initial dip occurs during the last approach step in which case he has attained a great horizontal speed but, by dipping late, there must be a large direction change and therefore a great loss of speed (Fig. A) or (2) if the dip is occurring in the last 3 to 4 approach steps, then the jumper simply attains a small horizontal speed but by dipping early he necessarily incurs a smaller direction change and therefore suffers a small loss of speed (Fig. B).

Valeriy Brumel's initial dip occurs in the last two steps. Thus he can take advantage of the approach to obtain sufficient horizontal speed and in dipping he has enough room to incur a very slight change of direction and thus a very small loss of speed. As especially favorable for the change of direction (for conservation of speed), it turns out that Brumel is already introducing a slight increase in elevation to the trajectory of the body's center of gravity during the last step (Fig. C).

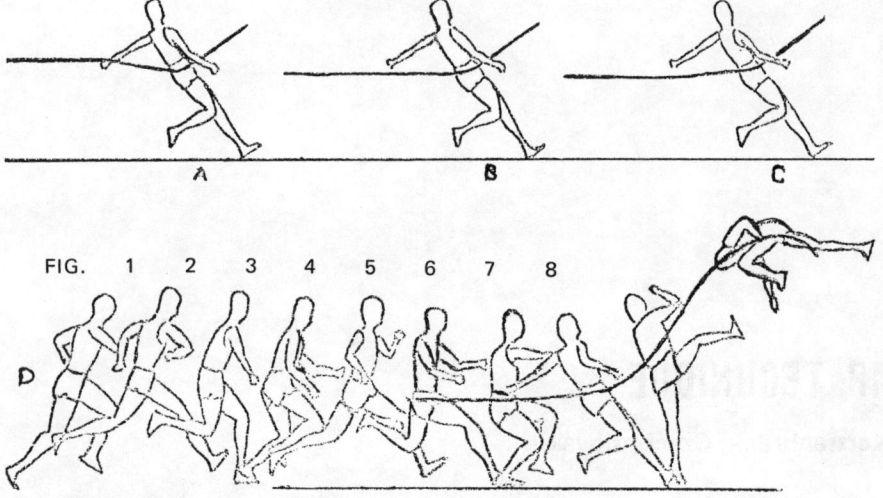

We shall investigate the aforementioned assertions by means of a photographic sequence of Valeriy Brumel's world record leap of 228 cm (Lehka Atletika 4/64, USSR). The photograph is especially advantageous since the approach is at right angles to the lens and parallel to the bounded trajectory. Small distortions of the pictures by parallex can be neglected, as long as exact numerical results are not required. To clarify the motion, a motion study was prepared (Fig. D) from the cinegram by tracing the pictures in their actual spatial sequence.

It must be noted that for a world record leap (almost at the limit of human performance) everything must be blended to the highest degree of perfection. By following the photographic sequence, it is seen that Brumel's last approach steps are carried out in a special manner; this is precisely what I want to make the reader cognizant of.

Even in the third from the last step Brumel approaches the bar in normal running position (Fig. 1). However, in the flight phase of this step we already notice an unusual extension of the lower leg (Fig. 2). The landing clearly occurs before the body's center of gravity (Fig. 3). In the extension to the penultimate step the leg is not straightened out much. The take-off leg swings far forward. A lengthened step occurs with the landing far in front of the body's center of gravity (Figs. 4, 5, 6). The airborne phase is shortened to a minimum. A comparison with the background (parallel oriented bar) shows that at this point Brumel dips and that the center of gravity of his body is now moving parallel to the ground. To continue to remain low, the subsequent roll must be accomplished from an extremely bent support leg (Fig. 7). It is to be noted that up to now the upper body has remained erect. The last step, which is significantly shorter than the preceding, occurs without a significant impression—hardly has the foot of the standing leg left the ground, than the heel of the take-off leg, which is extended far forward, is already touching the ground (Fig. 8). Thus, during this step an easy ascent of the jumper becomes apparent. Simultaneously Brumel draws his uppper body and both arms back.

The technique of the last steps merits special attention. By rapid straightening of the knee joint of the extended leg, the braking moment of the straddle position is diminished markedly and the subsequent sharp knee bend makes it possible to avoid raising the body's center of gravity. Thus Brumel was able to maintain a large part of his horizontal speed, especially since he was capable of increasing the number of steps per second in this very difficult position. In the vernacular of training we have designated this technique of the final approach step as "carry up."

According to measurements by Dyatchkov, the horizontal speed decreases in the last stride in spite of an increase in the number of strides per second. This is a result of the unfavorable position of the body's center of gravity at the point of ground contact and the consequent limit to the opportunity for stretching. Dyatchkov further believes that the high number of steps per second provokes special impulses in the relevant cerebral center which are fundamental for explosiveness in the subsequent take-off stretch.

The configuration of the approach which is described here should actually be regarded as the most successful. The practice of it should be worked into a methodical training:

Outdoors or indoors we attempt to cover a distance of 10 to 15 meters in the manner described, at first by walking, then by running. The strides are flat and extended. The swinging leg is extended far forward, the knees are straightened quite rapidly, all without the jumper's pelvis being elevated. It is important that the upper body remain erect up to the last stride. It is only during the last stride that he simultaneously takes the arms and back back. If the jumper were to lean back earlier, there would be a further reduction of the approach speed. Also the body's center of gravity would thereby be shifted back and would be in an even more unfavorable position relative to the point of support (the contact foot). Thus the overtaking of the support point would be delayed and the possibility of extending the stride would be reduced.

When the technique of the approach steps is absorbed, we try in a similar manner to increase the stride frequency (number of strides per second). In this case the stretching factor should be stressed.

Further we try to dip during the fluid run and to practice the "approach" with take-off indicated. When this is also absorbed, we try jumps over moderate heights. Finally, the approach is practiced in moderate jump competition.

# THE HIGH JUMP TAKE-OFF

By Fletcher McEwen, Australia

*In this article Adelaide coach Fletcher McEwen sums up the importance of the take-off in the high jump and gives his views on how it can be improved by a double-arm action.*

High School coaches often find athletes with natural jumping ability but extremely poor technique. The faults which occur most often are the anticipatory lean-in towards the bar at, or before, take-off and a poor leading leg action due to an upright body position at take-off. If the jumper is to be successful in later years these faults must be eliminated and this usually involves a complete relearning of the technique with emphasis placed on the approach run and take-off. As the relearning requires basic understanding of learning processes and the mechanics of the high jump, I will begin with a brief resume of both.

## THE LEARNING PROCESS

Dyatchkov states: "The process of the independent perfection of technique is very laborious and is achieved by a break-down of the old dynamic stereotype by overcoming the motor rhythm which had been learned." When the coach endeavors to alter an athlete's technique he must break down a "motor image pattern" which has been constructed as a result of the athlete's previous jumping experiences. As this process occurs a new "motor image", which corresponds to the altered technique is substituted. This process is usually slow, has many setbacks, and requires a sound knowledge of itself by both the athlete and the coach. Without this understanding mutual lack of confidence may result in discarding the new technique too early because results don't come quickly.

Since the learning process is difficult and time consuming, it is best tackled during the off-season. The athlete is then free of the distractions and stress of competitions, which may be the cause for a complete regression from the partly established skill back to his old technique. He should refrain from competition and also from jumping for height for the same reasons. Often, when the learning process is only partially completed, the heights which can be jumped by the athlete may be much less than those which he cleared with his old technique, but he must realize that this is only temporary.

The strangeness, or awkwardness, of the new technique can be reduced if the learning process incorporates imitative exercises, first in parts and later in a collective build-up to the whole jump. Some of these will be described later, but an extensive treatment can be found in Dyatchkov's article "High Jumping" (Track Technique, No. 36, June, 1969).

## MECHANICS

The alterations in technique have to be mechanically sound and well understood by the athlete and the coach. Basically the high jump consists of a run-up, a change of momentum to achieve a vertical velocity and a mid-air rotation to allow the athlete to clear a bar. The focus of the jump is the take-off where the change of momentum is executed. The requirements of the take-off are summarized by Dyson as: "During the take-off the jumper must (1) impart maximum vertical velocity to his center of gravity commensurate with (2) acquiring just sufficient body rotation (i.e., total angular momentum) for his subsequent layout."

To attain a vertical velocity the athlete exerts a force on the ground, a force which is bigger than that which supports the jumper's weight. The reaction to this force produces an upward acceleration in the athlete, thereby causing a change in momentum which results in the required vertical velocity. Since this force is a reaction provided by the ground, no force other than gravity acts on the athlete once he has lost contact with the ground. Hence, any change of momentum can only be made at the take-off and the path of the athlete's center of gravity is completely determined as soon as he loses contact with the ground.

Obviously the key to the high jump is the take-off which determines the success or failure of a jump and improvements will be made by aiming to maximize the change of momentum at this stage. It can be done by increasing the size of the force acting at the take-off and by lengthening the time of contact with the ground while the force is being applied. Only limited improvement can be made by working on bar clearance.

## THE TAKE-OFF

An efficient high jump take-off requires both of the above aims to be met. By using a heel to toe rolling action of the take-off foot, contact with the ground is maintained for as long as possible. A vigorous and coordinated swing of the free leg and arms provides the downward force on the ground. To allow for an efficient swing of the free leg the body is inclined backward. If this is not done then the swing of the leg will be inhibited. Two other factors which affect the take-off must also be considered. Firstly, the direction in which the forces act and secondly, the speed with which these actions are performed.

The athlete must aim to have all the changes of momentum directed vertically upwards. If this is not done then the height reached by his center of gravity will be reduced. It is therefore important that his body is aligned with a vertical plane through his run-up, which must be straight, so that the direction of change of momentum is not altered and height lost. Usually a deviation towards the bar from this position produces a tendency for the jumper to roll too early or even knock the bar with his upper body. The faster these operations can be performed the greater will be the forces acting, and the greater the height cleared. The limiting factor here is the athlete's strength. If he is lacking in sufficient strength then he will be unable to perform the desired actions at speed.

## THE IMPORTANCE OF ARMS

The modified technique is taught concentrating on the take-off and in particular the action of the arms. Once this has been done the rest of the jump can be built around it. Although the swing of the free leg is the most important contributor to vertical lift, benefits can be gained by teaching the take-off action around the arms. The arms are the center of co-ordination of the jump and thus are an obvious basis for learning. In addition, several other benefits can be obtained when the arms are correctly used.

Preparation for the take-off begins with the transition from a normal run up to one with knees slightly bent as the athlete runs on his heels and his center of gravity is somewhat lowered. The transition begins in the third last stride and is accompanied by an increase in speed. In passing through the second last stride the athlete moves quickly over his right foot and into the last stride. His speed and the increased length of this stride promotes the desirable body lean at the take-off, and is accentuated by the action of the arms.

When the last stride begins the right arm is usually forward and left arm back. The right arm is kept forward and raised slightly while the left arm comes through. As the athlete's torso passes over the right foot both arms are held in front of the body at about chest height and, as the stride continues, are brought down backwards in a circular motion during which the inner wrist is turned outwards. Then, as the left leg is planted and the right leg begins its full swing, both arms are swung forward and upward in unison with the leg. The left arm will stop just over the head of the athlete while the right arm continues to move a little higher. As the body lifts the left arm is allowed to tuck into the torso and the right arm reaches over the bar to promote the body roll.

This arm action will reinforce the movement of the legs past the upper body by opening out the chest and shoulders. The backward lean will come naturally without forcing and the athlete will be able to concentrate on his free leg swing. It is important that the arms are turned outwards as they are taken back. Failure to do this might result in the head being thrown forward as a reaction to the arm action.

Timing will also be improved since the jumper has a better idea of what is happening when the swing of his free leg and arms are synchronized. Once the timing is established the jumper can concentrate on his take-off explosion. Since the left arm is also swung forward and upwards the athlete is now usually more inclined to remain in the plane of the run-up and so the tendency to lean towards the bar is reduced and often eliminated.

Most of the benefit in a double-arm action is gained through a greater take-off force being applied in the best direction. However, the movement of the arms themselves contribute to vertical lift as they are accelerated upwards. It must be remembered that the arm action is not the most important part of the take-off, it is only a convenient center of attention about which the technique can be built.

## EXERCISES

The acquisition of this technique is best done in stages. The process should incorporate the use of imitating exercises of increasing complexity until the entire jump technique is mastered.

The first stage is done while the athlete stands still. The arms are moved backward as described earlier. At the end of their circular path they are immediately driven forward and upward. This exercise illustrates clearly the advantages of opening out the shoulders. It can be modified by having the athlete standing with both arms held in front of his body as he begins the arm action and plants his jumping foot in front of his body. The dip at take-off will be stimulated by a slight bending of the knees and settling of the hips. The backward movement of the arms should cease once the jumping foot is planted.

The next step is to combine the swing of the lead leg with the arms, and after this has been established further strides can be added as the jumper gains confidence. When completing the exercise the athlete should be lifted off the ground but it is important that his take-off foot lands in the same position.

Much benefit can be gained by short run-up jumps (three to five strides) either over the bar or ending with a take-off where the aim is to kick the lead leg as high as possible. At all times when the exercises are attempted care should be taken to see that all aspects of the run up and take-off form are kept as near as possible to the ideal. Once the exercises have been practiced the athlete attempts his new technique on a full run.

# AN INTERPRETATION OF FOSBURY TECHNIQUE

By Claude Labescat, France

*In this article Claude Labescat analyzes "Fosbury Flop" in great detail, drawing attention to the use of centrifugal force created by the curved run-up as the major novelty of the technique.*

## THE RUN-UP IN GENERAL

The run-up in the flop is immediately noticeable because of its curved characteristics. The approach on a bend forces the jumper outwards in the curve which appears to be counteracted by the vigorous push of the outside leg. This is clearly reflected in the stress it causes on the ankle and knee joints. (Jean Becchio, a friend of the author and a 6'6" flop performer, states that he has had his shoe laces broken and once even his shoe split under the stress. Further, he often complains of fatigue in the joints of the free (swinging) leg.

The jumper is apparently strongly influenced by the centrifugal force he has created by a curved approach run. He makes use of it at the take-off when the force is maximal and it appears that using the centrifugal force during the flight is the real novel characteristic of the flop technique.

By using a straight approach, the lift of the center of gravity depends on the forces applied at the take-off and velocity of the run-up. To convert the horizontal velocity fully into height requires an absolutely vertical take-off. In this case the jumper's center of gravity would be lifted at the right angle to the take-off plane and he would land exactly at the take-off spot, leaving the problem of clearing the bar unsolved. In reality, because of physical and mechanical limitations, the conversion of horizontal velocity into a completely vertical lift is impossible. However, in the flop technique a near-complete conversion appears possible because the centrifugal force, created by the curved run-up, assists in clearing the bar.

## THE RUN-UP IN FOSBURY'S TECHNIQUE

Here the first problem is to establish the run-up curve, depending on the approach speed of the jumper, his body mass and his muscular ability. We start by attempting a straight path which converts into a curve just before the take-off, called by us the "take-off curve". Later we shift the starting point of the approach by moving it further inwards in relation to the landing pit. This establishes a run-up path starting with a large radius before it converts into a "take-off curve" with a smaller radius (Fig. 1). The approach consisting of two curves appeals to athletes more than a straight start which swings into the "take-off curve", because it allows for a gradual adjustment to the bend and better balance. Further, the changes of the starting point allowed for better acceleration, brought the jumper longer under the influence of the take-off curve, and increased the number of strides before the take-off.

Jean Becchio, mentioned earlier in this article, had in December the following measurements for his run-up (see Fig 2):

1. Distance of starting point, measured at right angles to the bar, was 16.50m (AA). Start of the "take-off curve", measured in the same manner was 6.00m (BB) and had a radius of about

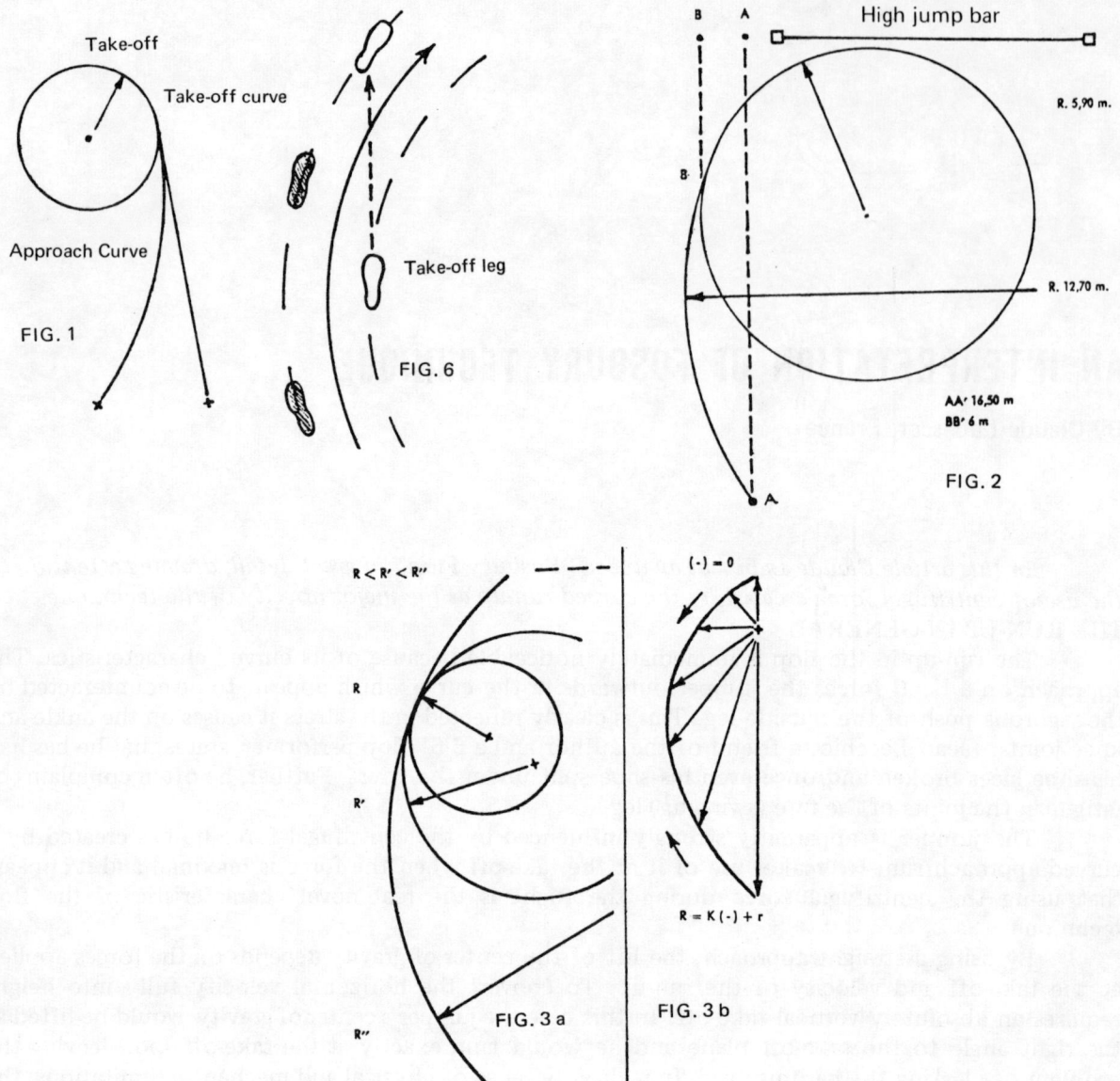

FIG. 1

FIG. 6

FIG. 2

FIG. 3 a

FIG. 3 b

5.90m. The radius of the early curve was about 12.70m.

As the centrifugal force $f = m\frac{R}{v^2}$, an overshort radius for the "take-off curve" appears unsuitable. The jumper has the choices to adjust it by changing the run-up speed, the radius of the "take-off curve" or both. Best results should come by using a wide bend with great speed, which allows for maximum forces to be applied at the take-off. At the same time it must be considered that at the same speed the centrifugal force increases according to the shortening of the radius, which suggests two forms of approach: 1. We combine several circles with continually decreasing radius (Fig. 3a); 2. The approach takes a spiral form, with the radius decreasing towards the take-off (Fig. 3b).

The last choice has an advantage in allowing the jumper to make his approach without being influenced by an over-strong centrifugal force.

We have already drawn attention to the effect of centrifugal force to the outside (swinging) leg in the last three strides. The placement of the outside leg counteracts the force and keeps the jumper within the set path. At this stage the basic principles of high jumping, lowering the center of gravity and keeping the take-off foot in line with the approach, apply (Fig. 4, Fosbury 1-3).

The jumper faces the strongest centrifugal force at the moment the take-off foot is placed down and the swinging leg starts to move. At this stage the center of gravity shifts from the vertical

FIG. 4

over the take-off point towards the bar. The jumper, provided the take-off forces and his free leg swing are in line with the run-up, is influenced by his horizontal speed, acting at a tangent to the take-off circle.

Using certain counteracting movements at this stage allows a near vertical beginning of the flight. First the bent swinging leg is lifted powerfully up and, in relation to the "take-off curve", inward. This improves the take-off and stops the jumper being driven forward towards the landing pit (Fosbury 4-7).

We believe that the movements of the swinging leg increase the centrifugal force further, because at the moment the take-off foot lands the center of gravity is behind the take-off point and the swing (with the hips being inside the curve) adds a rotational motion. The jumper lengthens his approach curve by shifting his center of gravity to a curve with a very short radius (Fig. 6) and thus increases the centrifugal force. At the same time the shift of the center of gravity increases the radius of the "take-off curve" and allows the jumper to continue his run-up movements during the free leg swing. (Fosbury 5 and 6).

The other counteraction to the centrifugal forces comes from shifting the center of gravity towards the take-off curve. During the last stride it follows in a virtually straight line from the previous stride (Fig. 6). This allows for a slight shift of the center of gravity (Fosbury 5 and 6), which during the take-off, because of the centrifugal force, is brought straight above the take-off point for an ideal and optimal vertical lift (Fosbury 7).

## THE ROTATIONS

The rotation around the longitudinal axis, assisted by the run-up, is achieved mainly by the movement of the swinging leg towards the run-up curve. The jumper takes off vertically, rotating around the longitudinal axis until he finds himself, at the moment the clearance starts, with his back towards the bar. We have experienced that some beginners have the tendency to over-rotate, which appears to be the result of a poor head position during the flight. In fact, Fosbury rotates his head after leaving the ground gradually towards the direction opposite to the swinging leg (Fig. 7).

This appeared mechanically wrong at the first glance because the general body rotation of Fosbury is from left to right and the opposite rotation of the head seemed to increase it (action and reaction). However, it could be explained by the chain of actions and reactions starting from the head. The head rotates from right to left, influencing an opposite movement from the shoulders, which rotate from left to right, and in turn are responsible for the equal and opposite reaction of the hips (Fig. 7).

Fosbury uses a synchronized arm action during his run-up which makes his take-off similar to that of the long jump. The opposite arm to opposite leg movement continues during the take-off action until the shoulders begin with an upward backward movement (Fosbury 6 to 14). The arm on the take-off leg side is lifted upwards in a bent position while the opposite arm is brought relaxed backwards (Fosbury 5 and 6). At the end of this motion both arms get as close as possible

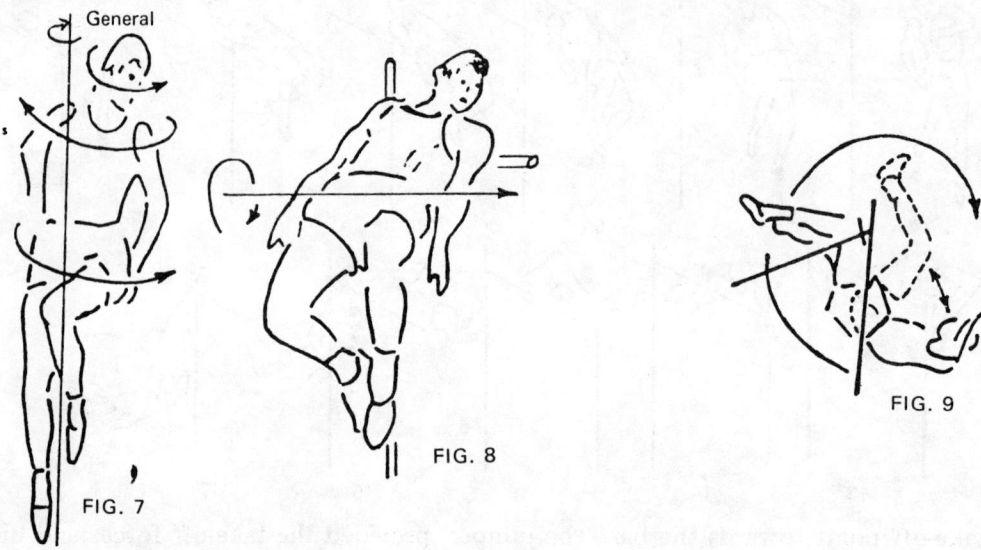

FIG. 7  FIG. 8  FIG. 9

to the longitudinal axis of the body to assist with the rotation. At this stage the arm on the take-off side becomes relaxed and both arms are now close to the body (Fosbury 7 to 11).

The rotation of the head begins as late as possible and becomes obvious only after the jumper has left the ground (Fig. 8). It has a double task in breaking, or keeping up, the rotation around the longitudinal axis when the jumper reaches the bar with his back. It also creates, or improves, the rotation around the transverse axis. The movement is closely related to the action of the shoulders, as the slight turn of the head towards the swinging leg makes the upper body follow and creates a rotation of the hip axis. The movement is generally controlled by the eyes as the jumper keeps the bar constantly in sight until it is cleared.

## CLEARANCE

A relaxation of the whole body becomes obvious immediately after the take-off. Both legs hang relaxed as the shoulders start their extension and rotation. This relaxation creates a passive stretching of the body. It is characteristically shown by Fosbury in the lower part of the legs hanging at a less than 90 deg. angle to the thighs and the relaxed and dropping shoulders. (Fosbury 14). This allows for a movement of the hips at the moment the bar is crossed.

The passive rotation can be improved by dropping the head and at the same time bringing the arms down towards the landing pit. (It is not done by Fosbury). A hollow back position would also be an advantage at the stage when the jumper is on his back and the bar is cleared up to the middle of the thigh.

The clearance of the lower leg is achieved by bending the hips and assisted by contracting the abdominal muscles (Fosbury 14 to 16). This action reduces the angle between the upper body and thighs and increases the rotation around the transverse axis as the mass of the body is moved closer to the axis. (Fosbury 16). Fosbury follows this by stretching his legs so that the lower part of the legs are brought high over the bar.

This has a disadvantage because it reduces the rotational force, as does the shifting of arms. The last is obviously a preparatory movement for the landing. Mechanically it appears advisable during this phase to increase the rotational force by bring the chin to the chest and knees towards the upper body (Fig. 9). This would mean that, starting from a certain height, the rotation should be completed, so that a full sommersault is performed and the jumper lands on his knees. As this causes the hips to drop, the action can only be completed after the hips have crossed the bar.

The above discussion doesn't mean that the flop has an advantage over other forms of high jumping. It is one of many possible techniques and has, compared with the straddle, several advantages and disadvantages. The straddle is more economical and allows for a better bar clearance as the center of gravity is closer to the bar. On the other hand, the flop has an advantage at the take-off. Mathematically it allows for a lift of the center of gravity 20 to 40cm higher than a jumper from a straight run-up. Although the bar clearance of the flop is at the moment inferior to the straddle, there are possiblilities to improve it in the future.

# TEACHING THE FOSBURY FLOP

By Hans Steiner, Germany

The "Flop" exhibits a relatively uncomplicated jumping technique which actually gave birth to the important principle: the necessity of eliminating the "bar-crossing cult".

Having sneaked into the Straddle Technique, this cult has eradicated (or weakened) the consciousness of the take-off and approach that are inseparably connected to each other.

To get into the typical backwards Flop position that has a definite consequence on the further phases of the jump, it is important for the beginner to achieve this position through a rotation at the take-off.

The learning of the slightly arched-back position (which must coincide with the flight curve), and, above all, the mastering of the continuation of this arch until a natural completion, is subject to two psychological factors with the beginner: fear and restraint. Every effort should be made to start the beginner on the jump proper, possibly without any further delay, and to ration, after careful observation, those individual exercises that will help eliminate the typical faults. Stressing the importance of the approach and take-off once more, I want to outline a few more preliminary practice progressions.

**Approach**

On the floor or on the dirt track, a nine to eleven strides long curve will be drawn. This curve bends only slightly at the start, but more strongly towards the end and corresponds to the course recommended by Labescat. (see previous article)

The youngster is required:

1. To run along the outlined path briskly in an upright position, and with natural strides.

2. To accelerate lightly at the beginning of the sharper curve (this spot may be marked with cross-lines).

3. To tilt his whole body, towards the inner curve.

4. To allow himself to gradually decelerate beyond that part of the curve where he had accelerated.

For the following reasons, the bar will be used only after the above listed exercises have been done repeatedly.

A good percentage of beginners that had been observed, above all, oriented themselves to the bar by their eyes, and with this their head, during the last third of their approach. The consequence of this is a turning of the head which in turn causes a jerky and restricted approach, a premature and rushed inclination of the upper-body towards the bar and finally, right from the beginning, an incomplete rotation about the long axis of the body. Therefore at the next exercise: the full approach with the bar on, special emphasis should be placed on the athlete's liberating himself inwardly from the attracting power of the bar, by running past it unaffected and without taking notice of it.

**Take-off**

1. Take a three strides approach, take-off and pop-up (without clearing the bar), emphasizing the placement of the take-off foot. Carry out a simultaneous quick knee lift of the swinging (kicking) leg.

Watch the following: take-off leg remains stretched (straight) until after landing; opposite arm performs a powerful action!

2. The same exercise with five, then with seven strides approach.

3. The same again with three strides, but now the kicking (free) leg and knee, with the whole body, performs a light rotation in the direction of the knee-swing inwards & upwards. The head turns slightly in the opposite direction.

4. The same again, this time with five strides approach, along the slightly curving path and with a somewhat stronger rotation (at take-off).

5. The whole exercise, now with a complete approach and a rotation of approximately 100 degrees, about the long axis of the body.

6. Approach and take-off along the pre-drawn curve with the bar on, with strong consideration of the elements learned about the approach, a decisive (clean-cut) body rotation, complete stretching, and an optimum switching from horizontal to vertical lift should be closely concentrated on. (Again: no clearance!)

**Flight phase and landing**

Besides the incomplete rotation about the long axis of the body, there is a further, conspicuous fault seen in nearly every beginner: a squatting posture, a "letting-the-bottom-hang-low" above the bar.

It is certain that the reason for this is not only the immobility of the hips, but, above all, it can be traced back to a known or unrealized fear of landing on the upper part of the back. The caused restraint reflects a "tucking-in" which prevents the acquisition of the arched-back position. The premature relaxing (abandoning) of the arch into a "tuck-in" (letting-the-bottom-hang-low) invariably leads to a backward somersault which may be traced back to the same cause.

To eliminate these restraining factors that are psychological in origin, the following preliminary exercises can be of great assistance:

1. Simple rotation jumps on a soft rolled up mat on which the landing occurs on the back or even in a "tuck-in" position.

2. Two partners stand up on the mat, back to back. One grabs the other's wrist and, bending over, pulls him forward on his back, until the other somersaults and lands on his feet, bent slightly in the waist.

3. Two partners build a bridge, holding each other by the hand. A third athlete can use this back support and perform the same movements as in exercise 2.

4. In case a flick-flack belt is at hand, a back handspring can be practiced. Here I should like to point out emphatically that no back handspring should be learned, but rather, by three to four such jumps, the psychological barriers of fear should be abolished.

For the mobility, stretchability of the hips, the following exercises are recommended:

1. The above-mentioned exercises 2-4.

2. Medicine ball throws backwards against the wall, watching the ball after it has been released.

3. The youngster, powerfully and quickly outstretching from a squatting position, slings a medicine ball backwards and upwards at a marked spot on the wall at one meter height and four meters from the point the ball is thrown. While in these throws he repeatedly watches the ball, his body occupies the typical Flop position. The whole musculature of the legs, front part of the body and the hips are strongly burdened down.

4. Exercise for the general mobility of the hip: the youngster hangs from the rings that are set low enough so that the knees almost touch the floor. Then he sets his legs and hips into a rotation so that the body is brought, from the legs, into a continued circular motion. (Like a Hula...)

5. The youngster stands up showing his back to the landing pit, bends his knees slightly, and swinging both arms, jumps up-and-backwards, concentrating mostly on keeping his pelvis elevated. It is advisable to reemphasize this between jumps with such high jumpers who do not bring

up the pelvis high enough.

After both approach and take-off are well established, and after the above-recommended preliminary exercises have been carried out, in proportion to the fault more or less intensively, the Flop proper is begun.

Because beginners often have a flat, long flight path, special care should have been taken to make the mats overlap on the right and left of the jump stands. The height of the landing mats should not be under 60 cm. If on the other hand, the mats are too high, the arch position cannot be attained due to a short falling height.

Because no two jumpers show the same jumping style, the coach will soon realize that it would be wrong for him to insist on a standardized, detailed execution of technique. Depending on body weight, jumping power, temperament, constitution, vitality, mobility, skill and other various attributes, the approach and take-off will be different in styles of technique.

It is interesting to note that the very beginner who previously appeared clumsy and untalented, shows a good start at learning the Flop. On the other hand, agile and lively beginners are often seen carrying out hasty movements at jumping. This haste results in their going into the arch position too early. The consequence is that the jumping power cannot be utilized fully. Besides this, because of excessively horizontal momentum at landing, the body rolls over backwards.

To correct these faults that appear time and again, one should turn to the above-mentioned fifth exercise: backward jumping, during which, according to the methodical reference, great care should be taken to maintain tension in the hip during the entire flight path, the curve of which should be steep.

Jumpers who practice on artificial surfaces complain continually that the friction between shoe and floor at the placement of the take-off is too strong. It is certainly more advantageous to turn in the toe of the take-off foot lightly at placement on the inner curve so that the friction, also present on the traditional dirt track in a lesser degree, will be avoided, though this would lend a smaller turning impulse.

A few more words about the health aspect of the Flop. One may safely assert today that, with a correct landing on the shoulder (upper back), the jump is not dangerous. Nevertheless, often it is a long way to perfection. From the very beginning the coach (teacher) should keep a watchful eye on the landing.

An over-rotation at take-off or a landing on the neck produces an undue strain on the spinal column, and the unnecessary and colossal force, concentrated at one point on the spine and ligaments, is comparable in its effect to a pocket knife that is snapped closed. Because of a faulty leverage position on the spine, the Hantel technique similarly creates an enormous strain.

If such technical mistakes are found in the jump, the jumping practice should be interrupted at once and exercise No. 5 should be repeated. Then, after 2-3 jumps, if no improvement is accomplished, the practice for this athlete should be terminated for that day so that not only the health hazard, but also the wrong kind of movements may be avoided. After two-three days, especially in case of young beginners, it may be much easier to start from scratch again so that perhaps this time correct movements and completion of the jump may be achieved.

**Summary**

The principles of any systematic beginning should be as follows:

1. To set out from the rudiments of the technique and also from a theoretical basis and from experience that is coordinated with a suitable movement plan.

2. To be aware through careful observation of the individual physical and psychological prerequisites of the athlete which again presupposes the intuition and willingness of the coach; and to make deviations from the stereotyped, theoretical movement-picture (the accepted technique).

3. To observe in detail and analyze the psychological demands (challenges) that force a technique on the athlete and with this to be able to eradicate certain restraint processes.

It is recommended to place emphasis on the following difficult points in the Fosbury Flop:

1. Approach exercises with emphasis on:
    - brisk speed
    - slight acceleration in the last third

- leaning into the inner curve
- ignoring the bar so that no tension during the approach occurs.
2. Jumping practices with the following goal:
    - to learn the elementary take-off position
    - to introduce the turn (twist, rotation)
3. Exercises for the preparation of the flight-and landing phases:
    - to put an end to the fear of the backwards jump and the landing
    - to make the hips mobile for the arched-back position
4. The total jump should serve as a basis for an intensive correction, and with the use of special exercises to bring about an improvement of the faults.

# LATEST DEVELOPMENTS IN THE FLOP

By the editors of *Modern Athlete and Coach*

*There is little doubt that the "Fosbury Flop" is rapidly gaining popularity and attempts to find the best possible teaching methods for this new high jump technique are being made all over the world. In this article the editors of* Modern Athlete and Coach *attempt to summarize the latest developments in teaching teaching progressions.*

## INTRODUCTION

It appears that at present there are still conflicting views on the biomechanics of the flop. Several authorities, including Labescat and West Germany's Dietrich Martin, stress that the curved run-up creates strong centrifugal forces which, by allowing a near vertical take-off, is the main advantage of the new technique. Labescat claims that it can be mathematically proved that this makes it possible to lift the jumper's center of gravity 20 to 40 centimeters higher than from a straight run-up.

Martin agrees in general with Labescat and draws attention to the fact that, besides the horizontal and vertical vectors at the take-off, the centrifugal force, created by the approach curve, is biomechanically significant. The center of gravity of the jumper is forced up by the centrifugal force directly over the take-off foot, making an optimal take-off possible. Several other authors, including Dr. Grundlach from Leipzig, believe that the centrifugal force at the moment of the take-off, provided that the take-off forces and the swing of the free leg are in line with the run-up, allow for an ideal vertical lift.

On the other hand Klement Kerssenbrock, Czechoslovakia, who has written several analyses on the flop technique, disagrees. He sees no significance in the curved approach and regards it more as a psychological advantage to prepare for the following rotation. He also claims that the vertical lift in the case of Fosbury actually passes his center of gravity on the right.

Karl-Peter Knebel, finds more significance in the speed of the flop approach than the actual formation of the curve. However, he agrees that practical experience at the Sports Institute, University of Heidelberg, has indicated that a curved run-up allows the jumper to get into a better position for the characteristic take-off action used by the flop jumpers. By using a curved approach the jumper's body is brought nearly parallel to the bar. A straight run-up places the body under a sharp angle to the bar and requires a greater rotational impulse which would detract from the efficiency of the take-off action.

It is interesting to note here that film analysis from Fosbury's jumping in Mexico City and the world record jump by Valeriy Brumel have shown that Fosbury is not as fast as he appears to be. Actually Fosbury approaches the bar at the same speed as Brumel who, admittedly, used a very fast run-up for a straddle jumper.

Brumel himself, in a recent interview with the Estonian journal Spordileht, was reluctant to comment on the flop technique. He thought that, while it apparently suits Fosbury, the technique appears mechanically inefficient. Brumel didn't recommend the flop for young Soviet high jumpers and thought that the landing position would never allow an athlete to produce his best. "I think that the way you land in the flop must create a subconscious fear of injuries which will restrict an all-out effort," said Brumel. He also felt that Fosbury himself, provided the American had mastered the straddle technique, would have jumped at least an inch higher in Mexico City.

## THE APPROACH

Despite different opinions on how the centrifugal force, created by the run-up, acts on the take-off, the curved approach has been universally accepted as a fundamental of the Fosbury technique. The most frequent method to develop the run-up is to mark the curve on the ground for the early learning sessions. This consists of two parts—the approach curve with a large radius and the take-off curve with a much smaller radius. As the jumper gets accustomed to the curved approach the starting point is gradually shifted further inwards in relation to the jumping pit until the most suitable curve for the individual has been established.

The measurements from three methods are included here to assist with the marking of the run-up for learning stages. The first is by Labescat, who combines two different curves for the run-up, because he believes that a start on the curve appeals to most athletes better than a straight start which swings into the take-off curve. The second sketch shows how the approach curve has been laid out by Martin. He uses small gymnastic boxes to guide the jumper and two different starting points, one for the beginners, the other for those who have already made some progress. A slightly different curve has been recommended by Kerssenbrock, starting on the curve and straightening a little before curving again just before the take-off.

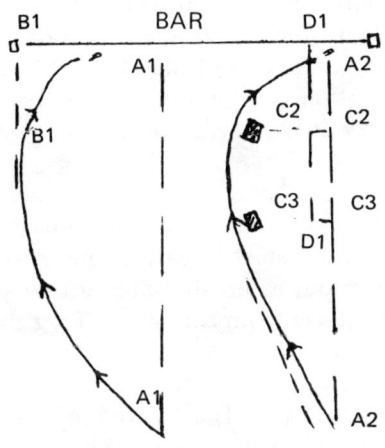

FIG. 1
The approach curves by Kerssenbrook (left) and Martin (right). Approximate distances are:
A1 to A1 20 ft., B1 to B2 10 ft., A2 to A2 10 m., C2 to C2 3 m., D1 to D1 5m.

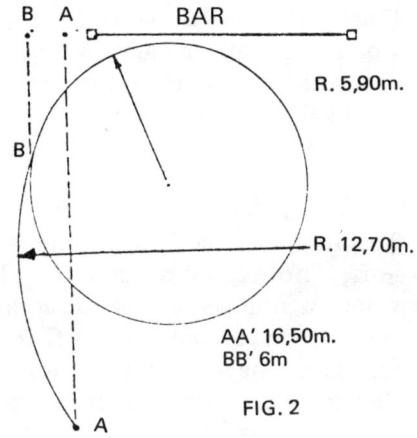

FIG. 2
Suggested approach curve by Claude Labescat, based on two different joining circles, The distance from the start to the bar in right angles is 10.50 meters.

In general, it is suggested that the approach should be executed with normal running strides, following a strictly marked path in the learning stages. As the curve is increased, the run-up becomes faster and the jumper is taught to adopt a slight inward lean. His attention is drawn to the fact that the outside leg must counteract the centrifugal force which increases with a sharper curve and the increase of the run-up speed.

To become accustomed to the unusual approach some preliminary exercises can be used with advantage. These could include running in circles, running in the form of figure "eight", accelerating runs in the snake form, etc.

## THE TAKE-OFF

One of the problems of the Fosbury technique is to avoid being driven forward, and achieve a near vertical lift at the take-off. This is accomplished by lifting a bent swinging leg up and, in relation to the take-off curve, inward. It must also be observed that the rotation round the vertical axis of the body is achieved by the movement of the swinging leg towards the run-up curve. This makes it important for the beginner to establish the correct rotation right from the start.

It appears therefore advisable to avoid teaching the typical Fosbury flight before the correct take-off and rotational impulse have been established and the early jumps should emphasize only the curved run-up and take-off actions. All landings when the bar is used should be simply in a sitting position but it must not be overlooked that the take-off leg has to remain stretched until the landing takes place.

It is important for the beginner not to be carried away by the details of the bar clearance. His action in flight depends largely on the rotational factors at the take-off to achieve an efficient position after leaving the ground. The failure to achieve a sufficient rotation at the take-off results usually in clearing the bar in a manner resembling the scissor jump and not completely backwards as required by the flop technique.

As in the other forms of high jump techniques, the flop learners start developing their take-off usually from a three-stride approach before graduating to five and seven stride exercises. At first the emphasis is on the correct placement of the take-off foot and pick-up of the swinging leg knee, which is combined with a powerful action by the opposite arm. After initial action has been established and repeated with five and seven stride jumps it is time to introduce the rotation. The swinging leg knee is brought upwards and inwards and the whole body rotates slightly in the same direction. At the same time a slight rotation of the head to the opposite direction can be introduced.

Finally the newly developed take-off action is combined with the already established curved run-up, observing that a rotaion of about 100 deg. around the vertical axis of the body is achieved for a correct start of the clearance action. Care must be taken that the take-off is about the same distance from the bar as in the straddle jump. A take-off further back indicates that the novice has not yet established a satisfactory vertical lift and is driven forward towards the bar.

## THE CLEARANCE

The flight in the flop technique can be divided into two phases. The first phase following the take-off, is noticeably relaxed. Both legs hang as the shoulders start to extend and rotation. This passive rotation follows a series of complicated rotational impulses created at the take-off, which decide the behavior of the body in flight. The main impulse starts from the take-off leg through the horizontal axis of the lower body towards left.

The second phase, which brings Fosbury to his remarkable position over the bar, is the direct result from the passive stretching of the body after the take-off. The relaxed legs and dropped shoulders allow for the movement of the hips at the moment the bar is crossed. The clearance of the lower leg is achieved by further bending of the hips to reduce the angle between the upper body and thighs. This, in turn, increases the rotation as the mass of the body is moved closer to the rotational axis. The whole clearance action starts by the upward movement of the lower leg.

Two points appear important in teaching the flight phase of the flop. First the jumper must avoid bringing up the legs after the take-off. He should attempt to relax and leave his legs hanging. There should be a definite relaxation in this phase, following the active behavior in the clearance phase and not vice versa, as is often the case in the learning stages.

The other noticeable fault is the bar clearance in a position with the seat and hips dropped. This is not caused by lack of mobility of the hips but by fear of landing. Unfortunately it makes a bend in the back impossible and the clearance inefficient. Here again the correct rhythm in the execution of the flight is important. First the relaxing phase, while travelling towards the bar, then the active phase of the clearance. The last requires action from the hips which helps to lock the hip joint and secures a safer landing. The opposite sequence by beginners often, because of relaxation in the final phase of the jump, allows the rotation to continue and makes a safe landing difficult.

There are several preliminary exercises recommended by various authors to prepare the novice for the flight technique. These can be executed by using a trampoline, springboard or by simply landing on a high and soft pit. The jumps from the trampoline are from a standing position. No crossbar is used for exercises from a springboard or landing in a high jump pit or pile of mats. Basically all the exercises stress backwards rotation, relaxation of the lower legs after the take-off and correct landing. After some confidence has been gained the leg action is stressed. Here it is recommended to avoid lifting the legs too early and too high. The legs should not be moved up too vigorously as this would be reflected in a lowering of the body, a typical position in dislocating the bar with the seat.

There has been considerable discussion concerning the correct position of the head in the flight phase. In Fosbury's case the head is kept slightly forward towards the chest and Labescat feels that his rotation could be improved by dropping the head and at the same time bringing the arms down towards the landing pit. Others disagree and see no advantage in the position. Toni Nett explains that the movement of the head, as used in a backward somersault, would be of no benefit in the flop and is not even used in gymnastic movements today.

## TEACHING METHODS

It is obvious that the methods used in teaching the flop should be divided into the run-up, take-off and bar clearance phases. Most authorities agree that these parts should be taught in the order here presented, starting with the run-up, because of the relative simplicity of the flight action and its dependence on the proper approach and take-off.

It is important for the beginner to get into the typical backwards to the bar position of the flop and this is only possible by creating sufficient rotation around the vertical axis of the body at the take-off. The take-off itself depends largely on mastering the curved approach and the movement of the swinging leg during the lifting action. Nevertheless, as soon as the jumper goes through the take-off movements and becomes airborne, he is worried about his landing. For this reason some authorities, including Kerssenbrock, recommend to begin with preliminary flight exercises before the run-up is tackled, or teaching the movements in the air and the run-up simultaneously. Kerssenbrock, for example, suggests in his five-stage teaching progression the following order:

1. Preliminary exercises for the flight, landing on mats placed on a gymnastic form; 2. Teaching the curved approach and take-off action with emphasis on the rotation and free leg action but landing on the meanwhile dropped swinging leg; 3. The flop, combining the approach, the take-off and the basic flight, but landing on a gymnastic form; 4. The flop over a bar, landing in a normal high jump pit, but being assisted by two helpers who drop and remove the bar in the middle of the flight; 5. The flop over the bar under normal high jump conditions with the first attempts over a very low bar.

Martin, who prefers a trampoline for preliminary exercises, recommends the following sequence:
1. Learning the curved approach, using a marked path; 2. Learning the correct rotation and take-off, landing on a high pit in a sitting position; 3. Learning the flight action, first on a trampoline, then with the use of a mini-trampoline and landing on mats placed on gymnastic boxes; 4. The full flop over low heights under normal high jump conditions.

A good conditioning program and safety precautions have to be emphasized whatever learning sequence is preferred. It is too late to think of conditioning when teaching of the flop technique has started. Like in any other form of high jumping the development of take-off power and agility must come first.

There has been a lot written on the danger of injuries when the flop technique is used. It is true that some danger exists but this can be minimized by correct technique and a safe landing pit. It is obvious that a jumper, landing on the back and shoulders, has little to fear, provided the pit meets the minimum requirements. It must have sufficient height to reduce the distance of fall and the danger of over-rotation. It must also be soft to compress at least about 12 inches to reduce the deceleration impact.

Of course, the proper landing technique must be constantly observed and stressed in the learning stages. It is advisable to return to preliminary exercises of landing immediately the beginner is found landing on his neck or over-rotating.

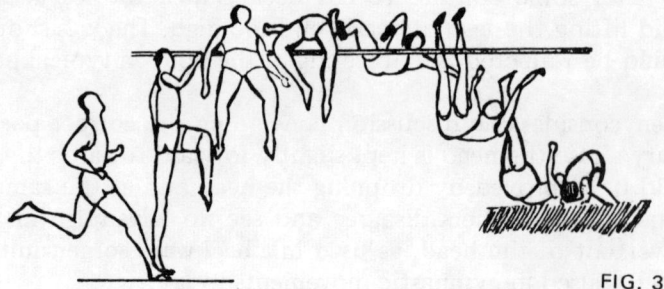

FIG. 3

32

# SHOULD HIGH JUMPERS USE THE STRADDLE OR THE FOSBURY FLOP?

By Prof. Carlo Vittori, Central School of Sport, Rome, Italy

Do you recall that day in Mexico, a few years ago, when Fosbury "flopping" so well, won the Olympics, leaving everyone gaping? I remember on the field—I was serving on the jury—seeing a "red-jacket" perplexed and shocked fingering through the Rules handbook maybe in the hope of coming across some niggling point to legally justify such an improbable and hitherto unheard-of way of jumping, though not so crazy as all that if it managed to secure an Olympic victory.

The question at stake might have been expressed as follows: 'Yes, but if we don't take expensive measures to ensure an absolutely smooth landing (the . . . Lem . . .), what about the neck vertebra? . . . A weak protest, if one only thinks of the pole-vault!

"Only he can do it"—the world went round—"being what he is, with his unique power of co-ordination; you don't find two like that" . . . Such was the effect of his high-speed approach, the difficulties of his actual achievements were underrated.

Then there was the analysis and the discussion, others made the attempt, and the thing began to be a success.

In the last four years, keen as he is to try out everything, Vittori has concentrated on high jumps, encouraged by the successes and progress of the jumpers who have been trained by him.

He is facing the "Fosbury" problem with frank devotion, with the excellent intention of neatly focusing the problem in discussion: Is the "Fosbury" as a style of jumping unconditionally more effective or is it preferable only for "some" jumpers, in view of their particular features as athletes and energy-wise?

The right way to state the problem is to find the right solutions for each of these. This is what I am happy to note in this little report, the conclusions of which, while justifying the coexistence of "straddle" and "flop," are more than of merely practical value, since they help to save time and to provide a sound basis for experiment and to keep discussion permanently open and on the right tracks.

In my opinion these are questions we should have asked as soon as we became familiar with this new high jump technique: Which jumpers should use the Fosbury Flop and which the straddle? As is often the case with something new, general interest is focused in the immediate application rather than on objectively examining the phenomenon. Thus, sight is lost of the study of the laws governing it.

In search of truth, much research has been started in various directions, all with the simple aim of showing that the flop is in every way superior to the straddle. This has still further convinced those who had already begun to use the flop to utilize it to an increasingly greater extent.

What concerns me is the risk of losing so many possible straddlers.

I doubt that the "flop" is unconditionally more effective than the "straddle" on the ground that the center of gravity is better positioned during the crossing of the bar.

It is a known fact that to jump 2.24m. an athlete of 1.90m. must raise his center of gravity about a meter, i.e., impart to his body a vertical velocity which at the moment of take-off from the ground is about 4.10 m/sec., regardless of whether the "flop" or the "straddle" is used. If there is a problem of choice, this only concerns the physiological type which can best use one or the other technique in order to improve the result.

The first technique research is aimed, therefore, to pick out those athletes who are especially able to get the best advantages from the "flop", while it would be well to follow up and decide the others by the "straddle".

Let us now consider some of the basic principles which may be valuable for a better understanding of the "Fosbury" phenemonon and to avoid falling into unqualified generalizations.

With regard to the moment before take-off, in particular the time of contact with the sole of the take-off foot, while the athlete is imparting to his body the necessary force to make it take off, the time for the great heights of the flop is about 14 hundredths of a second, while that for the "straddle" is about 22 hundredths. Clearly two athletes of the same weight and build, to get the same vertical speed with different take-off times, would have to impart different amounts of force to their bodies. In the flop, where this time is less, the force would have to be greater. On this basis, flopping is seldom justified because ground contact with the takeoff foot during take-off of the best floppers may range between quite narrow amounts, i.e. from 13 to 15 hundredths of a second, (the condition for making a really good jump), while the take-off time for straddlers may range more widely, between 18 and 24 hundredths of a second. It is obvious, thus, that the flopper is a special biological type, whereas the straddle technique may be used by a greater number of athletes.

To my mind, the biological feature of a flop consists in the different way in which the neuro-muscular system works, which is seen in the ability of the nervous system to promptly issue a series of stimuli of higher intensity and in the ability of the muscular system to respond accordingly.

The features essential to the muscle formation of a flop are elasticity and a nimbleness. These qualities permit building up during a minimum time-period the surplus energy which will be added to the energy deriving from geniune muscle contraction, so the jumper can get the vertical speed he requires. In simpler and perhaps clearer language used in sport, this is the ability of the muscle system to "break out" or "explode", which may be seen in any motor process in which the lower limbs are used as a system of propulsion.

On the other hand, it is the short take-off time that leads one to think that the propelling action must involve a strong elasticity factor. It is worth noting what Fosbury's coach, Bernie Wagner, said on this point, that he had never seen a high-jumper with so rapid an overall action (Sports Gazette).

In very rapid movements, in which touch-down time is very short, this particular factor is increasingly more noticeable. One need only think of the sprinter, whose touch-down time is about 8 hundredths of a second, to realize how his high output is to be ascribed to an "accumulation" of elastic energy during the movement-building phase, when the muscle stretches in a state of contraction before shortening. The subsequent step restores the balance (+). In other words, the sprinter's running action is largely achieved by elastic reactions of the muscle-structure of the lower limbs. As the touch-down time diminishes, in order to build up forward movement, so the elasticity factor and its effect is increased. Athletes having these natural features are highly likely to be able to successfully employ the flop.

The straddler's muscular structure may be less elastic, have marked features of "slow resistant strength" [i.e. able to maintain high levels of energy-output longer though taking longer to reach these levels], so that he may get equally good results. Our two Italian athletes Crosa and Azzaro are classic examples. Witness the difficulties that the Swedish high jumper, Nilsson, found when he tried to use the orthodox "straddle", in which the kick of the leading limb is made with the leg straight. This movement, which is more difficult than that done with the leg bent, as performed by Nilsson, takes longer so that as a result it also lengthens the movement of the take-off limb (shock-absorption/thrust) which is done in perfect timing with the former.

After a year of trying, Nilsson had to go back to 'kicking' with the limb bent. The failure was due to the greater extent of movements in the final touch-down phase which clearly also lengthened his take-off time, and did not allow him to take full advantage of his muscular "explosion" capacity. This he achieved better of course with shorter and more rapid movements closely linked to the 'kick' with the lead leg bent. It may be considered that if the "flop" had been to his liking and if it had been known, Nilsson would have had the biological features to become an excellent flopper and may have achieved better results than those he did. His take-off time, in fact, is 15 hundredths of a second (Dyatchkov: "High Jump Technique") which is about equal to that of Fosbury.

The flop offers another chance to those who, while they have the above-mentioned neuro-muscular features, are unable to use a straight lead leg at take-off in the straddle, and thus they may reach a higher result with Fosbury's revolutionary invention.

Let us now compare the two final touch-downs of the "long jumper", the Fosbury flopper and the straddler, which is very important to correctly choose the biological type to use the flop. The photos show how the positions achieved by a "Fosbury" in building up tension on the last-but-one touch-down are more like those of a "long-jumper" than of a "straddler". The time for take-off (14 hundredths of a second for Fosbury and about 11 hundredths of a second for a long jumper) are closer to each other than are that of a "straddler" (viz. 22 hundredths of a second to that of a "long jumper"). The flop in fact needs, above all, high speed at the take-off to build up a parabola the horizontal component of which reaches values almost double that of the straddler and allows him to get clear of the bar. The straddler, on the other hand, performs fuller and more marked movements in the final stages at a speed of about 8 m/sec. so that at the point of take-off he reaches a more backward-inclined position, which is essential to create a more vertical parabola owing to a lower horizontal component value and to a higher exit angle. The forward launch of a straddler is about 2.60m. because of the mode of clearing the bar, which is the particular technical feature of this style.

The flop jumper as a biological type resembles the long jumper and, generally speaking, the movements of the final steps are alike. This comparison is borne out by the news that has reached us on the fleeting appearances of Elliot, the flopper who was seen jumping at Formia, in a high jump contest in which he got results of 8 meters, in spite of the wind.

More should be said on the biological type, to illuminate a number of points made on the achievements of youths and several athletes owing to their general application of the Fosbury technique, to declare it to be superior to the straddle. Apart from the mistake of raising an argument that might well confuse the real aim, one thing is sure: youths of 12-13 years often do not yet have sufficient muscular strength to use the classical straddle. This usually becomes possible only at about 15-16. However, mature women, according to Hettinger (+), have a higher percentage of elasticity than of strength.

This would explain, as mentioned above, why youths and women find the "flop" more useful. But matters are rather complicated for youths, when the development brings about important changes in the muscle structure and working at the age of 15-16, when and only then, it is possible to say which of the two types—"explosive" or the slow resistent strength—they belong.

But if we had already applied the "flop" technique to a large number of boys, we should have to admit to being mistaken at least for those who, on maturing, have acquired the biological features of the "straddler".

Which amounts to saying that at least time has been lost. Applying the "Fosbury" technique more generally with women is basically justified, with the due exception of women whose nervous and muscular features allow them to do a practically orthodox straddle. The lack of strength in women is more clearly shown in the take-off moment or in the marked tension-change of the limb at the last-but-one touch-down: these steps being very irksome and difficult to execute.

Clearly all these points are justified by the fact that the aim of the techniques is to raise the average of the results of high-level performers rather than that of the mediocre.

### Conclusion and Points to Note

1) Youths should specialize in the high jump later (whether "flop" or straddle) which should be begun at about age 15-16. In the earlier years it would be better to engage in general

muscular and technical preparation. Of great value for this purpose are "jumping exercises" which comprise the movements and the actual jumps of the long and triple jump with short run-ups, as well as all the exercises using the lower limbs with more or less rapid bend-and-stretch (softening-up) movements.

2) The "Fosbury" technique should be limited to those children who have the essential features for high jumping in the future, while the others should go on with the practice they have already had towards the straddle. There is still the question of how to find those who have "Fosbury" qualifications. A piece of practical advice would be: a) to note the behavior of young people in a number of expressions of movements such as exercises as under item (1), concentrating attention on the overall energy-use of the actions; b) make these youths also perform classic jumping movements, mainly long-jump, which should show their "explosive" ability. In the long jump take-off, they should do 6-8 fairly fast run-ups to be concluded with an actual take-off, without jack-knifing the body. It is enough for the coach to expect little of the athlete in regard to the speed of the overall action of run-up and take-off and the completeness of the extension of the limb on the last touch-down leading to the body up-thrust. The choice will alight on those youths who after a high-speed run-up and take-off succeed in jumping the highest.

3) The "flop" should be more widely used for women, for the reasons mentioned above.

The useless arguments that tend to center on deciding whether the "flop" is better than the "straddle" should be discontinued, because the two techniques exist side by side, each offering the chance of getting excellent results when they are used by athletes who have the right physical features to utilize them.

(+) See R. Margaria, L. De Caro "Fisiologia Umana", 4th Ed., vol. 2, Chapter 15, 1967, Villardi Medical Library.
(+) Toni Nett, Ulrich Jonath, "Kraftubungen zur Konditionsarbeit", Ed. Bartels & Wernitz.

# IMPROVING SPRING IN THE HIGH JUMP

By Adam Bezeg, National Coach of Poland

The improvement of spring in the high jumper is based on: (a) exercises aimed to increasing the power of the legs; (b) general jumping exercises; (c) special exercises; (d) jumping exercises with weights; and (e) exercises in jumping technique.

**Exercises Aimed to Increase Leg Power**

There are four types of well-established exercises:
1. Knee bends with weights on shoulders.
2. Jumps with complete flexing of legs.
3. Jumps with half-flexing of legs.
4. Calf raises (with weights).

These exercises are carried out in June and July, three times a week. The first load of weights must be equal to the (in knee-bends) previous season's personal best.

From here, the training scheme of established jumpers is as follows: (a) bends with weights on shoulders (70% of previous year's record) up to weights equal to the record. Five repetitions per set; (b) Jumps with complete flexing (50% to 70%). Five repetitions per set; (c) jumps with half flexing (50% to 70%). Three sets of five to ten repetitions; (d) Toe raises (80% to 100%). Two sets of ten to twenty repetitions. All exercises are continuous until the first signs of fatigue appear.

Each week the load is increased by 5 to 10 lbs. for each of the exercises. The recovery time is to be determined individually (by the coach).

At the end of July the load is not increased any more but in exceptional circumstances may be continued to be raised until mid-August.

The preliminary exercises then give way to more dynamic exercises. In July the number of flexion repetitions per set (3 to 5), may be reduced but a maximum load is used. These "heavily loaded" exercises can be carried out once a week or even once every two weeks.

Calf raises are abandoned from the beginning of August, they are replaced by jumping exercises with weights and special exercises.

Beginners may undertake the same training, but modifying the loads thus:

| Exercises | Men | Women |
|---|---|---|
| Knee bends | 60% | 50% |
| Jumps with complete flexing | 35% | 25% |
| Jumps with half flexing | 35% | 25% |
| Toe raises | 70% | 60% |

For these exercises the load is increased every two weeks by five per cent.

The leg strengthening work in the competitive season consists of exercises (2) and (3) and every two or three weeks a few bending and stretching exercises with weights on shoulders are added. The exercises are omitted before important competitions.

Beginners, during the competitive season, continue with exercises (1), (2), and (3) but use reduced weights.

**General Take-off Training**

Take-off training starts from the first day of the year and continues to the last. It consists of hard work on the lift-off drive. This drive can be increased by over-loading (for example, bicycle tires filled with sand and suspended on the shoulder; special belts; vests filled with sand, etc.) the jumper in training.

The load is decided according to the age of the jumper, his body build, number of years of training, and also the stage of training in the current year. The principle is to increase the weights from year to year in order to make the leaps more difficult, but without interfering with the movements of the jumper.

The jumper, during the performance of the take-off exercises, avoids adopting an unsuitable kind of take-off for his particular jumping demands.

A vertical take-off inevitably leads the jumper to a recognition of his technical defects provided the action is done at adequate angles (not forgetting the leading leg).

| Exercises | XI | XII | I | II | III | IV | V | VI | VII | VIII | IX | X | Total |
|---|---|---|---|---|---|---|---|---|---|---|---|---|---|
| Technique work over the bar | - | - | - | 60 | 100 | 130 | 160 | 80 | 100 | 140 | 90 | 40 | 900 |
| Special Jumps | - | - | 100 | 150 | 250 | 150 | 100 | 120 | 100 | 60 | 100 | 70 | 1200 |
| Jumps over the bar (loaded) | - | 100 | 200 | 400 | 700 | 200 | 400 | 200 | 200 | 400 | 200 | - | 3000 |
| General take-off work | 150 | 400 | 600 | 850 | 600 | 200 | 400 | 150 | 300 | 200 | 50 | 100 | 4000 |
| Total | 150 | 500 | 900 | 1460 | 1650 | 680 | 1060 | 550 | 700 | 800 | 450 | 210 | 9100 |

This table contains statistical averages over three years of training by the Polish elite and may therefore serve as a model for established jumpers. It is understood that the annual total may vary in relation to physical conditioning, motor factors and physique.

Below is the table for beginners:

| Exercises | XI | XII | I | II | III | IV | V | VI | VII | VIII | IX | X | Total |
|---|---|---|---|---|---|---|---|---|---|---|---|---|---|
| Technique work over the bar | - | 60 | 100 | 120 | 140 | 160 | - | 100 | 80 | 150 | 80 | 60 | 1050 |
| Special jumps | - | 100 | 100 | 140 | 160 | 100 | - | 80 | 60 | 100 | 60 | 20 | 920 |
| Jumps over the bar (loaded) | - | - | - | 300 | 400 | 200 | 300 | 150 | 400 | 300 | 150 | 100 | 2300 |
| General take-off work | 350 | 650 | 1000 | 800 | 600 | 350 | - | 250 | 500 | 500 | 300 | 200 | 5500 |
| Total | 350 | 810 | 1200 | 1360 | 1300 | 810 | 300 | 580 | 1040 | 1050 | 590 | 380 | 9770 |

**Special Lift-off Exercises**

This work emphasizes the "launching" of the leading leg. It is important to work on jumps in which the high point to be reached with the head, with one hand, or with both hands, is fixed.

During these jumps the exact highest point reached would be checked as it will help to judge the power of the take-off. These jumps can also be carried out over obstacles (vaulting box): (a) over low obstacles (land on the trailing leg); (b) over high obstacles (land on both feet).

The starting load for established jumpers in June is 40% and in August is 60% of personal best. The maximum load is reached one month after the start. The load at the time of competition is reached to 25 to 30 per cent.

# PERSPECTIVES IN THE IMPROVEMENT OF SPEED-STRENGTH PREPARATION OF JUMPERS

By Yuri Verhoshanski, U.S.S.R.

Evolution of the views on methods of speed-strength preparation is characterized by periodic repetition of a complete cycle in creative thought. The beginning of such a cycle gives immediate success through cognition of the complex motor mechanism in sports technique. This helps determine means of strength preparation corresponding to the motor specifics of the given exercise and because of this, naturally raises the effectiveness of the training. However, in measuring the growth of sports achievement, this effect appears less significant. We then go to raising the volume of the training work until further increase becomes impossible. And now, we again return to analysis of sports technique with the hope of seeing the falling of a new "Newtonian apple." With this, we begin the new cycle of searches and this time on a higher scientific level, having behind us much practical experience.

Many years ago, the universal method of developing jumping ability was jumping exercises, the volume of which from year to year has steadily and unbendingly increased. In the end, thanks to improvement of research methods, there appeared overwhelmingly great dynamic efforts by sportsmen and the universal method for strength preparation was with weights. The use of weights brought determined success but very soon the swiftly growing sports achievements using this means of strength preparation became less effective. Not taken into consideration was that work with the barbell had reached a very great volume. Devoting the necessary attention to the basic exercise simply never happened. And now we are already hearing voices questioning the advisability of exercises with weights for the track and field athlete. Together with this, there is again appearing increased interest in the dynamic mechanism of sports technique. What kind of new means or principles of strength preparation will we now find?

One thing is clear: in place of unwarranted searching for some kind of absolute means of strength development, it is necessary to direct one's efforts to the construction of a determined system of strength preparation—a system with maximum suitability for achieving the necessary effect with minimum expenditure of time and effort. From such a presentation of the problem, it becomes necessary to speak of the principle of dynamic correlation, which should guide in the construction of a system of strength preparation. The leading idea of such a principle is the necessity of correlating training methods with those needs of the organism required during fulfillment of the basic movement on a determined level of sports achievement. Adherence to the principle of dynamic correlation allows for objective evaluation of the effectiveness of the methods used, the working out of new means if required, and determination of the rational mutual ties between the methods and their consecutiveness in a plan covering many years.

We will now look over in a general way, how strength potential of sportsmen is revealed in jumps at various stages of sports mastery. In flexing the legs at the beginning of the take-off (phase of amortization) the tie-in with support is at maximum strength. After this follows the transition of the muscles to overcoming work (phase of active take-off). During extension of the legs definite acceleration is imparted to the body, after which strength of the related action with support begins to decrease. This entire complex action in the triple jump is completed in 0.13 seconds in which the amplitude of movement in the knee joint is up to a four-fold, dynamic reloading of the support leg.

Specialized study of jump dynamics showed that increased effectiveness in the take-off is tied in with development of the ability of the jumper to display the greatest dynamic effort in the least time. Of decisive significance here is the quality of his muscles in showing strong effort immediately after high mechanical loading in the phase of amortization. In this case, the muscles of the jumper should quickly switch to overcoming work and without delay impart to the body the necessary amount of acceleration in the required direction. Therefore, as the load in the phase of amortization increases, there is also an increase in jump results, and then it is possible to suppose that growth of sports mastery to a significant degree is stipulated by the so-called "reactive ability" of the muscles.

For quantitative evaluation of the reactive ability of the nerve-muscle apparatus of the jumper, an index was proposed by us characterizing the load of the support apparatus to a unit of take-off time, $R = \frac{Fm}{Pt}$. Such an index of reactiveness, where "Fm" is the mean sum of dynamic effort, "P" is the static weight of the sportsman, and "t" is the total time of take-off, satisfactorily evaluates the reactive ability of the nerve-muscle apparatus and can be used as a quality evaluation criterion for dynamic characterization of jump and strength exercises. It indirectly reflects the power and speed of dynamic effort in the take-off and the speed of switching the muscles from yielding work to overcoming work.

Research on the dynamics of the take-off by jumpers of various qualifications with use of the index of reactiveness confirms that growth of sports mastery is tied in mainly with development of the reactive ability of the nerve-muscle apparatus. For track and field jumps, this tie is expressed as almost a straight line relationship along the entire range of sports results and has a very high quantitative index of correlation (the greater the relationship between each of the studied factors, the closer the index approaches one). From this comes an important practical conclusion: to raise the strength potential of sportsmen, we must, first of all, strive for development of the reactive ability of his nerve-muscle apparatus.

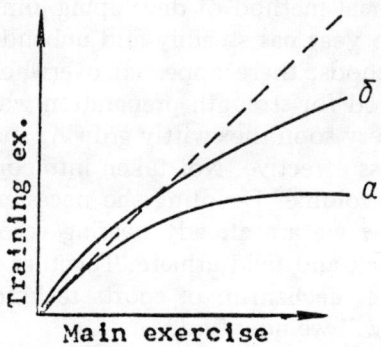

Drawing 1. Relationship between results in the main and training exercises (a - jump type, b - with weights).

We will now take a look at the extent to which jump exercises and exercises with weights occupy a basic place in strength preparation of the jumper and how they serve to increase his sports achievement. In Drawing 1, schematically presented is the experimentally found relationship between results in weight exercises and in basic sports exercises. Analysis of this relationship allows one to conclude that on the first stage of sports improvement, the usual methods allow for growth of sports achievement. However, further on, jump exercises serve to increase the sports result to a lesser degree than do exercises with weights. However, in its own turn this latter effect on the highest stages of sports mastery likewise decreases. This means, if we try to explain this phenomenon from the position of the principle of dynamic correlation, that the training function of weight exercises does not answer those needs which appear in conditions of fulfilling the jump. And so it appeared when a comparative investigation was carried out on the dynamic characteristics of those exercises which are used in practice by jumpers. Not a single training exercise was found which, according to the complex of dynamic characteristics, corresponded to the take-off in the jump executed on a high level of sports mastery.

With what, then, is it possible to explain the increase in reactive ability of the muscles according to measurements of the increase in the sports result and to know which method achieves this? It is obvious that one such method is the basic sports exercise executed for record for the given jumper's level of achievement (this was brought out earlier by V. Dyatchkov). However, for reasons known, this is not always possible to do. Because of this, it is advisable to search for means which by their own dynamic characteristics give adequate ties with the basic sports exercise showing a straight line relationship for the whole range of sports results (Drawing 1—the broken line).

But, before talking of this, we will try to find out why, with an increase in sports mastery, the effectiveness of exercises with weights decreases. It shows up that weight lifting, while stimulating the appearance of significant strength, at the same time slows down the speed of its development and frequently the speed of switching the muscles from yielding work to overcoming work. From here, it is logical to suppose that for development of reactive ability of the nerve-muscle apparatus, it would be ideal to have such strength training conditions that in the forthcoming work regime the muscles developed dynamic strength corresponding (by its complex characteristics) to the phase of amortization in the jump, and, at the same time, did not slow down the switching of the muscles to overcoming work. Such conditions can be artificially created if, for example, the sportsman takes off (forward-upward or upward) after a jump in depth from a determined height. By its own dynamic characteristics, and mainly by the striking character development of strength, the work of the muscles in these exercises is very close to the take-off in the jumps. Such exercises by themselves are not new and are seen in practice (jumping over hurdles and jumping off and jumping on gymnastic apparatus). D. Ioseliani, an all-around athlete, used these exercises in training and his outstanding jumping ability is well known. N. Ozolin used take-off after a jump from a not too high pedestal in preparation of ex-world record holder, L. Shcherbakova.

Later on, in research directed to the improvement of methods of specialized strength preparation, we studied all sides of this principle of strength development. In the course of laboratory investigation and scientific experimentation, the high effectiveness of the take-off after a jump in depth was shown for improvement of reactive ability of the nerve-muscle apparatus and a method for their use was worked out. (See *Legkaya Athletika*, No. 7, 1964.)

Now this method is used by many sportsmen and trainers. However, danger was brought about in conducting it as a universal means, and likewise, an ill-advised increase in volume and utilization in the training of beginning sportsmen. Tied in with this, it is necessary to once again stress the extra-ordinarily strong action of the take-off after a jump in depth on the nerve-muscle apparatus and to allow these jumps only for single-minded and systematic use on a high level of sports mastery.

And so, in drawing out the contour of a system over many years of specialized strength preparation of athletes directed to the development of jumping ability, it should, we believe, consist of several stages. We will say from the beginning that the division into these stages, according to sports classifications is clearly conditional, for as yet we do not have objective capabilities to do this in relation to the level of physical preparation of the sportsman.

The first stage corresponds to the Class III athletic sports classification. In this stage, mainly general developmental strength and jump exercises are used (with moderate loading) directed to all-sided development of the athlete.

The second stage corresponds to the Class II sports classification. In this stage, mainly exercises with the barbell or other weights are used (weight is 75%—90% of maximum). These exercises should resolve the task of further improvement in many-sided preparation and, likewise, insure the direction of strength development of the "working" groups of muscles and the capability for the "explosive" appearance of significant nerve-muscle loading.

The third stage corresponds to the sports classifications of Class I and Master of Sport. In this stage, the methods used are directed mainly to the development of reactive ability of the nerve-muscle apparatus during significant dynamic effort and speed of switching the muscles from yielding work to overcoming work. An example of such an exercise is take-off after a jump in depth from a height of 75 and 100 cm., of which the method of fulfillment was explained earlier. In addition, exercises with the barbell at maximum and near maximum weight are used to develop the ability of "explosive" display of significant effort and in maintaining the necessary level of strength preparation.

We emphasize that the single direction development of reactive ability should go through all stages of strength preparation, and to resolve this task the chosen methods should correspond to the level of physical preparation of the sportsman. Many years of test work on such a system allows us to recommend the following method for development of reactive ability of the muscles. On the first stage, good results are achieved from fulfillment of the complex of jump exercises in place (Drawing 2: 1—easier, and 2.2—a more complex variant). Such a complex is fulfilled in every training lesson—in the warm-up or in the main portion. Each exercise is fulfilled in series ten times, with a rest between series of from 1.5—2 minutes.

Used in the second stage is an effective complex of exercises united according to the principle that basic exercise for the development of reactive ability is fulfilled in a background of heightened excitability of the central nervous system, brought about by preliminary fulfillment of exercises requiring great power. The complex is composed of the following exercises:

**First Group:**
1. Squats with a partner on the shoulders—ten to twelve times.
2. Squats with the barbell on the shoulders—80 to 90% maximum weight—two to three times.
3. Skips with the barbell on the shoulders—30% maximum weight—eight to ten times.
4. Jumping out with 32 kilogram dumbells—eight to ten times.

**Second Group:**
1. Jumping upward after a leap on both feet, and at the same time reaching for an object hung high—six to eight times.
2. Jumps over five to six barriers, take-off with both legs—two to three times.
3. Five skips on one leg from a five step run—one to two times on each foot.
4. Five to seven take-offs in movement, imitating the take-off in the long jump or in the high jump.

One exercise from each group is included in the complex. For example, at the beginning of the preparatory period, one or two exercises from the first group and one or two exercises from the second group are included. In the middle preparatory period, three or four exercises from the first group and three or four exercises from the second group are included in the complex. The complex is fulfilled from two to five times, depending upon the character of the training. During the rest between repetitions of the complex, exercises for relaxation are fulfilled. These exercise groupings appear as good preparation prior to application of the take-off after the jump in depth for Class I and Master jumpers.

In the limits of this article we can only illuminate the most general and essential details of the strength preparation system conducted over many years and directed to the development of jumping ability. Of course, this is only first, and far from being completed, trial to resolve this long-time urgent problem. Further research in this direction and study of practical trials are needed. This depends upon the resulting work of trainers which will save their students from non-useful and unjustified loss of time and work and will shorten their path to the summit of sports mastery.

(See "Yessis Review of Soviet Physical Education and Sports," Vol. 3, No. 3, pp. 75-78, for additional information on this topic. —Ed.).

# THE MATZDORF WINDMILL

By K. Kerssenbrock and Dr. K. Spilar, Czechoslovakia

While we often hear that techniques in track and field events are already completely developed, top-performances inevitably bring with them some elements which make the previous techniques appear less economical and less effective. As a rule such new elements assert a positive influence only if they are accompanied by a higher level of physical condition—especially of strength, speed and coordination.

In referring to a new style or technique I do not mean only the revolutionary changes—like the Parry O'Brien "back-technique" in shot put or the flop of Dick Fosbury—but also the variations which occur within a well-known style. The stages of development in straddle-technique belong to this latter category. In each of these stages athletes have discovered and overcome limitations in style in order to surpass existing records. Thus in the last 15 years a high speed run-up and strength in the take-off have received most attention. The bar clearance has been recognized as depending naturally on the run-up and take-off. And now arrives the new world-record holder, Pat Matzdorf, who has developed a special straddle-technique, which we propose to discuss here.

In order to better understand this technique a short explanation of biomechanics is necessary. As we see in films of high jumpers, or simply by eye on the track, various rotations are needed if an economical clearance of the bar is to be effected. These rotations may be acquired:

(1) While the athlete is in contact with the ground—a so-called direct rotation. This type of rotation stems from the influence of a lifting force which is directed a little to one side of the CG and is always more or less detrimental to the height attained by the CG. The rotation acquired has a direction like the purpose—leaning back produces a backward rotation and so on.

The athlete's body is able to rotate about three axes which run through his CG. The direction of each axis is constant. The vertical axis coincides with the jumper's longitudinal axis at take-off but in the layout position over the bar the same vertical axis coincides with the jumper's antero-posterior axis. The duration of this kind of direct rotation is infinite—it goes on until changed by another force or, in jumping, until it is stopped by landing. The speed of the rotation may be increased or diminished either by shortening or lengthening of the radius of rotation or by combination with an indirect kind of rotation.

(2) When the athlete is no longer in contact with the ground—a so-called indirect rotation which originates in response or "reaction" to a contrary "action" initiated after the jumper has left the ground. It therefore has no negative effect on the height of the lift. The direction of rotation is contrary to that of the jumper's initial action; the axis of rotation is not constant but passes through the CG; the duration of rotation is equal to that of the action which provoked it; and the amplitude and quickness of the provoking action influences the extent of the rotation.

This explanation is based on Newton's Third Law concerning the action and reaction. If I stand on the ground and make a swing of my right arm around to the left, the swing will turn me to the left, because the reaction was cancelled by the stability of the support. If I make the same motion while in the air, the same swing of the arm will turn me to the right, for the reaction cannot be cancelled in the absence of a supporting surface.

The center of gravity moves in (or beside) the body to accord with the direction of movement of the body parts. This is very important for an understanding of the problem in clearing the bar. Thus every motion of an extremity upwards means also an elevation of CG upwards. However, since the trajectory of the CG during flight is determined at the moment of take-off, an upward motion of an extremity causes a lowering of the general body-mass. Similarly, a downward motion of an extremity causes a raising up of the general body-mass. So there is always an advantage to be gained if a necessary lifting of an extremity during the flight can be compensated by an intentional lowering of another extremity. Now we are able to explain what the high jumpers try to do to restrict their use of direct rotation as much as possible—because it is to the detriment of the take-off-impulse—and to better exploit the take-off. They try to replace the direct rotation by the indirect rotation if possible. Dick Fosbury successfully tried it in his flop and Pat Matzdorf is doing the same thing in his straddle.

Matzdorf's world record is too recent and the development of Matzdorf himself has been too rapid for an analysis to have been made of his technique. We did not find much information about his performance, style and training in the track and field literature. Some details we knew by the kindness of Mr. Fred Wilt, and some others from reading an article by J. Hendershott, quoting observations of Matzdorf's coach, Bill Perrin. Some peculiarities were published in the German journal "Leichtathletik" in 1971. The greatest help for our investigation was a 16 mm film taken at 128 frames per second by Orra D. McMurry, and put at our disposal by Fred Wilt.

The angle from which the film was taken unfortunately did not allow us to determine the stride-lengths or to find the exact frames showing the jumper's CG at the turning point between the supporting-phase and the driving-phase of each stride. In comparing Matzdorf's run-up technique with that of Brumel we must therefore be satisfied with knowing the stride-frequency and the duration of the last two run-up strides. As for their metric length, Matzdorf makes the last stride much longer than the penultimate one, contrary to Brumel who (in his 2.28m leap in 1963) had a penultimate stride of 2.5m and a final stride of only 2.0m. On this important difference depends the quite different take-off preparations of Matzdorf and Brumel. Whereas Brumel's right foot left the ground without the ankle being extended (Fig. 1) Matzdorf's right foot makes a tremendous drive up onto the toes in order to accelerate his CG to a horizontal speed near 7 meters per second (cf. Brumel 7.24 meters per second just before take-off). According to our supposition, Matzdorf accelerates the horizontal speed of his CG from the penultimate to the final stride, while Brumel

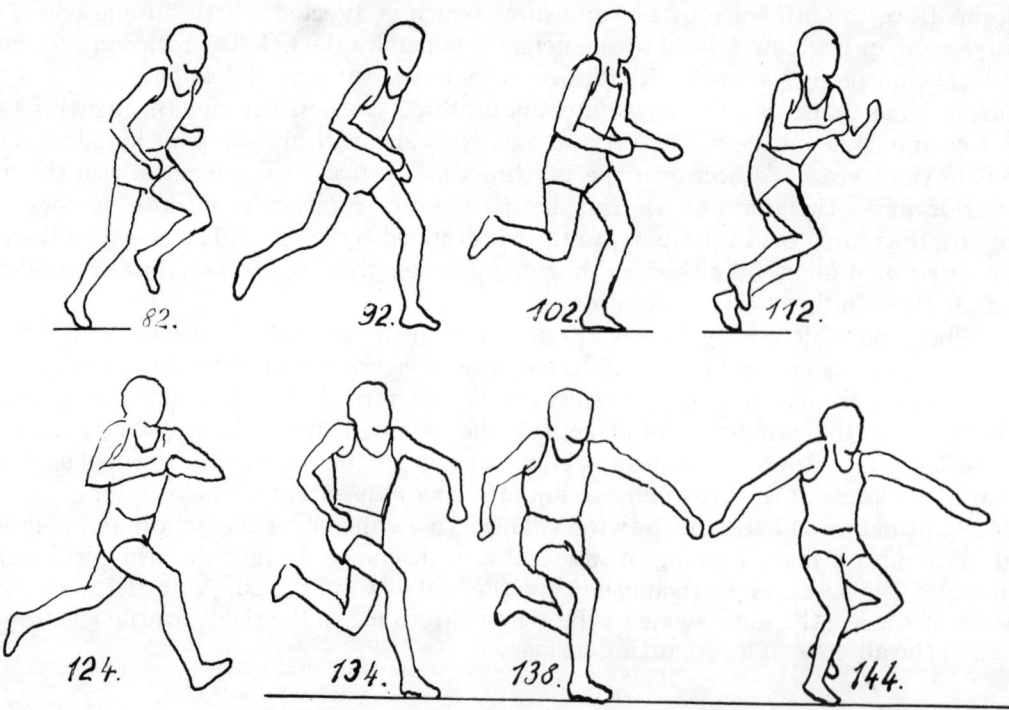

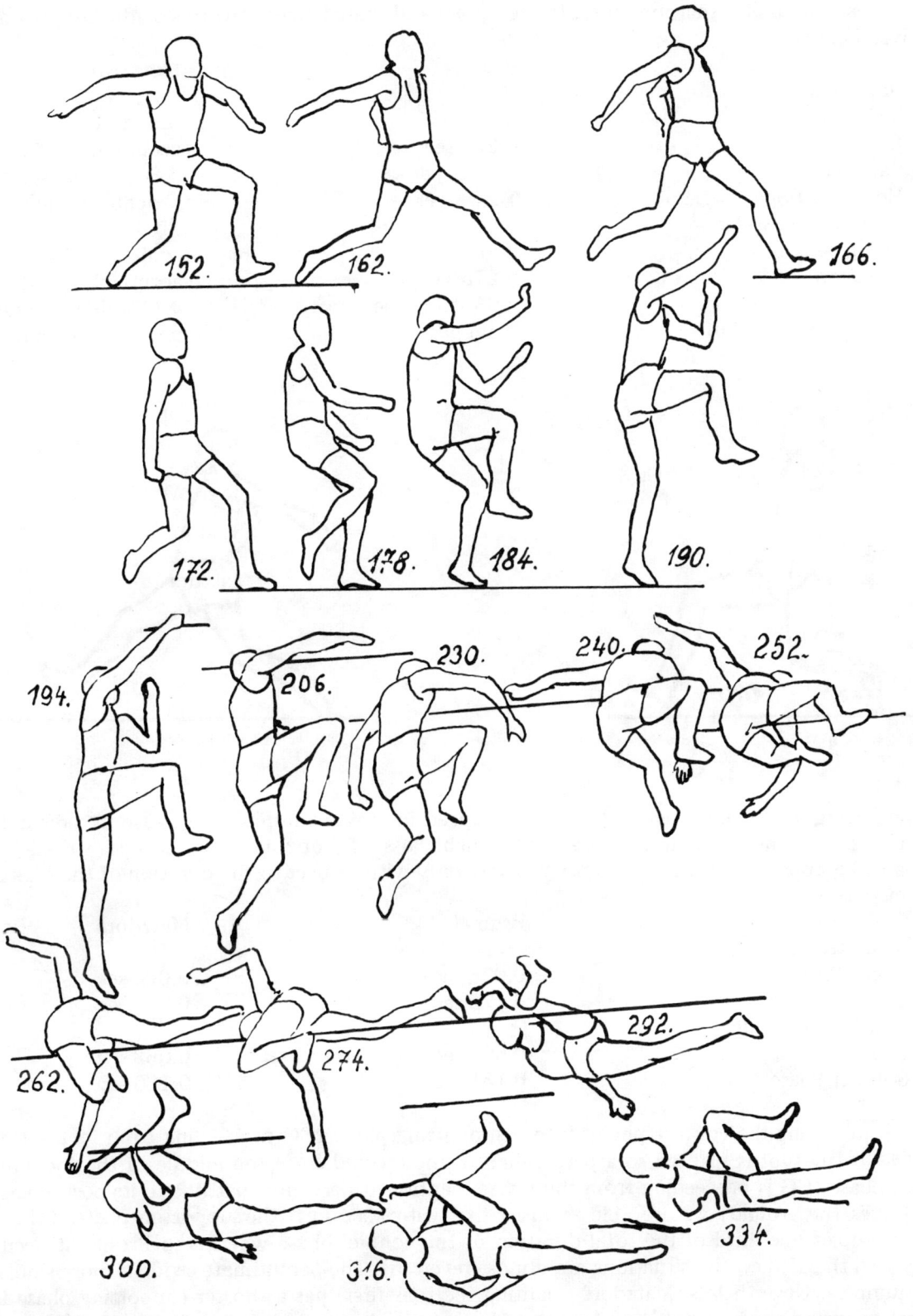

loses 0.26m/per sec from his "speed-provision" of 7.5 meters per second *in moving from the penultimate to the final stride without distinct ankle-drive*. The reader will better appreciate the purpose of these variations by having a brief look at Figs. 1 and 2 showing Brumel and Matzdorf respectively near the end of the driving-phase of the final stride.

The corresponding information about the temporal and spatial characteristics of the last two strides are given below:

|  | **Brumel** | **Matzdorf** |
|---|---|---|
| **The Final Stride:** | | |
| Metric length | 200 cm | probably 193 cm |
| Duration | 0.250 sec | accurately 0.272 sec |
| Cadence | 4 steps per sec | 3.6 steps per sec |
| Horizontal Speed of CG | 7.24m per sec | probably 6.95m per sec |
| **The Penultimate Stride:** | | |
| Metric length | 230 cm | probably 156 cm |
| Duration | 0.275 sec | accurately 0.243 sec |
| Cadence | 3.63 strides per sec | 4.11 strides per sec |
| Horizontal Speed of CG | 7.5m per sec | probably 6.5m per sec |

Fig. 1
Brumel

Fig. 2
Matzdorf

Having determined that Matzdorf's CG speed increased (despite a decrease in cadence) and Brumel's stride-cadence increased (despite a slight loss of horizontal CG speed), we may now compare the approach rhythm but unfortunately only with respect to the duration of the flight and contact phases:

|  | **Brumel** | **Matzdorf** |
|---|---|---|
| **The Final Stride:** | | |
| Flight Phase | 0.078 sec | 0.024 sec |
| Contact Phase | 0.172 sec | 0.248 sec |
| **The Penultimate Stride:** | | |
| Flight Phase | 0.094 sec | 0.063 sec |
| Contact Phase | 0.181 sec | 0.180 sec |

In dividing the contact phases into a supporting phase (CG proceeding from its position at the instant the foot is planted to a perpendicular line erected from the middle of the foot) and a driving phase (CG is proceeding from the above-mentioned perpendicular line to its position as the foot leaves the ground) we are able to insist that with Matzdorf the supporting phase of the final stride occupies one-third of the total duration of the contact-phase whereas in Brumel it occupies nearly two-thirds (i.e., the situations are almost reversed). The penultimate stride is more similar in both jumpers. Nevertheless, Matzdorf (planting the toes first) has a shorter supporting phase than Brumel (planting the heel first). As a result of his planting his feet further in front of his CG, we see an interesting phenomenon in the longer flight phases of Brumel. The planting foot moves backwards a little just before planting and the other foot "tries" to come nearer by the knee of the lead leg being brought towards the other knee as if the jumper desired to alternate his legs in flight. However, Brumel used to do it better in jumps other than in his recently-broken world record and for that reason we preferred the choice of a frame from the film of a former world record of 2.27m set in the autumn of 1962. The most admirable thing is the fast maturing of Matzdorf's approach. What Brumel took many years to perfect Matzdorf found "overnight". However that might be just a bit of good furtune.

The differences in the methods of jumping may be seen in the preparations for the take-off into the last stride—Brumel's right ankle and knee do not extend to push the body from the ground, but rather the right hip extension which thrusts the pelvis forward is entirely responsible for tearing or pulling the right foot from the ground. The extent of this movement of thrusting the pelvis forward is distinctly smaller in Matzdorf and in this lies the origin of the different swing of the lead leg in the subsequent take-off.

Both jumpers use a double arm swing, but in a little different manner. Brumel begins the swing of bent arms a little later in the last stride. Especially in his 2.28m leap he brings the right arm back very late and very little. During the forward swing, the right arm stays bent to 90° at the elbow while the left arm begins slightly bent at the elbow and finishes sharply bent at the elbow with the fist at the height of the chin. Matzdorf brings both arms back while still on his penultimate stride and this undoubtedly involves a certain loss of speed. Because he begins his forward swing from well back and with his right arm quite extended at the elbow, he develops plenty of energy to add to the swing of his bent lead leg. The difference between the bent leg action of Matzdorf and the straight kick-up of Brumel's lead leg is well known. The duration of the take-off of Matzdorf. This shows that the combined effect of the swing of the lead leg and arms is similar in both cases when we know that the only other factor making the take-off "harder" or "stronger," the horizontal speed of the CG, is also similar for both jumpers. The method of the planting the foot (heel first, and knee nearly extended) on the take-off point is the same for both jumpers as too is the immediate planting of the sole of the foot in the next frame of the film (barely .01 sec after the heel plant). Unfortunately it is not possible to distinguish the exact duration of the amortization (or "cushioning") phase of the take-off and the phase of active extension in the take-off. Both best-ever jumps (the 2.28m of Brumel and the 2.29m of Matzdorf) had take-off times of about 0.21 sec and the dividing line between the bending and extending of the knee was probably in the middle of this time. The difference of 0.07 sec between the take-off time for Matzdorf's record jump and that for his 7'2" jump in the same competition seems incredible. The difference between Brumel's longest and shortest take-off time in a competition was never much more than 0.02 sec. No reason was found for Matzdorf's long "sleeping" in his 7'2" take-off (0.28 sec!). However the record jump seemed to have a shorter amortization phase than this long antipode. Yet in this part of the jump—so similar in most of the best performances of each of the two jumpers—Matzdorf brings us a surprise which is difficult to explain. In the succeeding phases he surprises us even more and we must confess we hesitated for many hours over whether the principles of his actions were right or wrong. Finally we became convinced that Matzdorf was technically right and utilized his speed and strength as effectively as possible.

During the take-off Matzdorf naturally had to develop the direct rotation necessary for the later bar clearance. From the angle at which the film was taken it seems reasonable to suggest that he acquired the rotation around the antero-posterior axis and around the vertical axis (his longitudinal axis in the take-off position) and the impulses for them with every consideration for the inevitable loss in lift. The rotation around the antero-posterior axis was established by a slight leaning of his left side towards the bar (which seems, from the angle at which the film was taken, like a small forward-lean at the end of the take-off) and the rotation around his longitudinal axis (his vertical axis at the moment of take-off) was obtained by the dragging of his bent lead-leg swing. He most probably did not establish any rotation around the horizontal axis passing from left to right through his CG (when the jumper is taking-off) but instead obtained the previous two kinds of rotation and was satisfied by the indirect rotation around the horizontal axis from left to right for the difficult bar-clearance.

Matzdorf's unique bar-clearance technique is based on a system of rational movements, in which the upper and lower parts of the body including the extremities succeed each other alternately in their functions. It is almost incredible how rationally Matzdorf makes the preparations necessary to get the job done. The whole trace of his actions reminds us of the function of a wheel and the work of the extended arms looks like the movement of little shovels on a windmill. Every individual rotation is preceded by a contrary rotation, a contrary rotation which permits the possibility of obtaining an even greater rotation than would otherwise be the case (this, in accord with Newton's 3rd Law). Unfortunately it is inevitable that we should express it by an example: to obtain a mighty chop a woodcutter needs a preparatory movement in the opposite direction; in this way the extent of his final action is governed by his previous "stretch-out". The objective in all this is to obtain a wrapping of the body around the bar by provoking an indirect rotation. Matzdorf's efforts in this direction are an unmistakable sign of sparing the direct rotation-impulse at take-off and spending the maximum of the lifting-power on the vertical elevation of his CG.

After being torn from the ground, the take-off leg is correctly allowed to hang for a moment. When the upper body approaches the level of the bar the take-off leg begins to bend at the knee and hip. This lift of a certain part of the body-mass is immediately compensated for by a lowering of the arms—the right arm over the bar, the left arm in front of the bar. The resulting bent body-position accelerates the rotation by shortening the radius and, due to the direct rotation-impulse around the horizontal (antero-posterior) axis the legs approach a horizontal position. It is important to note that the pelvis is rather in a horine-position while the arms are trying to bring the shoulders into extreme torsion so that their axis is perpendicular to the axis of the pelvis (an axis passing through both hip-joints). The bent take-off leg position under the bar—as if the knee were stuck through the vertical plane of the bar—is an inevitable result of this torsion. The pelvis of the jumper is lying on its left side in front of the bar and the shoulders are twisted in a contrary direction behind the bar with the right shoulder behind and below the bar. The arms are stretched out wide and moving like little shovels of a windmill in a clockwise direction; and the body is lying quite horizontally—no diving of the upper body is observed at any point in Matzdorf's jump!!—additional proof of the economical use of leaning to the left at take-off to obtain direct rotation.

The most critical point follows now when the second leg is to be brought over the bar. The action is based on a rapid rotation of the pelvis and a drawing of the left leg, very bent at the knee and hip, over the bar. The rapidity of these actions is tremendously influenced by the contrary motion of Matzdorf's arms, shoulders and the simultaneous lifting of his head and stretching of his lead leg. All the existing "biomechanical means" are exploited to achieve the main task of all, the bar-clearance—or, more specifically, preventing the take-off leg from striking the bar with the inner side of the thigh. However he had a close shave—he touched the bar and it vibrated very dangerously but finally did not fall down.

During the descent the arms continue their action with the left one coming in front of the body while the right one comes close to the right hip and a little behind. The rotation around the longitudinal axis goes on accordingly and the jumper lands on his back. The head, which tends to cross the bar perpendicular to it, comes nearer to the left of the bar than the legs in the landing due to the continued direct rotation around the vertical axis—direct rotation established during the take-off, especially by dragging the right hip forward through the bent lead leg swing. These late upshots of the rotation, which have no effect in deciding the success of the jump, are cancelled by the landing.

In conclusion it is possible to say that Matzdorf's technique is characterized by a full utilization of the lifting forces with the minimum of direct-rotation impulses. In comparison with the technique of Brumel it has considerable advantages in this respect whereas Brumel's technique was excellent above all for the applying of extraordinary strength and speed. Brumel's straight lead leg swing was completely compensated in Matzdorf's jump by a double-arm swing of maximal extent and by a totally extended right arm. Brumel's bar clearance seems to be less complicated and maybe allowed more performances near the limit of Brumel's physical potential. On the other hand, while Matzdorf's technique is very effective it is complicated and requires a full physical and psychical condition. Although the voluntary actions are completed by certain instinctive movements (which must be considered as lucky improvisations) all of these movements are based on rational principles and from the lower heights to top performances vary only in their amplitude. The relative lack of consistency in the young record-holder's performances during last season can be understood in view of the above facts. Unfortunately we cannot be sure about Matzdorf's stride-length and the precise horizontal speed of his CG in the run-up and we would be glad if we could read further contributions by other authors (especially Matzdorf's coach) containing exact information about his fantastic technique. We are afraid our investigation could not avoid errors in view of the limited scope of our information. We rely at this point on the aid of other interested authors.

POLE VAULT                    *Credits*

*Developments in Pole Vaulting,* by Richard V. Ganslen. An extract from a paper presented to the American Association for the Advancement of Science, Dallas, Texas.

*Comparison of Rigid and Flexible Pole Vaulting Technique,* by Kenneth O. Bosen. First publication.

*Teaching Beginners to Vault in Ten Easy Steps,* by Tom Olsen. Reprinted from *Track Technique,* No. 21, September, 1965.

*Some Basic Principles of Fiber Glass Pole Vaulting,* by Denis Watts. Reprinted from *Athletics Weekly,* Vol. 24, No. 11, March 14, 1970.

*Pole Vault Technique,* by Gerhard Jeitner. Originally published in *Die Lehre der Leichtathletik.* This English translation, provided by the College of Artesia, New Mexico, Charles Solberg, Athletic Director, appeared in *Track Technique* No. 28, June, 1967.

*The Keys to Successful Vaulting,* by Walter R. Welsch. First publication.

*Five Serious Misconceptions about the Attributes of Fiberglass Poles,* by George Moore. Reprinted from *Track & Field News,* September, 1971.

*A Summary of Physical and Techical Characteristics of Outstanding Vaulters,* by Pete Boudreaux. First publication.

# DEVELOPMENTS IN POLE VAULTING

By Dr. Richard V. Ganslen, U.S.A., author of "Mechanics of the Pole Vault"

*(This is part of a paper presented to the American Association For The Advancement of Science at Dallas, Texas, entitled, "Scientific Training Techniques and Modern Methods of Track and Field Skill Execution".)*

**Pole Vaulting:** Pole vaulting has benefitted, but hasn't really been revolutionized, by better poles. Better poles were introduced in 1855 when the bamboo pole was first tried. No doubt, some track buff predicted a sensational change in vaulting records at that date, but it took another 30 years to get the record much past the 9 foot vaults reported by Guts Muths in 1792. Hugh Baxter, a huge man, was the first future national champion to use the bamboo pole which he discarded immediately, perhaps because of his size. He used to enjoy talking about the English pole climbers who used very heavy poles weighted at the bottom end like ash trays to clear 11-12 feet. When the movement of the upper hand was eliminated from pole vaulting, pole climbing was eliminated.

In the 1930's an aluminum alloy pole was invented, but its lack of elasticity eliminated it from contention with the bamboo pole used until the end of World War II. In 1946 the writer began testing a new steel pole manufactured in Sweden which, with its American counterpart, remained popular until the early 1960's. The fact that Don Bragg broke not less than 15 of these poles attests to the fact that they were far from perfect. In 1948 the writer tried to explain the pole dilemma in an article for a national sports magazine entitled, "The Pole Makes the Vaulter." It is sometimes quite astonishing for many uninformed track enthusiasts to learn that the fiberglass pole was produced for pole vaulters in 1948! The fundamental difference in techniques utilizing the fiberglass v.s. steel poles was described by Ralph Higgins and the writer in 1960. According to Browning Arms Corp., manufacturers of the Silaflex Pole, this article produced a vertical line on their sales charts thereafter.

SENSATIONAL or a SENSATION: One of the most devastating kinesthetic sensations associated with fiberglass pole vaulting is that terrible sinking sensation one experiences when the fiberglass pole bends. The sensation is drastic enough to markedly affect the confidence and timing of the vaulter, particularly if he learned to vault on a steel vaulting pole. The fiberglass pole bends 100-110 degrees in .256 of a second after foot contact with the ground is lost. To overcome this psychological problem, Bill Perrin invented a device to simulate the "pole sink", and this device is now widely marketed.

Pound for pound, pole vaulters are the strongest, most agile and highly coordinated athletes on the athletic field. Pole vaulters have been world ranking decathlon athletes—Richards, 26 foot broad jumpers, Meyers of Colorado, 6 foot 7 inch high jumpers like Guinn Smith and Boo Morcom, 9.7 sprinters, Pemelton, Hansen, and Morcom, champion divers, hurdlers, triple jumpers, football players, gymnasts, and javelin throwers. Houvion of France, 5'9" and 160 pounds, routinely presses 200 pounds, snatches 230 pounds, and cleans and jerks over 250 pounds. Dave Tork, slightly under six feet tall and weighing 155 pounds, and the first man in history to vault 16 feet outdoors, could do a bend-arm pull over while lying on the floor *with 300 pounds.* One does not easily run a 10.5 hundred while carrying a 17 foot pole weighing 7 pounds with 15 feet of the pole extended in front of the body without strength. Modern pole vaulters, in addition to their sprint and endurance training, spend many hours lifting weights. The weightlifting is often supplemented with gymnastics to preserve flexibility and develop timing.

*Pole vaulting poles do not have any energy in them* that is not created by the vaulter during the course of his plant and take-off and which derives from his run. The principal advantage of the fiberglass pole is that it permits the vaulter to hold one foot to 18 inches higher on the pole at the moment of take-off and with some vaulters holding two feet higher than they could have held on a steel pole. The use of the super flexible poles was introduced by Sueo Ohe of Japan in the 1936 Olympic Games and used by him consistently in Madison Square Garden in 1937 to exceed fourteen feet.

The greatest problem, *always*, in the pole vault, is to get the pole into the box smoothly while running at top speed without having the pole torn out of the vaulter's hands. AFTER 15 YEARS OF DILIGENT PRACTICE, CORNELIUS WARMERDAM WAS ABLE TO SUCCESSFULLY HOLD THE POLE AT APPROXIMATELY 13 FEET 9 INCHES AND ACHIEVE 15 FEET 7½ INCHES IN THE POLE VAULT. Today, school boys, after one year of practice, routinely hold the pole at 14 feet and champions hold the pole over 15 feet from its bottom end with their top hand. A hand grip on the pole in excess of 13 feet two or three inches was considered quite sensational on a steel vaulting pole and most vaulters could seldom exceed 12 feet 8-9 inches. The high grip on the pole is only possible because the pole bends so terrifically upon impact with the box and permits a smooth transfer of linear to angular moment. Thus, the modern vaulter does less work at the start of the vault and more work at the terminus of the vault than his predecessor. Pole vaulting poles always bent a lot, but often after the vaulter was in mid-air, and their snap-back was quite rapid and invisible to the naked eye. Spectators like fiberglass pole vaulting because, perhaps, they subconsciously hope that the pole will break. One modern vaulter and world record holder has broken as many as 15 fiberglass poles in a season, a not-inexpensive indulgence with poles at $50-$60 each.

Two modern innovations in vaulting are the *elimination of the hand shift* of the pole, to facilitate the bending of the pole, and *$600 polyvinyl foam rubber landing mats*, to absorb the landing shock. Today, the vaulter need not concern himself with how he is going to land before he leaves the ground, a problem of some concern when a pile of wet sand was usually considered adequate. A number of back injuries in recent years may be due to this casual approach to landing or the poor distribution of the work in pulling with one over-extended arm.

# COMPARISON OF RIGID AND FLEXIBLE POLE VAULTING TECHNIQUE

By Kenneth O. Bosen, former Olympic Coach of India

## INTRODUCTION

Briefly, the problem in this event is to be able to get one's self off the ground and over a high cross bar with the aid of a pole.

The use of various types of vaulting poles has greatly influenced the emphasis of technique in vaulting. As far back as 1855 vaulters used heavy wooden poles with metal tripods at the end to assist them in clearing heights up to ten feet. Some years later the bamboo pole came into use and remained in top class competitions for many years. Warmerdam of USA cleared 15'7¾" in 1942 using a semi-flexible bamboo pole. About this time sports goods manufacturers started experimenting with the manufacturing of light-weight aluminum poles. By 1947 the Swedish steel pole came into popularity, but the lighter weight aluminum poles continued to be in use all over the world.

Actually the present-day pole made of Fibre-glass was used by vaulters as early as 1948. The Fibre-glass pole of those early days was not very dependable, since it broke very easily. This lead to its being discarded by most vaulters. About 1954 two famous American vaulters, Dooley and Uelses, used specially prepared Fibre-glass poles which gave vaulting its much needed impetus. This stimulated the manufacturers to start experimenting and produce better, more flexible, and lighter poles. As a result of this experimentation and the acceptance of this Fibre-glass pole by the I.A.A.F. we today find many supper flexible Fibre-flass poles in use which has resulted in vaults over 17 feet, and one over 18 feet at this writing.

## SELECTING A POTENTIAL VAULTER

A good pole vaulter is usually an above average all-around athlete. This event requires very good all-around physical ability and conditioning. The stress on speed, strength, endurance and coordination are important factors for successful vaulting. But the dexterity and coordination of a gymnast is a necessary qualification in order to perform the complicated sequence of movements that are executed during a vault.

Since the introduction of the Fibre-glass pole with its extreme flexibility and particular characteristics, the need for tall persons to take up this event is no longer a must. The more rigid metal poles require tall persons to take to the event since the advantage of height increases the pendulum action of the suspended body on the moving pole, emphasizing a long pendular swing phase. The flexible Fibre-glass pole, has now made way for even short persons to achieve championship class vaults.

The long pendular swing hardly exists any longer. Emphasis is now placed on a short swing-up phase, which gives the compact type of vaulter a chance to excel.

## BASIC FUNDAMENTAL PRINCIPLES

(a) **Building an unstable body momentum.**

The establishment of momentum by a well graduated approach run provides a supplementary force to the force of the vaulter at the take-off and remaining phases of the vault.

(b) **Changing of this horizontal momentum to a vertical direction.**

The momentum of the approach run is changed angularly into height by the use of the vaulting pole, which is planted at the end of the run-up into the vaulting box for the take-off.

(c) **The coordination of body momentum with body force.**

This refers to the use of the vaulting pole with its end in the box as the muscular force of the vaulter is applied at the take off on completion of a smooth shift, plant and take off with a minimum loss of speed.

(d) **The efficient use of the resulting impetus to achieve the desired results:**

The forces combined at the take off are efficiently used in a vault only when pole momentum is maintained to its maximum. It is with attempting to achieve this that the actual technique of vaulting is largely concerned.

## THE ESSENTIALS OF CORRECT FORM (FOR RIGHT HANDED VAULTERS)

(a) **The Hold and Pole Carry.** The manner in which the pole is carried influences the speed of the approach run by as much as a 0.1 second for 50 ft. Therefore, it becomes necessary that the vaulter carry the pole in a comfortable manner so that it does not interfere with the normal rhythm of running.

For a right handed vaulter the pole is usually held with the left hand in front of the body, holding the pole with palm facing downward. In other words, the left hand acts as a fulcrum and holds the pole lightly while pressure is applied with the right hand, which is behind the body, towards the top end of the pole.

The left arm is flexed at right angles and holds the pole loosely away from the body. The fore-hand is usually nearly parallel to the ground with the wrist held straight, not cocked. The right hand, which is toward the rear or top of the pole, holds the pole mainly by the space between the inverted thumb and forefinger, which presses downward on the pole. The elbow forms an approximate angle of 100 degrees. Both the front and rear elbow angles depends largely on the extent of the hand spread on the pole as well as the angle of pole carry.

The hand-spread on the pole is usually what determines the comfort of the pole carry. If the hands are spread too wide it makes the shift difficult, though the pole itself feels lighter during the carry. If the spread is too small, control of the pole is difficult though the shift may be through a smaller range on the pole.

Usually the spread of the hands on pole is between 24 to 36 inches. This again is directly related to the comfort of the carry and the height and the angle of the pole in the approach.

Basically there are three angles of pole carry.

(i) **The high carry:** In this method the tip of the pole is above head height. The acute angle made by the pole brings the common center of gravity of the pole and vaulter closer to the medial plane. Thus the pole feels lighter. This affords a closer hand-spread than is normal. The main objection of this type of carry is that the height of the tip of the pole causes the need for exceptional timing in the shift and plant.

(ii) **The medium carry:** This is the most widely used and recommended method of carry by most vaulters. The tip of the pole is usually at about head height and directly opposite the left shoulder. This makes the pole appear almost cross-wise from right to left shoulder in the carry. This position permits the shoulders to remain square to the front and is conducive to shoulder and arm relaxation in the approach.

(iii) **The low carry:** This is the least used type of carry since the low position of the pole forces a wide hand spread and makes the shift and plant difficult to execute. The low position of the pole causes the pole to feel heavier and may therefore result in tension of the upper body, thus hindering the speed of the approach.

Among champion vaulters, the pole is usually carried initially in a high position. After the vaulter has accelerated to a certain extent, the tip of the pole gradually lowers to the medium carry position. This method is widely used among experienced vaulter who can control the pole well. The method of pole carry, like the other aspects, of form in vaulting, is an individual skill that is modified to suit the particular vaulter. Morcom of the USA used a pole carry in which the pole was straight up for most of the run-up. Bob Richards used a carry in which the pole was almost horizontal for most of the run-up. Laz of the USA carried the pole across the runway.

These individual aspects of form do not differ from the fundamental fact that the vaulter must coordinate the work of holding and carrying the pole with the rear hand, and allow the left hand to do the minimum work possible in this respect. If the grip of the left hand is over-emphasized, the vaulter will experience difficulty in shifting the hand during the plant. Furthermore, gripping with the left hand indicates that either the angle of carry and hand-spread are not correct or that the pole is too heavy for the particular individual.

(b) **The Approach Run.**

(i) **The starting position:** The importance of developing a uniform starting method for each run-up cannot be over-emphasized. If a vaulter is not consistent in his starting method there will be considerable variation of the starting strides, which in turn will lead to difficulty in arriving at the take-off correctly.

Generally, the best basic starting position is to toe the starting mark with both feet slightly apart. With the pole in its carrying position, lean forward from the ankles in a controlled loss of balance, thus forcing a high knee pick-up and acceleration.

The length of the run and the number of over-all strides used determines which leg has to be brought forward for the first stride. For an even-stride approach, the jumper must take the first step with the right foot if his left leg is the take-off leg. An athlete using an odd number of strides is required to start with his take-off foot for the first stride.

(ii) **Speed and length of run-up:** The length of the run in vaulting is of no particular consequence, but the character of the run is vital to successful vaulting. The vaulter's run must be powerful yet smoothly accelerated. The run shall be long enough to permit the vaulter to reach top speed seven strides before the take-off yet not so long that the vaulter begins to decelerate at the take-off. Preussger of Germany used a run of only 98 ft. to vault 15'9½" whereas Tork of the USA used a run of 152 ft. to clear over 16 ft. The factor which determines the length of a run are the vaulters' reaction time and ability to accelerate within a given distance.

The emphasis in approach speed must always be on the use of maximum controllable speed and not simply on maximum. Generally speaking, beginners tend to run too far and too fast, making coordination difficult due to the low height of the bar and fast speed of the approach. The most important single factor in the run is what a vaulter does with his speed after he gets to the vaulting box for the take-off and not how fast he is en route to the take-off.

(iii) **General aspects of the run-up:**

(a) The length of the run does not determine the ability of the vaulter to vault high. It is the ability to use whatever speed he has gained from the run-up in the actual take-off that really matters.

(b) The vaulter must not concentrate on accelerating to build up speed right up to the time of the take off.

(c) The last three or four strides are almost flat-footed and the vaulter is nearly erect during the shift and plant.

(d) Due to the brief period of preparation before the take-off the last stride may be slightly shorter than the preceding one.

(e) In order to bring the body-weight over the take-off foot, vaulters sometimes toe out on the next to last stride at the take-off.

(f) An off-balanced vault is usually attributed to a failure of the vaulter to shift his weight on to his take-off leg.

(g) Vaulters using a fiber-glass pole must maintain a consistent hand grip and approach speed in order to get a consistent bend in the pole.

(h) Use of a smooth, powerful and controlled run. Do not punch the pole back and forth in the run. Rhythm in the run-up comes from the shoulders and not a back and forth jabbing of the pole.

1. The final two approach strides and pole plant.

## SHIFT AND POLE PLANT

There is nothing that is more significant to determine the success or failure of a vault than a smooth and efficient pole plant. The factors influencing a successful pole plant are not too difficult to enumerate. The plant should be early,—easy, smooth, forceful and in the right direction. No amount of time devoted to perfecting a good plant is ever wasted.

The trend of teaching vaulting when using a *rigid* pole is to shift the hands as close together on the pole as possible. When both hands are close together on the pole there is a better distribution of the work done by the arms, resulting in better pushing power and reach over the cross bar. Furthermore, to aid the leverage of the pole to the vertical, the long arm position with hands closed together gives a longer pendular swing of the body, which conserves the angular momentum of the rigid pole.

The present-day trend is to keep the hand slightly apart on the fibre-glass pole. The vaulter does not shift the hands completely. Those who use the fiber-glass pole claim that they get better balance and pressure distribution when their hands are spread over a wider area on the pole, which in turn gives a certain leverage to create a pole bend. Fibre-glass vaulters claim the hand spread also helps them to get a consistently deep bend on the pole, which is not possible when the hands are completely shifted. All fiber-glass vaulters, however, do not agree on the necessity for a wide spread of the hands to get a deep bend of the pole. Some feel that perhaps the inconsistency of the flexible nature of the pole is more at fault than the vaulter's form. However, a wide hand-spread is used by almost all fiber-glass vaulters.

However, irrespective of the type of hand-spread used by vaulters using rigid or flexible poles, the technique of planting the pole remains almost the same. For practical purposes the pole plant may be divided into three types—under-hand, modified or side-arm, and over-head. A pole plant is seldom purely over-head or under-hand. It is usually the modified or side-arm type that is most commonly used.

The pole plant should be started when the vaulter approaches within one and a half or two strides before the take-off. The shift, if present, and the plant must be completed before the take-off leg is grounded for the take-off actions. It is of vital importance to get the pole into the box before the take-off foot grounds. The action of planting the pole in the box must not slow down the run and upset the balance of the vaulter.

During the approach run the vaulter must watch the box at all times and must reach forward with the pole to an optimum extent to contact the box. Reaching out early for the box will feel awkward for the inexperienced vaulter. Once the feel of getting set on the pole with plenty of time for the take-off is experienced, the shift, plant and take-off actions will become more efficient.

## TYPES OF POLE PLANTS

(i) **Under-hand plant:** In this type the rear hand comes through very low, almost level with the right hip. It may be described as an under-hand scooping motion. The right hand must pass very close to and almost touch the right hip. All the work of planting the pole in any style of plant originates with the rear hand.

The shoulders must be kept square to the pit at all times during the approach and plant. If they twist to the right to make the plant, it clearly indicates that the plant was started too late. The principle emphasis on the under-hand plant is that all the motion of planting the pole is upward in coordination with the swing from the take-off leg.

(ii) **The modified or side-arm plant:** In this method, upsetting the vaulter's balance at take-off may easily occur. In order to execute this type of plant, there is usually a tendency to throw the pole out to the side as it passes the body in making the plant. The rear hand usually passes the body at a point between hip and shoulder level in this method. Loss of balance is a consequence of a poor pole plant. It is therefore necessary for the coach to stand in front or directly behind when a vault is being made in order to check on the alignment of both the pole and the take-off foot during the shift and plant.

(iii) **Over-head plant:** This method has gained popularity as a direct consequence of the fiber-glass pole. Vaulters using this method claim that they get a better bend in the pole and more leverage. For consistency in the pole plant and to bend the pole more effectively, the over-head plant has certain advantages. This plant works well for some vaulters because the angle at take-off for a flexible pole is more forward and a flatter swing takes place. In other words, the shock of planting the pole in this manner (which, in the case of top class vaulting, is nearly 1000 lbs. pressure) is absorbed by the flexibility of the pole and less of it by the vaulter's arms and shoulders than is the case with a rigid pole.

(iv) **Establishing the take-off point:** Though it is possible to locate the take-off point from a stationary position, this is not the true take-off mark simply because it is measured from a static position. The location of the true take-off point can only be determined from examining a number of successful vaults. In other words, the true take-off point is not static but dynamic, because as the speed of the run increases, the take-off point may alter somewhat accordingly. Only if a vaulter uses the same grip and runs at the same speed for every successive vault can the take-off point remain absolutely constant.

If there is a big variation in the take-off point on successive vaults it will upset the vaulter's timing entirely. If the take-off is too far away from the box it will cause the vaulter to swing down or drag his hips at the take-off. If it is too close, there will be a jerk at take-off which will cause the grip to slip on the pole. Especially with the rigid pole, a close take-off may be disastrous.

Because fiber-glass vaulters use a wide hand-spread, the true take-off point will not be under the top hand, which is normal for the rigid pole, but at some point between the lower and upper hand-grips, since they remain spread apart on the pole. That is to say, the top hand will be above and actually behind the head, while the true take-off point will fall perpendicularly between both hands down though to the vaulter's take-off foot. Competent vaulters have been known to adjust to takeoffs as much as one foot in front of and behind this point and still complete successful vaults.

## FACTORS AFFECTING HEIGHT OF HAND-GRIP

(i) **The rigid Pole:** If a vaulter grips too high on the pole it is difficult to lever the pole to the verticle due to the increased distance of the suspended weight of the body away from the fulcrum of the box. If the grip is too low for a particular height to be vaulted, it causes too fast a swing and therefore leaves no time for coordinating the other parts of the vault. There are many factors influencing the height of the grip on the pole, some of them are as follows:—

(a) **Speed:**— In general, if all other things are equal the faster the approach the higher can be the grip on the pole. If this increased speed is properly coordinated at take-off it will help to lever the pole to the vertical in spite of a higher hand grip.

(b) **Strength (Power):**— Strength (the ability to exert force) and power (rate of work or force x velocity) are important factors because it takes considerable power to change horizontal momentum of the approach to a vertical direction through the medium of the take-off and pole.

(c) **Coordination:**— Coordination and good timing help to overcome the shock of the pole hitting the vaulting box, besides being of great assistance in linking the speed of approach with the forces of take-off.

(d) **Height of the vaulter:**— The taller vaulter has the advantage of a higher reach over a shorter vaulter who has the same speed and strength characteristics. For a rigid pole, a taller vaulter with a higher grip will have a longer pendular swing, which is a definite mechanical advantage.

(e) **The method of pole shift and plant:**— The method of pole shift and plant may also influence the height of the hand grip. A well-executed shift and plant gives greater speed force conversion at the take-off and thus influences the height of gripping the pole.

Starting from the beginner stage we normally find that the top hand-grip is about 2 feet above the cross bar, while there is no shift of the hand when the pole is planted. As strength, technique and experience are gained, the grip is gradually lowered to a level with the cross-bar and then gradually down to a point about 2 feet below the cross bar. For example, normally if the height of the cross-bar is ten feet the hand-grip on the pole will be the same as the cross-bar. If the height of the cross-bar is below ten feet, the hand-grip height may be about one foot above the cross-bar. If the height of cross-bar is above 10 feet 6 inches the hand-grip would normally be about one foot below the cross-bar. C. Warmerdam of USA used a grip of 13 feet, 11 inches to vault 15 feet 8½ inches. This is a difference of 1 foot 9½ inches between the height of hand-grip and cross-bar. Bob Richards also of US used a 13 foot 6 inch grip to clear 15 feet 6 inches giving him a difference of about 2 feet. In a study by Warmerdam comparing the height of the vaulter and the height of hand-grip on the pole with that of the height of the cross-bar it was found that men under 6 feet used an average grip of about 13 feet 4½ inches while men over 6 feet used an approximate grip of 12 feet 8¼ inches. This is with reference to rigid poles *only*.

(ii) **Flexible Pole:**— Every known fiber-glass vaulter reports the use of higher hand grips than do rigid pole vaulters. Warmerdam's hand-grip of 13 feet 11 inches on a bamboo pole is a noteworthy performance as compared to the hand-grips used by famous metal pole vaulters such as Don Bragg and Richards who used hand-grips of 13 feet 6 inches to vault under 16 feet. As compared to the vaulter of the rigid pole era, fiber-glass vaulters such as Tork used a 13 foot grip on a metal pole and after shifting to a fiber-glass pole was able to increase his hand-grip to 14 feet 6 inches and later to 15 feet 2 inches. The use of grips over 14 feet with flexible poles is today as common as the use of a 12 foot 6 inch grip on rigid poles.

The reason for such increased height in hand-grips is obviously due to the extreme bend of the pole, which reduces the radius of the true axis of the pole by as much as 2 feet at takeoff, thereby making it possible to maintain and change the horizontal speed of the run-up and gain efficient leverage of the pole to the vertical.

## ESTABLISHMENT OF APPROACH CHECK-MARKS

After having made a number of successful vaults and the approximate take-off point has been located, the next step is to establish check-marks (if necessary) near the starting end of the run-up. It is necessary to bear in mind that having check marks placed close to the take-off point is not desirable because the vaulter has enough to do during the crucial last steps without considering check-marks. Vaulters using approaches measuring over 120 feet usually have one check-mark about 8 to 10 strides from the starting mark. Any subsequent check-marks used should be located well away from the take-off area.

## THE ACTION OF THE TAKE-OFF

A vaulter's aim is to gain height through the use of speed in the approach and the pole at the take-off. He must never forget that he is trying to change the linear momentum of the approach run into angular momentum for height. Therefore, in order to effect change of direction of the body, a certain amount of force must be used. For this purpose the present day vaulters use a forward-upward spring at the take-off, rather than a prolonged swing with the pole as was advocated when rigid poles were in use.

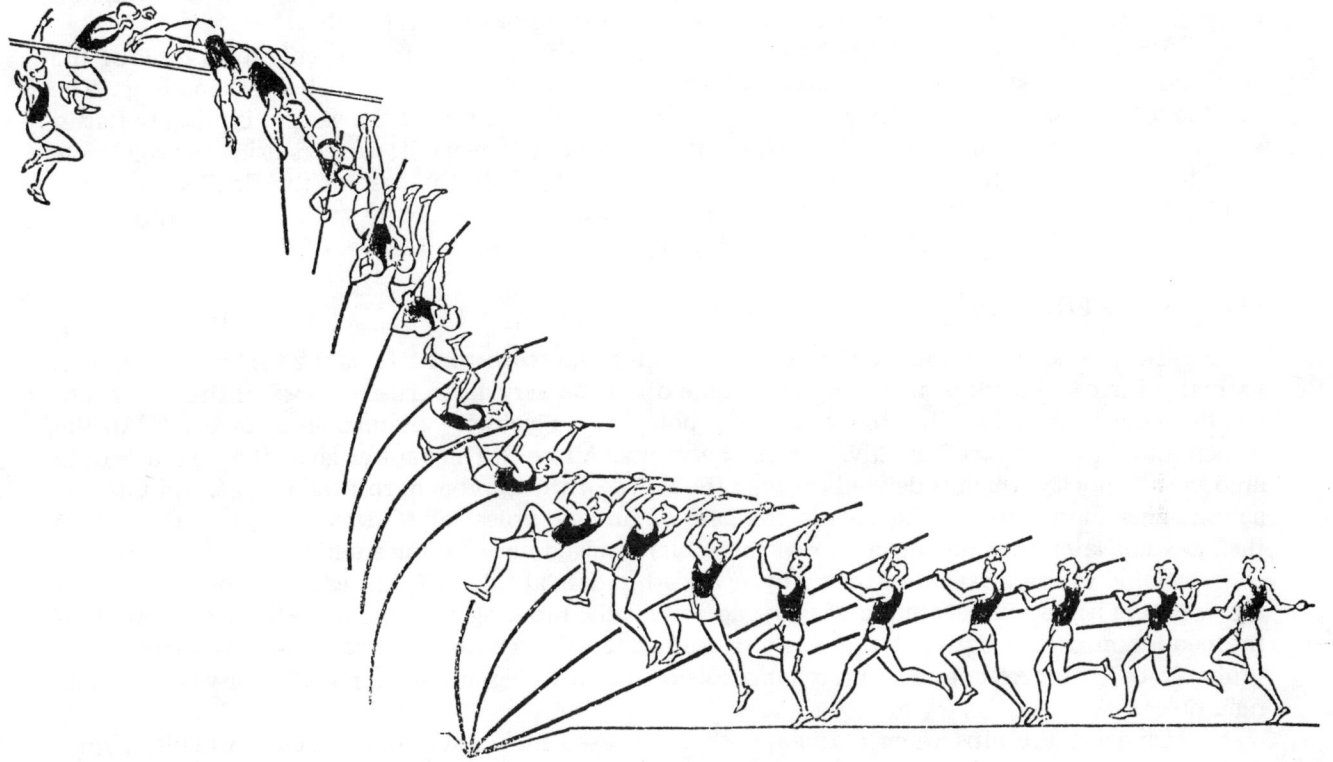

2. The complete vaulting action

Vaulters using rigid poles must accentuate the actions of the lead leg in a vigorous high knee pick up and drive. The faster the run-up, the more the stress on the lead leg action. The extent of the swing can be controlled to a large degree by properly using the free leg at the take-off and immediately after. In order to get a longer swing the knee of the leading leg is driven vigorously up and forward. If the swing is to be shortened, the knee motion is not accentuated but is given its optimum lift at the take-off, before an early swing-up begins.

The action of the take-off leg and foot plant are identical to that of long jumping. The exception here is the need for a precise alignment of the take-off foot and pole in the box, since it is a vital factor in conservation of the take-off forces as well as the balance of the total vault.

Vaulters using the fiber-glass pole have a more complicated action to deal with at take-off. Due to the flexibility of the pole, the initial take-off action is a drive forward toward the back of the pit as the pole begins its big bend. In order to stay behind the pole and not lose control of the bend, the vaulter must shorten the body pendulum quickly, drawing the legs up into a "Kip-up" position. In other words, the action of the lead leg is such that it sweeps forward-upwards as in long jumping, but does not continue upward until the take-off leg also catches up with it. All this happens in one smooth motion, so as to avoid any drag of the hips and especially the take-off leg.

When using a rigid pole the swing is prolonged after the take-off, and the swing up action is delayed since the body, which is kept long, keeps pace with the movement of the pole. With a fiber-glass pole, the body will tend to rush ahead of the true axis of the pole unless the vaulter does something to control it. The bringing in of the legs into a "Kip-up" position is therefore the key element to control the speed of the body moving forward in relation to that of the flexed pole's reduced axis.

The principle contradiction of actions at the take-off when using a fiber-glass pole is that in order to make the pole bend the vaulter must drive hard toward the back of the pit but then once the pole bends and the vaulter leaves the ground he must compensate for the hard forward drive by staying behind the pole so as to prevent too much linear momentum from causing him to swing past the pole's true axis too quickly and thereby upset the timing of the total vault.

Vaulters using a rigid pole have a steeper take-off angle due to the centrifugal force of the swing and the resistance of the vaulter which is exerted through his arm being kept long. The flexible fiber-glass pole bends at the take-off so that the flight curve of the vaulter is initially flatter as compared with the stiff pole. Conversely, at the climax of the vault, vaulters using the rigid pole have to work harder to keep the pole moving to the vertical. In the case of the flexible pole, the vaulter is already in position to complete the vaulting action, but merely waits for the whip-out or catapult action of the pole, thereby taking advantage of the speed and thrust of the pole.

## THE SWING PHASE

The average duration of the swing phase for vaults up to 14 ft. is 0.24 of a second. This naturally forces all actions after the actual take-off to be very fast. The purpose of the swing is to get the pole into motion for the vault. The pole has no velocity of its own at take-off. All the velocity that the pole gets is driven from the vaulter himself. The vaulter gives the pole a certain amount of velocity which is derived through the speed of the approach, shift and plant, and take-off action, plus the flexion of the pole in the case of flexible poles. This stored energy in the pole is then at some later stage (at the climax of the vault) received back by the vaulter.

Some vaulters execute a swing by using a hip drag at take-off through delaying the take-off leg. Vaulters using this technique of swing agree that the hip drag adds significantly to the length of the pendulum of the body. If there is any gain, it may be with short vaulters. The swing could probably be better executed by more emphasis on the lead leg action, especially for vaulters using rigid poles.

Dragging the hips when a fiber-glass pole is used makes successful vaults difficult. With a flexible pole the swing is very short and fast and the body pendulum tends to rush past the pole's true axis very quickly. Therefore, to prevent loss of control of the body, due to the short duration and high velocity of the swing, it is necessary to get into a swing-up position as quickly as possible. Dragging the hips makes this quick swing-up in fiber-glass vaulting most difficult.

## FACTORS CONTROLLING THE SWING IN FIBER-GLASS VAULTING

The first factor is the stiffening of the left arm at the take-off or immediately thereafter. This is made easy due to the hand-spread and particularly due to the lower hand position on the pole. It is not absolutely necessary to use this method alone, but some top-class fiber-glass vaulters have found this technique of stiffening the lower arm to be effective in stopping the forward momentum of the body so that it does not swing past the true axis of the pole too early. In so doing, the burden of supporting the swing and the weight of the body is placed upon the top hand-grip. This makes it necessary to have well developed arms and shoulders to withstand the strain and shock which is involved in suddenly stiffening one arm while allowing the other arm to support the entire weight of the body.

The second controlling factor is the rapid lift of the take-off leg, which is sometimes termed as the left lead-leg action (for right-handed vaulters). This left lead-leg action has two positive effects. Firstly, it prevents the hips from dragging in the swing, and secondly, it helps the vaulter to get into an early "rock back" positions. Since both legs are used to swing up, it helps to bring the hips up quickly and not drag them. Furthermore, the fast lift of the take-off leg also helps to keep the centre of gravity close to the true axis of the pole.

When using a rigid pole, the optimum delay of the swing phase keeps the pole going up to the vertical much easier. The rock-back is therefore slightly later but of equal importance to a successful vault. With a flexible pole the true axis of the pole is not in the same position as that of the rigid pole. Therefore, the early rock-back action does not have as much tendency to stop the forward speed of the pole as it would be in the case of a rigid pole.

3. Takeoff point in relation to hand-grip.

## IMPORTANT POINTS RELATED TO THE ROCK-BACK PHASE OF THE FIBER-GLASS POLE

The following points are a summary of the vaulting technique with a flexible pole:—

(i) The initial bend of the pole depends upon the amount of the handspread after the shift (if any) and plant, together with a stiffening of the lower arm in order to help to maintain the bend of the pole.

(ii) There must be specific emphasis devoted to lifting both legs in the rock-back phase.

(iii) The rock-back and lift of the legs helps to lift the hips and thereby brings the centre of gravity under the hand-grip.

(iv) A back head drop will help materially to achieve a better rock-back action but this is difficult to perform if the vaulter does not time the action of pulling so that it is as late as possible in coordination with the catapult action of the pole.

(v) In order to use a fast and hard rock back on the pole it is much easier and faster to bend both the knees and hips together into a "Kip-up" position.

(vi) The vaulter must not pull up with the arms during the rock-back action. Any pull that is exerted by the arms at this stage will cause an exaggerated bend in the pole which will have the tendency to stop the forward speed of the pole.

(vii) The natural resistance of the stiffened left arm to prevent the body from rushing forward after the take-off causes an exaggerated bend in the pole which will bend still further due to the hard rock-back action.

## TIMING THE PULL AND TURN

Due to the early rock-back action a vaulter using a flexible pole must remain on his back longer than a vaulter using the prolonged swing action and short, fast rock up action of a rigid pole. Due to the lack of whip the stiff pole causes the vaulter to speed up the rock up action in coordination with the pull and turn. But with a flexible pole the vaulter must wait for the pole to begin its straightening-out action before he begins to pull and turn.

If the vaulter pulls on the pole when it is in its deep bend phase, the pull that is exerted will cause a further bend. The force of the pull will stop the forward speed of the pole too early. With more rigid poles (including poles that bend slightly) the straightening action of the pole is very fast and forceful and as such any early pulling efforts on the pole do not spoil the pole's speed altogether.

No matter what type of pole is used, once the pull is started it must be of maximum effort and as directly parallel to the long axis of the pole as possible. For fiber-glass vaulters, the force of the pull-up gives them a shooting-up action with legs first, straight up into the air without turning. The rigid pole forces the vaulter to turn his legs in coordination with the pulling action of the arms so that the action of the lead leg is a twisting up-shoot over the cross bar as the turn is being made.

The action of shooting over the cross-bar is more or less a forward-upward whip-out action in the case of a flexible pole, whereas with the rigid pole the final thrust is more or less only upward due to the timing of the vigorous two hand push-up on the pole. If a vaulter using a flexible pole turns face downwards too soon, he will fly into the cross-bar since the straightening flip of the pole will thrust him into a forward direction and not upward and forward.

With a flexible pole the action of the pull must begin as the pole straightens. Therefore the reaction of the pulling force exerted by the vaulter will be greater than if the vaulter were pulling on a rigid pole. In this way the vaulter takes back the energy he gave to the pole at the take-off and in so doing gets a sensation of being catapulted into the air.

With a rigid pole this catapulting action is not present due to the lack of pole flexion. For rigid poles the pull-turn and shoot over the bar are started sooner and coordinated with the general over-all action of the vault. In flexible pole vaulting, the pull is delayed to the last possible moment, giving the pole time to unbend. It is for this reason that vaulters using flexible poles are forced to keep the vaulting standards deeper toward the pit (from 18 to 24 in.) on their best vaults.

4. The swing and rock-back phases in fiber-glass vaulting

## IMPORTANT POINTS ON EXECUTING A PROPER PULL AND TURN

(i) If the pull is exerted when the hips are still parallel with the ground and the centre of gravity is in front of the true axis of the pole, the vaulter will shoot forward into or under the bar.

(ii) The hips must swing up above the horizontal, along with the lead leg drive-up action before the pull is initiated.

(iii) The vaulter has three forces which may help him in executing the pull properly:
(a) the unbending of the pole
(b) the speed and force of the pulling action itself
(c) the driving action of the legs coupled with the arm pull which helps the legs to shoot over the bar.

(iv) For rigid poles the pull and turn actions are usually a coordinated upward-twisting action of the lead leg swing-up. For flexible poles the turn action is delayed until the last possible moment, just before the hips come up to the cross-bar, after the pole completes its unbending action.

(v) Therefore the turn is later but much faster for flexible poles than is the case with the coordinated pull-turn action of the rigid pole.

(vi) The principal forces that initiate the turn come from:
(a) the spread of the hands on the pole
(b) a vigorous twisting action of the lead leg drive-up
(c) combined with a twisting action initiated from the hips.

(vii) The leg drive must be up along the long axis of the pole for a successful hip lift and twisting action of the lead leg.

(viii) The position of the hips at the time the pull is exerted is an important factor in achieving a good turn and push-up on the pole.

(ix) Any mistake in timing the pull and turn action will bring the vaulter too close or too far away from the cross-bar at the top of the vault.

(x) If a vaulter's jumping style is consistently the same for each vault, the replacement of the vaulting uprights to suit the timing of his pull and turn is the final point determining the success or failure of a particular vault.

## THE PUSH-UP ACTION

Vaulters using a rigid pole usually shift the hands closely together which permits a more efficient push-up on the pole, since the distribution of weight is almost even over both arms. The wide hand-spread used by flexible pole vaulters makes any effective push-up difficult, due to the uneven weight distribution over the spread arms. The upper hand bears the full burden of the push-up because the lower hand (left arm) is too low on the pole and is almost straight by the time the pull and turn are completed.

An effective push-up in any type of vault is a combination of the pull and turn action on the pole, which originates with a well-timed swing-up action. A failure to shoot-up over the bar can always be traced back to some earlier action in the vault and very seldom to the lack of effort on the part of the vaulter.

The push-up action should be as vertical as possible to get the best lift of the body and arms in order to clear the center of gravity of the vaulter over the bar. The push-up action is directed downwards along the length of the pole which offers a solid support for a brief moment as it reaches the vertical. The success of the push-up depends on how much hip-elevation the vaulter gets over the bar while he keeps his body weight as much as possible over his shoulders and close to the pole. In other words, the hips and trunk should be thrust up at such an angle that it brings the vaulter's weight over his flexed arms. The vaulter is now in almost what is termed as a hand-stand position. Actually, this difficult position is maintained only for a fraction of a second, during which time the push-up action of the two arms is coordinated with a breaking of the body at the hips, as the legs drop over the cross-bar down towards the pit. The explosiveness of the push-up is directly related to the power of the pull and turn action. In good vaulting, the vaulter never feels any sensation of pushing-up with his arms even though he is actually performing the action of pushing the arm outwards along the length of the pole. This action of pushing while on a moving support is only possible provided all the phases of the vault preceding the push-up were well coordinated.

## POLE RELEASE

After completion of the push-up, the previously flexed arms of the vaulter have been vigorously straightened. The major portion of the body is traveling up and over the bar, while the fingers hardly maintain contact with the pole and flip it back towards the runway.

In a well-timed push-up the pole is close to the right shoulder as the arm straightens with both elbows facing outwards and thumbs turned inwards. Such a position of the arm may avoid dragging the cross bar down, for an otherwise successful vault.

Since one arm is above the other on the pole, on completion of the push-up the lower hand loses contact a fraction of a second before the top hand, which straightens later and therefore leaves the pole last.

With the wide hand-spread used by fiber-glass vaulters, the lower hand automatically leaves the pole earlier than the top hand. When the hands are closer together, the timing of the pole release may be almost simultaneously, as is the case with some vaulters who use a very close hand-spread. There are some cases of vaulters who release the top hand before the bottom hand. This is usually the result of an off-balanced vault.

## CLEARANCE STYLES OVER THE BAR

There are three major styles of bar-clearance in vaulting:—
(i) The jack knife (ii) arch style and (iii) the fly-away style of clearance. All forms of

variations by individual vaulters are modifications of these three basic methods.

(a) **The Jack Knife Style:** This method of bar clearance originated in the days when vaulters used heavy poles. The vault depended largely on muscular strength due to the comparatively slow run-up and heavy poles that were used. The grip was low, so as to give a faster swing-up and thereby help the heavy pole to rise to the vertical. This type of bar clearance was necessary because the vaulter lost most of his forward speed, and in order to save the vault and ensure a successful bar-clearance he had to time the drop of his legs with a push-up of the arms as the hips were lifted high over the cross-bar in an inverted "V" position. The timing of such a clearance must be very precise. The placement of the uprights at the exact spot is of great importance to a complete clearance without knocking off the crossbar. This type of bar clearance is not in use today, since the days of the heavy pole and slow run-ups have been replaced by better and lighter poles, and longer and faster approaches.

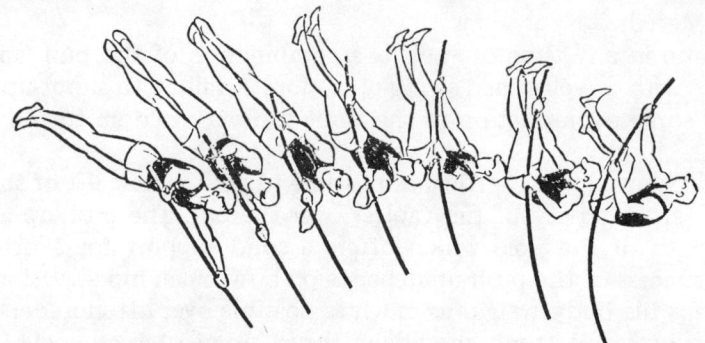

5. The rock-back, pull-up, and turn phases
in fiber-glass vaulting

(b) **Arch Style:** This is the most commonly used method of bar clearance and suits most average vaulters, since it is relatively simple to execute. It permits clearance even though the uprights may not be placed with precision, or even if the timing of the vault is slightly incorrect. Besides, in this method, the vaulter is able to use a higher hand-grip, making the push-up easier. Present-day vaulting technique is a variation which combines the arch and fly-away, and is called a modified arch or arch-fly away type of clearance.

In this style of bar clearance the legs do not drop very much and there is no breaking at the hips as is done in the jack-knife. Instead, there is an arching of the body as a whole, which lifts the bulk of the body over the bar. The effectiveness of this method depends on the hip elevation gained from a hard pull-up and fast turn while the legs are still driving upward.

(c) **Fly-away style:** This is a difficult action to perform over a high cross-bar since it consists of forming a modified arch position and then at the prescribed moment quickly unarching the body to clear the bar. A vaulter using this type of bar clearance must possess good lower-back muscle development in order to be able to hold the legs up after the hips lift and the upper body is flung up and backwards along with the arms. The clearance is therefore a precisely-timed action in which the body is comparatively flat while the lower legs are kept up in coordination with the upward action of the arms. The placement of the upright depends on the approach, speed and power of the rock-back action, which is used to elevate the hips.

## THE LANDING

On completion of the bar clearance a fall from 16 to 18 feet or more can be rather disastrous. A well-timed vault and properly excuted take-off should bring the vaulter up and over into the pit with the vaulter either facing the runway or with his right side to the runway. A poor landing position is directly related to an off-balance clearance, which in turn indicates that there was something wrong at the take-off. It is necessary that in landing from such heights, emphasis be laid on relaxation of the body so that the vaulter may break the fall in the pit with a less jarring effect. To make oneself rigid is to be jarred badly and may result in injury. To facilitate good landing and improve vaulting technique, it is imperative to provide soft, built-up landing areas. Present-day landing pits are made of various forms of foam rubber, which is most effective in avoiding injuries.

## SPECIFIC EFFECTS OF A FLEXIBLE POLE

i) A vaulter can hold higher on a flexible pole than is possible on a rigid pole, due to the flexion of the pole.

ii) Due to the extreme bend of the pole, the take-off action must be forward-upward, as is the case in long jumping, so as to give maximum potential energy to the pole in the form of pole flexion which is taken back by the vaulter during the clearance over the cross-bar in the form of catapult action.

iii) The vaulting upright must be placed further back behind the vaulting box (even up to 2 feet) so as to provide enough time and space within which the hurried actions of the pull, turn and push are coordinated with the whipping action of the pole.

iv) The swing itself hardly exists, but the swing-up and rock-back must be stressed so that the center of gravity of the vaulter is brought close to the true axis of the pole and thereby avoid halting the speed of the forward movement of the pole. By so doing, the flight path of the center of gravity is flatter to begin with, but has a very sudden rise at the end.

v) To get an optimum pole bend, a vigorous, well-executed swing-up and rock-back action must be executed.

vi) Vaulters who are normally poor in the swing-up action when using a rigid pole may derive benefit from this when using a flexible pole.

vii) For a constant bend the weak side of the pole should be marked.

viii) The use of a spread hand-grip helps to the lever the pole into its big bend and prevent the vaulter's center of gravity from passing the true axis of the pole too early.

ix) With the fiber-glass pole, less work is done initially by the vaulter, in contrast with the amount of work done at the end of the vault.

x) An essential skill for vaulters using a flexible pole is to master the timing of the pull-up, turn and push-up actions with the catapult action of the pole during bar clearance.

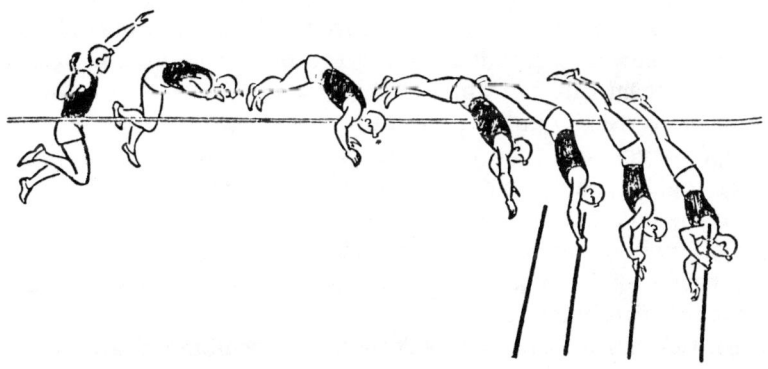

6. The push-up, pole-release, and bar-clearance

# TEACHING BEGINNERS TO VAULT IN TEN EASY STEPS

By Tom Olsen, U.S.A., former President, Thermoflex Inc., Salina, Kansas

Assume the beginner is a "right-handed" vaulter. This means his right hand holds the pole above the left, the left foot leaves the ground last at take-off, and he swings to the right of the pole.

1. Stand a 10-ft. pole vertically in front of you. Place the right hand on the pole at head height and the left hand 18 inches below the right. Both thumbs are up. This will be your handhold.

2. Place the "planting" end of the pole on the grass 3 ft. in front of you. Now spring forward, taking-off on the left foot. Pass the right side of the pole, using the arms and pole to give support as you go forward. Carry the pole with you as you land facing the same direction as at take-off. Repeat this five times.

3. Repeat the exercise in (2) five times, but walk into the take-off.

4. Jog into the exercise described in (2) and (3), but raise the handhold about 2 inches each time. Swing loosely forward with arms somewhat extended. Repeat this until you can hold the pole a foot above the highest handhold you can reach. Avoid letting the top (right) hand slide down the pole as you take-off and swing forward.

5. Stand on a chair. Hold the pole vertically, grasping it as high as you can reach, with hands placed as in (1). Place the pole 1 to 3 ft. in front of the chair and swing forward to the right of the pole with arms somewhat extended, taking the pole with you as you land facing the same direction as at take-off. Repeat this five times.

6. Stand the pole vertically in the pole vault box. Take a handhold as high as you can reach. Walk back far enough so you can take three paces forward to plant the pole and swing forward. Stand with both feet together, and pole nearly horizontal, pointing toward the box. Walk briskly forward, starting with the left foot. As the right foot lands, slam the pole into the box and bring the arms overhead with an underhand, forward-upward sweep. Take-off on the left foot, and swing forward past the right side of the pole to land facing the same direction as at take-off, taking the pole with you. Repeat this five times.

7. Repeat (6), but run into the take-off instead of walking. Start with your feet together at a point far enough back so you can run in using a 5-stride approach, taking the first stride with your take-off or left foot. Each time you repeat this, raise your handhold 1 or 2 inches. Soon your handhold will be 1 to 2 feet above the highest height you can reach with the pole standing vertically in the box.

8. With your handhold 1 or 2 ft. above the highest standing grip you can reach, start using a seven-stride approach. Start with the left foot and take-off directly behind the pole with your left foot vertically beneath your right hand. As you improve, accelerate the last three strides. Spring into the take-off, leading with a vigorously bent right knee before hanging in an extended position momentarily. As the left side of your chest approaches the pole during the swing-up, roll back and bring your knees as close to your handgrip as you can get them. This will place your back horizontal to the ground. Think of getting your hips higher than your shoulders. Permit the arms to remain

relatively extended during this roll-back. As you improve, you can give yourself additional height by pulling downward through the length of thy pole as your knees come to your handhold, and as the pole approaches the vertical. Land facing the same direction as at take-off, carrying the pole with you. Repeat this five times.

    9. Use a proper pole carry down the runway. The planting end of the pole should be no higher than eye level, and may point very slightly to the left. Your hands remain about 19 inches apart, right hand behind right hip with fingers pointing down, pressing downward on the pole at the fork formed at your thumb. The left hand is placed palm down on top of the pole, with thumb beneath supporting the pole. If you find it more comfortable to carry the pole with a wider handspread, then it will be necessary to shift the left hand toward the right as the pole is planted.

    10. Place the bar at 2 ft. and start vaulting. As you approach the bar after take-off, "scissors" the right leg to the left over the left leg, and the left leg backward-upward to the right, turning your body left so that you cross the bar face downward. Push the pole back toward the runway as you clear the bar. Raise the cross-bar 3 inches each time you clear it. Try for a more pronounced roll-back each time. Soon you will be vaulting well over 8 ft., and ready to learn refinements of technique and details of fibre glass vaulting.

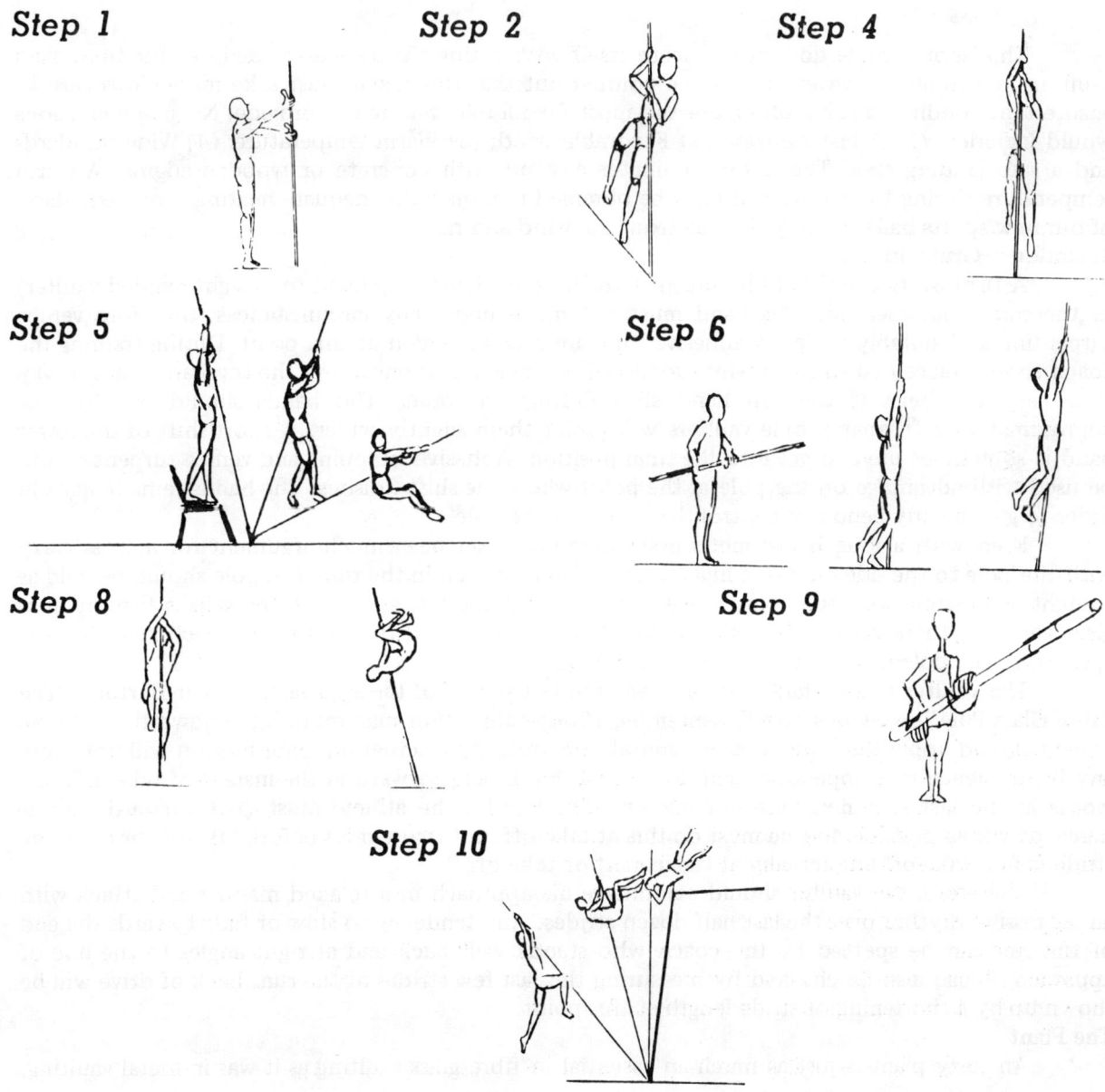

# SOME BASIC PRINCIPLES OF FIBER GLASS POLE VAULTING

By Dennis Watts, British Senior AAA National Coach

This short article does not concern itself with listing the necessary facilities for fibre glass vaulting in Britain. However, it must be pointed out that the coach must take meticulous care to ensure that conditions for vaulting are the most favourable that he can provide. Normal conditions would include:—(1) A fast runway; (2) Favorable wind; (3) Warm temperature; (4) Wide standards and a safe landing area. The latter eliminates any pit with concrete or wooden edging. A warm temperature during the winter can only be obtained indoors with adequate heating provided. Many of our new sports halls are only shelters from the wind and rain.

### Technique—Grip and carry

A firm overgrasp should be taken with the right hand (top hand for a right-handed vaulter) as the run is commenced. This hand must not move under any circumstances, therefore venice turpentine and suitably wrapped adhesive tape are recommended at this point. During training the coach should place two strips of white adhesive, one below and one above the top hand. In this way it is easy to check if the top hand slips during the vault. The hands should be 60 cm. or approximately 2 ft. apart; some vaulters will prefer them slightly wider. A short shift of the lower hand is sometimes used to get into the final position. Adhesive wrapping and venice turpentine can be used with advantage on the pole at the point where the shift finishes. The hands remain apart in order to get an early bend and control that bend on the pole.

Even with a long heavy metal pole there has never been much argument for a cross carry with the pole to the side or even a high carry to avoid tension in the run. The pole should be held as straight as possible with the point roughly in line with the left eye. Since the grip is firm in fibre glass vaulting, there should be little or no shoulder movement during the approach run. Specific speed with the pole must be worked for in training.

The vaulter must attack the box over the last strides of the approach. Trevor Burton ("The Fibre Glass Pole", *Athletics Coach*, September 1966) states: "For maximum force down the pole the athlete should apply his force in a horizontal direction. Any actual jumping motion will not cause any bend. Hence it is imperative that the athlete be driving forward at the instant of take-off. The words in the last sentence were not chosen idly. Firstly, the athlete must drive forward with as much power as possible and he must do this at take-off, not two strides before take-off or even one stride before take-off but actually at the instant of take-off."

Therefore, the vaulter should commence his approach in a relaxed manner and attack with an aggressive rhythm over the last half dozen strides. Any tendency to slow or fade towards the end of the run can be spotted by the coach who stands well back and at right angles to the line of approach. It can also be checked by measuring the last few strides of the run. Lack of drive will be shown up by a shortening of stride length at this point.

### The Plant

An early plant is just as much an essential in fibre glass vaulting as it was in metal vaulting.

In fact, if the vaulter fails to get an early plant in modern vaulting, it is impossible for him to retrieve the situation. In order to obtain a good plant, the pole should be lowered over the last few strides of the run. Assuming the vaulter is right-handed and, therefore, grips the pole with the right hand on top and springs from left foot, the pole should be going forward into the box as the right foot completes the penultimate stride. This means, of course, that the right arm is going forward with the right leg (contrary to normal body mechanics in running), the right hand reaching a position in front of the hips. The pole strikes the back of the box and is driven up in front of the vaulter; he is now in a position to drive into the pole before breaking contact with the ground. A good plant can only be mastered by constant practice and a pole vaulter may require as many as 3000 vaults a year during the crucial stages of his career. This broken down may mean that the athlete who is working to improve his technique may well have to take as many as 60 vaults a week.

**The Take-Off**

The left foot should be directly under the top (right) hand at take-off. The left elbow and wrist should be kept in and behind the pole from the beginning and the arm should be pushed forward throughout the vault, the vaulter attempting to keep away from behind the pole. Some vaulters tend to let the lower arm go through and then push off the pole again in the 'rock back' phase. These two methods have been described as the American and European techniques but really this is an individual matter. Pentti Nikula's lower arm went through but never past the pole. He then pushed away from the pole, never letting the lower arm bend at less than a right angle at the elbow.

**The Rock Back**

After take-off the right knee should remain bent and, if not already at hip level as in the case of Bob Seagren, it should continue to flex to this position. The left leg (take-off leg) should swing straight to increase the pull about the hands, then, as the vaulter rolls back, it must flex rapidly to join the right leg. There are other methods: for instance Pentti Nikula brought his right knee just above half-way to hip level and then dropped the lower leg and foot to join the take-off leg. Both legs then swung straight to increase the pull about the hands and improve the bend of the pole. He then tucked fast with the knees open (easier to tuck quickly), pulling the front of his thighs back towards his chest. When the tuck commences, it must be fast with the knees bent and thighs coming back towards the chest, the eyes directed at the top hand on the pole and **not at the bar**.

However, the secret of good vaulting at this stage lies not so much in what is happening to the legs but, much more important, the action of the hips rotating about the shoulders. If the hips are not above the shoulders and the body mass (centre of gravity) close to the pole and high during the recoil, then the vaulter will be thrown out and into the bar. It is at this point where all our young vaulters find grave difficulty. Their legs come up but not their hips and, therefore, as soon as the recoil starts their legs drop. The hips should be well above the hands and the body and legs close to the pole BEFORE THE TURN COMMENCES.

The pull should take place as the recoil finishes and this then automatically initiates the turn. The left arm must pull across the chest and the vaulter must 'take the pole with him' keeping it as close as possible to the neck so the final push from the right hand can be effective in a downwards direction. When the rock back has been completed and the hips are above the shoulders, the vaulter should extend the body up the pole with the hips still square to the front and wait-wait-wait until the recoil is finishing and then pull and turn. In this way he will be able to keep all parts of the body going up until he has broken contact with the pole and, though the pole, the ground. Now he is subject to action and reaction and can jackknife his body over the bar in order to raise the hips a little in the final moments of clearance.

The most common faults in vaulting are:—

(1) Late plant.
(2) Failing to stay behind the pole.
(3) Not rotating the hips above the shoulders.

Failure in any one or all of these important aspects means the vaulter is thrown out and into the bar as the pole recoils.

# POLE VAULT TECHNIQUE

By Gerhard Jeitner, Germany

Spun-glass poles were sanctioned officially for competitive events by the Rules Committee of the IAAF in time for the Olympic Games in Tokyo in 1964. This, however, merely recognized the fact that the the elastic pole—together with new conditions and forms of pole-planting troughs—had won acceptance in the practice of the sport despite all early objections and reservations. The innovation of the spun-glass pole went hand in hand with the explosive upping of the pole vaulting performances. This development is apparent from the improved world record as well as from the improvement in the Olympic record. But in the course of the last four years, almost all national records have likewise been bettered by a considerable margin, and the same applies to the performances of youthful vaulters (see Table 1).

Bamboo, steel and light metal have had their day. Now the material for the pole is a plastic fiber, often referred to as "fiberglass". This plastic pole is a tube rolled out of a nonalkaline spun-glass tissue bonded with a synthetic resin (i.e., an epoxy or phenol resin). The synthetic binder has outstanding elastic properties. The multilayered cross-section of the pole—the spun-glass tissue is wound around from eight to 16 times—provides the bending strength required to withstand the extreme mechanical stress of the jump. The resiliency of the pole naturally changes the sequential pattern of the athlete's movements during performance. The first phases of the jump coincide with the bending of the pole, and this elastic deformation, imparted to the pole by the athlete's technique and made possible by the resiliency of the material, results in a marked lowering of the overall center of gravity of the athlete's body and hence in the storing of a considerable potential energy. During the later phases of the jump, when the pole straightens out, a skillful correlation of the timing of the athlete's movements with the progressive straightening of the pole can assure a release of the stored energy with a minimum of loss. This enable the jumper to place his handhold higher on the spun-glass pole than is possible in the use of rigid metal poles. The higher handhold, in turn, opens up the possibility of greater vaulting heights. This is in essence the advantage of the spun-glass pole technique. The development may be characterized by a juxtaposition of some reported performance values established under the conditions of the metal-pole technique with values established in the use of the new technique (see Table 2).

In the technique of the spun-glass pole, an improvement by about 30 centimeters (11¾") in the height of the handhold may result in an improvement by about 50 centimeters (1'7¾") in the vaulting height. Technical flaws have so far prevented the full exploitation of the theoretically possible improvement in the push-up preceding the clearing of the crossbar and similarly of the possible increase in the height of the hand-hold. We may, therefore, look forward to further increases in performance.

It follows that the extraordinary improvement in the pole vaulting achievement figures in recent years is a result of the principle of pole flexure during the jump. Observations and measurements carried out during the Olympic Games in Tokyo allow us to assert that there has been no substantial change in the physical and constitutional qualifying characteristics of the pole vaulting athletes (see Table 3). The basic special prerequisites—for instance, the decisive speed attained during the last 10-meters of the approach—have likewise undergone no substantial change or improvement in comparison with the figures previously obtained with the metal-pole technique. This is apparent from an evaluation of the Olympic Games in Tokyo (1). Speeds of better than 1.10-seconds for the last 10-meters of the approach prior to take-off had been achieved with the medal-pole technique. This confirms once again that the improvement in the performance is to be accounted for by the new pole-manufacturing material and the resulting changes in athletic technique.

### Pole Flexure—A Critical Factor of Performance

Pole vaulting achievements with the use of spun-glass poles depend on the flexure of the pole in the course of the successive phases of the vault. The flexure of the pole depends, in turn, on a number of variables in the total performance. These are: 1. The athlete's movements during pole planting and take-off, transferring the approach and foot-stamp energies to the pole (i.e., bending of the pole), and also the athlete's movements during the ensuing phases of body upswing and jack-knifing up to the moment of maximum pole flexure. 2. The approach speed and the foot-stamp energy. 3. Individual body parameters of the athlete, such as weight, height and reach (2) (the latter determining the possible height of the handhold on the spun-glass pole). 4. The type of pole used (3), i.e., the hardness of the pole which depends essentially on the wrapping layers of the plastic-fiber tissue and the quality of both the resin and the necessary chemical hardening agent. The efficient vaulting performance requires that a pole offering great resistance be bent to the highest degree possible within the limits set by the athlete's technical skill and the speed of his approach. Maximal bending of relatively soft poles involves the risk of pole snapping and affords no guarantee of an adequate body upswing during the phases of pole straightening. If the various factors contributing to the bending of the pole are to blend in smooth interaction, the athlete must know the hardness of the pole. This may be expressed in the form of a single bending coefficient (f) which can be precisely determined for a specific load and point of application of that load and by the observation of the maximum pole flexure occurring in the course of an individual pole vaulting event (4).

### Extent of Pole Bending

For the purpose of determining the maximum pole bending occuring in the course of the vaulting performance, various methods have been proposed. Dzhachkoff (5) measures the bend of the elastic vaulting pole by determining the distance between the chord from the point of the pole to the handhold (see Figure 1) and the pole-curvature tangent which is parallel to the chord. In the case of elastic bamboo poles, he cites on that basis flexure values between 40 and 100 cm. (1'3¾" and 3'3½"). Felde and Wolf (6) measure the maximum pole flexure as the bending angle (B) which is formed by the pole-curvature tangents in the point and the handhold on the pole and which it is easy to observe in practice (see Figure 1). In terms of this measuring procedure, Nikula obtained in 1963, using an American pole (16 to 160 HD) a maximum flexure of B approximately=107 degrees, while Preussger, working with the same pole, obtained a flexure of B approximately=93 degrees. In bending-strength tests with poles manufactured in the German Democratic Republic (Type 4570-68) angles of between 135 and 140 degrees have been reached. Prihoda (7) expresses the pole flexure as the percentage ratio of the chord interconnecting the planting point and the handhold in the bent pole to the height of the handhold on the straight pole. The figures quoted for individual handhold heights and various pole types range from 17 to 24 per cent (1962) and from 19 to 24 per cent (1964) as the maximal chord-length reduction resulting from the curvature in the pole.

For the individual pole vaulter, the most immediately impressive representation of the pole flexure is doubtless the difference in length (given in cm.) between the point-handhold on the straight spun-glass pole, the vaulter can determine his "relative handhold height" at the moment of the greatest pole flexure.

### Curve Forms in Maximum Pole Flexure

In order to achieve the highest possible handhold and a dynamic vaulting performance, the vaulter in training needs to be interested only in the maximum pole flexure occurring in the course of the vaulting performance. This is easy to observe and to express. The same parameter can also be used to express the maximum permissible pole load. Expressed as a bending angle, the maximum is B approximately=100 degrees. Expressed as chord shortening, it is in the vicinity of 110 cm. (3'7¼"). The form assumed by elastic spun-fiber poles under the bending stress varies greatly. The differences result from the rolling layers and the cut of the plastic textile. This holds true in particular in the case of poles in which the lower portion is considerably more rigid than the upper portion, i.e., for instance for the pole types of the American Silaflex line with a length of 15 feet (4.57 m.). The curvature of the pole is influenced, furthermore, by the highly individualized transfer to the pole of the approach and foot-stamp energy and by the variable of the power impact of the front arm on the individual phases of the take-off and upswing into the L or jackknife position. When the bending is slight, a symmetric bending form is not at all impossible (see Figure 2, bending line 1). On the whole, however, a particular degree of bending can well be associated with different curve conformations (see Figure 2, bending lines 2 and 3). The strongest and most uniform bending would seem to be, in theory at least, associated with a semicircular bending curve (see Figure 2, bending line 4). However, the stress involved in such bending represents a punishment which no currently available spun-glass pole can take during the actual vaulting performance, and the vaulter, who wants to avail himself of the handhold height made possible by high-degree pole flexures (with B=90 and up to 100 degrees) must be content with the next harder pole type and strive to achieve with it the same or an even greater handhold height despite a somewhat lesser degree of flexure.

**Pole Bending Throughout the Total Vaulting Event**

The most important factors joining the approach and take-off speed and the mass represented by the body of the jumper in initiating the pole flexure have their flexing onset as early as the beginning of the take-off phase (see Figure 3, phase 1). The pole convexes forward under the impact of the approach and take-off energy. The subsequent pole-flexing phases are not uniform since the movements of the vaulter's body swinging on the pole release complex forces of heterogeneous effect patterns. Initially, the pole flexure increases slightly (Figure 3, through phase 3) oscillations superimposed on the steadily increasing flexure. During the phases in which the vaulter is clearly hanging below the pole, the beginning leg upswing (see Figure 3, phase 3) is associated with a more rapid increase in pole flexure. As the upswing is completed, the pole is subjected to an intense "pull", which forces it into maximum flexure (see Figure 3, phase 4). This is the time when poles are most likely to snap. As the phase of the leg upswing begins, the pole-bending process, characterized so far by an exclusively forward orientation, reveals a more lateral trend as the handhold and hence the mass of the athlete's body approach a position perpendicular over the planting trough, which is the pivotal point of support of the entire performance (see Figure 3, phase 4 through 6). The phases of progressively decreasing flexure of the pole and the final straightening of it in a fully vertical position require a perfectly coordinated timing of the corresponding movements of the vaulter's body. Every disproportion in this relationship is reflected in a more or less erratic course of the curve followed by the upper handhold until the vault is completed. (In Figure 3, this curve is roughly indicated by a dotted line connecting the handhold points in the seven major phases.)

**Critical Factors in the Continuity of Movement**

Pole vaulting with the use of spun-fiber poles has evolved from the metal-pole technique. This applies, in particular, to the continuity of movement which cannot be the same for the two types of poles and serves to explain why at present many of the world's best vaulters, utilizing the new technique, still reveal signs of individual compromises with the old. Nonetheless, specific criteria applicable to the new technique begin to be discernible. In order to show the main principles of the new vaulting technique, i.e., the bending and subsequent straightening-out of the pole, in their proper perspective, the vaulting performance may be subdivided into the following phases: 1. Approach. 2. Pole planting. 3. Take-off. 4. Pole bending (upswing of the vaulter's body to the L position). 5. Pole straightening (a. L position, b. stretching from L position, c. body turn and handshift, and d. throw-away of pole). 6. clearing of crossbar. 7. Landing. This subdivision of the vaulting performance is of theoretical significance but must not make us overlook that all the different phases are interlinked and interdependent. The critical factors associated in particular with the various phases in terms of the new technique include the following.

### The Pole Carry During the Approach

In the pole carry, and also during the ensuing take-off, a wide handhold (more than shoulder width) appears to be advantageous. The formerly practiced complete joining of the lower with the upper hand during the pole-planting phase, which coincides with the last approach strides, has become obsolete. The grasp of the pole (as well in regard to the distance between the hands as also in regard to the type of grasp employed) may thus remain unchanged from the beginning of the approach through the pole-planting phase to the beginning of the take-off phase.

### Pole Planting

The continued retention of a wide grasp implies, in turn, the need for an early and well-timed raising of the arms as part of the pole-planting phase, coincident with a straightening of the back arm, in order to assure during the take-off phase the transfer via this arm of the approach and foot-stamp energy to the pole and the bending of the pole.

### The Take-Off

The vaulter's body movements during take-off under the conditions of the new technique reflect particularly clearly the compromise with the movements conditioned by the use of a metal pole. On the basis of our observations of pole vaulters in action, we may distinguish three variants. First variant: The most characteristic trait of this take-off, which shows great similarity with the technique used in the past in taking off with a metal pole, is the upright body posture, the pole hugging the chest, and the resting (or overshooting) of the forearm on the lead side on the pole. The handhold is relatively wide. The point of take-off is vertically under the right (upper) handhold. This take-off is almost invariably associated with a dropping of the free leg during the ensuing phases of swinging from the pole. Representatives of this variant (see Figure 4, A) are, among others, Preussger, Lehnertz, Bliznyetsov and Fyeld. Second variant: In this technique—also known in Germany as the "Finnish or "Hangen take-off" because it was first seen in vaulters from Finland—the approach and take-off energy is transferred to the pole via the outstretched lead arm and a body posture of curved tension. The point of take-off is no longer directly under the lead handhold but some 30 to 60 cm. (1-2 feet) in front of it. The vaulter "under-runs" the take-off. The body leans over backward, the chest is pushed toward the pole, and the lead forearm clings to the pole. This variant (see Figure 4, B) is used by Hansen, Hein, Chase, Nikula, Ankio, Mustakari and others. Third variant: This variant is known in the training practice as the "Pennel technique". It is characterized by the fixed right angle which the lead arm forms with the body. This assures a rapid and direct transfer of energy from the approach and the take-off via both arms into the bending of the pole. The take-off point in this technique lies perpendicularly under a point midway between the handspread. Numerous vaulters have used this technique with good success (see Figure 4,C). They are Pennel, Pemelton, Reinhardt, Tomasek and (not invariably) Nordwig. The three take-off variants differ in their effects on the subsequent vaulting performance. The following descriptions of the phases of the vault must hence be viewed throughout the pole-bending and straightening phases in connection with the several take-off variants.

### The Phases of Pole Bending

The bending of the pole begins during take-off and the immediately ensuing post-take-off phases. In the first variant, the dropping of the free leg after the take-off has little significance. In the other variants, it has none. After the take-off, the upswing movements, involving a progressively more pronounced bending of the pole promoted by the swinging and stretching of the take-off leg, lead via the leg swing-up to the phase of maximum bending of the pole (see Figure 3, phases 1 through 4). In these phases, it is essential that the trunk should be bent back (while the legs are being pulled up) and that the arms (especially the lead arm) should be stretched out, in order to achieve as wide a separation as possible of the body from the pole. This separation enhances the bending of the pole still further.

### The Phases of Pole Straightening

L position: As the pole begins to straighten out, the vaulter has reached a phase which is both typical and necessary if he wants to exploit as effectively as possible the straightening of the spun-glass pole. The body posture is jack-knifed and resembles the shape of an L (see Figure 3, phase 5). The trunk is bent back. The pelvis is still below the lower handhold but in front of the pole. A vigorous bend in the hips brings the closed legs parallel to the pole. This phase, especially the position of the legs, is of critical importance for the subsequent vertical swing.

Extension of the L position: In order to force the vaulting movement into a vertical line, the pelvis must be brought up, by stretching the hips, close to the handhold of the lead arm and hence close to the pole which is still bent (see Figure 5). This "extension of the L position" occurs with most vaulters even before the body turn and the preparatory pull-up. For a more refined designation of the extension of the L position, i.e., the straightening out in the hips, the technical language has adopted the expression J position and I position (see Figure 5). In the J position, the hips are straighter than in the L position. In the I position, the hips are completely straightened out. A point of considerable importance for the subsequent swing-up in the Pennel technique is the release of the lead arm, which results in a reduction of the distance between it and the pole. This technical detail is important for the systematic development of the vertical swing-up, i.e., for the ensuing lift in the pelvis. Full awareness of these kinetic requirements (fixation during take-off, relaxation in the upswing) can lead in practice to a harmonious flow of the components of movement in the total performance.

### Body Turn and Shift to Push-up

The body turn which leads to the shift of the body into the push-up position is itself introduced by the arm pull-up. The timing of the pull-up and hence the starting position for this phase of the movement differ somewhat in that they may be derived from the L or J or I position and because they depend on the kind of take-off and on the timing of the ensuing phases up to the maximum pole bending as well as on the energy available for the pull-up. In spite of the differences in onset of the pull-up among world-renowned vaulters who use the spun-glass pole, there is a generally valid rule for the timing of the body turn. This turn and hence the shift to the push-up posture must not begin until the pelvis is near the upper handhold. The pull-up and the body turn coincide with the final phase of the straightening of the pole, i.e., they occur when the pole is in the straightening of the pole. It is then impossible to exploit fully the energy released by the pole as it straightens out.

### The Throw-Away of the Pole

Because of the spread between the handholds, the push-away of the pole requires arm and hand pressures on the two sides, respectively. The lower arm releases the pole first, with the result that the quick push-away executed by the upper arm constitutes the last impulse for the movements involved in clearing the crossbar (see Figure 3, phase 7).

### The Crossbar Clearance

From the dynamic sequence of the earlier phases to the vaulting performance with the use of the spun-glass pole, crossbar clearance in a curved shoot (see Figure 3, phase 8) follows as the natural effect of the straightening of the pole.

### The Landing

The landing-pit material which is currently in use (sponge or foam rubber) minimizes the perils of landing from great heights, helps to eliminate psychological inhibitions before the vault or the landing and provides a fairly reliable assurance that accidents due to pole snapping are rare. The special pit fillers currently in use have led to the development of a new form of landing, i.e., the vaulter no longer lands on his legs, but the soft material makes it possible for him to land in practically any form (sitting, rolling overhead, etc.).

Despite the fact that the world's best vaulters still differ in technical details of execution and furthermore, in spite of the fact that the coaches and the track and field instructors are not in agreement in their views regarding technical principles, it is possible—as we have tried to do in this article—to formulate a few generally valid statements of technical significance. If we are to succeed in clarifying the situation which is still characterized by a divergence of opinions, we shall require further investigations of the kinetic and biomechanical implications of the new vaulting technique utilizing the spun-glass pole in supplementation of the experience that can be derived from practical work in the training of beginners as well as in the coaching of mature athletes.

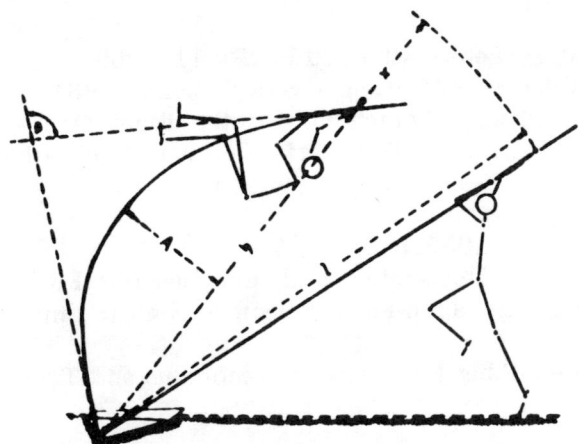

FIG. 1--Extent of Pole Flexure: l=handhold height (bendable length of pole; A=maximum "bracing height" of bent pole; x=chord shortening resulting from flexure of pole; h=length of chort of bent pole from point to handhold (l minus x)

FIG. 2--Forms of flexure Ordinate=direction of force; abscissa=direction of pole flexure

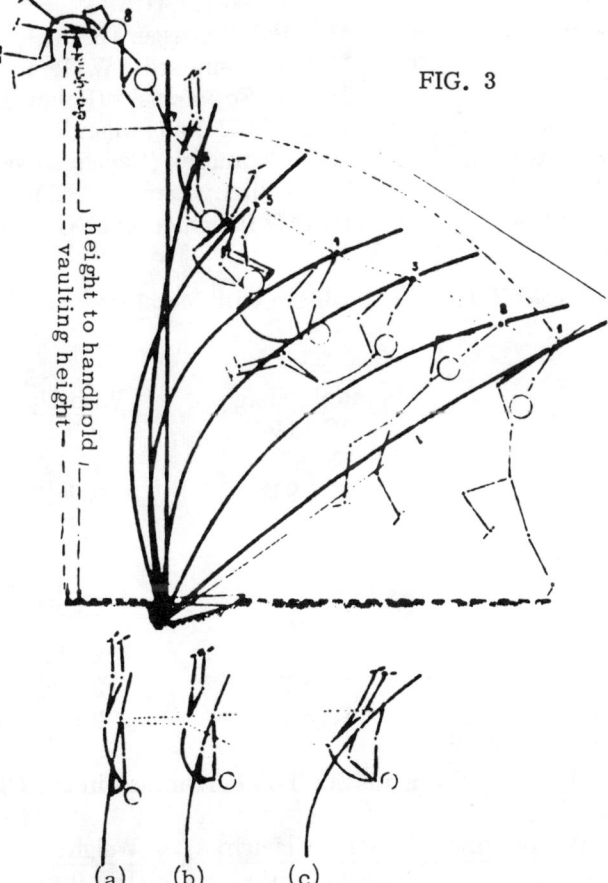

FIG. 3

FIG. 5--Raising of Pelvis in Extension of "L" Position (Jackknife): (c)=L position; (b)=J position; (a)=I position.

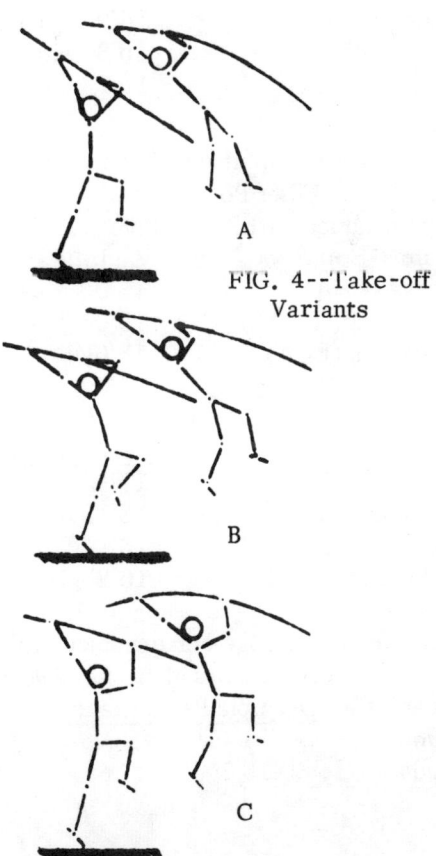

FIG. 4--Take-off Variants

Notes:

1. See Prihoda, Z.: "Pole Vaulting in Tokyo," Lehka Athletika 17 (2): 11, 1965.
2. See Leichtathletik (Track and Field Athletics), p. 386. Sportverlag (Berlin). 1964.
3. See Jeitner, G.: "Welcher Stab ist Richtig?" (Which Pole is the Right One?), Der Leichtathlet 12 (18/19), 1964 (Supplement "Der Leichtathletiktrainer" [Field and Track Athletics Coach]).
4. Ibid.
5. See Dzhachkov, W.M.: "Pole Vaulting," FIS, 1955, p. 9.
6. See Felde and Wolf: Entwicklung von Hockfesten und Elastischen GFK-Staben (Development of Highly Resistant and Elastic Plastic Spun-Fiber Poles), Technical University, Dresden, 1963, 1, 80f.
7. See Prihoda, Z.: Ibid., p. 14-and, "Spun-Fiber Poles Modify Technique and Training," Lehka Athletika 15 (3): 10, 1963.

TABLE 1: Pole Vault Record Trend

|  | 1960 | 1966 |
|---|---|---|
| World Record | 15'9" Bragg (USA) | 17'4" Hansen (USA) |
| Olympic Record | 15'5" Bragg (USA) | 16'8¾" Hansen (USA) |
| European Record | 15'3" Krasowski (USSR) | 16'10¾" Preussger (E Ger) |
|  | 15'3" Preussger (E Ger) |  |
| Youth World Record | 15'0" Brewer (USA) | 16'6¾" Wilson (USA) |
| National Records | 15'3" Preussger (E Ger) | 16'10¾" Preussger (E Ger) |
|  | 14'8" Lehnertz (W Ger) | 16'9¼" Reinhardt (W Ger) |
|  | 14'10¼" Wazny (Poland) | 16'5¾" Sokolowski (Poland) |
|  | 15'0" Landstrom (Finland) | 16'5¼" Nikula (Finland) |
|  | 14'9½" Tomasek (Czechoslovakia) | 16'5" Tomasek (Czechoslovakia) |
|  | 15'3" Krasowski (USSR) | 16'5" Bliznyetsov (USSR) |
|  | 15'1¼" Roubanis (Greece) | 16'1¾" Papanicolaou (Greece) |

TABLE 2: Comparison of Vaulting Height, Handhold Height and Push-Up with Metal Pole and Spun-Fiber Pole

Performance with Metal Pole:

| Name (Country) | Vaulting Height | Handhold Height | Push-Up |
|---|---|---|---|
| Bragg (USA) | 15'9" | 12'11½" | 2'9½" |
| Gutowski (USA) | 15'9¾" | 13'¼" | 2'9½" |
| Richards (USA) | 15'6¼" | 12'10¾" | 2'7½" |
| Preussger (E Ger) | 15'5" | 12'7½" | 2'9½" |

Performance with Spun-Fiber Pole:

| Name (Country) | Vaulting Height | Handhold Height | Push-Up |
|---|---|---|---|
| Pennel (USA) | 17'¾" | 14'3¼" | 2'9½" |
| Preussger (E Ger) | 16'10¾" | 14'1¼" | 2'9½" |
| Tork (USA) | 16'1¾" | 14'¼" | 2'1½" |
| Nikula (Finland) | 16'2½" | 13'5½" | 2'9" |

TABLE 3: Average Performance and Personal Data Based on the Six Top Performers in the Olympic Games at Rome (1960) and Tokyo (1964)

| Year | Pre-Olympic Performance | Olympic Performance | Age | Height | Weight |
|---|---|---|---|---|---|
| 1960 | 14'11½" | 14'11½" | 25.3 | 6'0" | 168-lbs. |
| 1964 | 16'7¾" | 16'5" | 25.3 | 5'11¾" | 167-lbs. |

# THE KEYS TO SUCCESSFUL VAULTING

By Walter R. Welsch, U.S.A., University of Florida

When coaching vaulters it is wise to concentrate on one phase at a time. There are five key phases in vaulting that may serve as points of concentration and once the athlete has mastered them he can coordinate them into a smooth, well executed vault. These are (1) the run, (2) the plant and take-off, (3) the vault, (4) the turn over, and (5) the fly-away. It is important that the coach pick out the major faults first and correct them before moving on to others. Practice makes permanent. It does not make perfect. Practice only improves a person if he does the correct thing over and over again. If he practices improper movements they become reflex actions which are more difficult to correct once he has them well imbedded in his mind.

Too often the run-up in vaulting is neglected. The key to a good run is high knee action. Watch any of the great vaulters carry the pole down the runway. They all have high knee action—they remind us of a trotting horse. This high knee action prepares the vaulter for the second key point—the plant. If the vaulter is not running with a high knee lift, he must change his leg action when he makes his plant. The body should be straight with a slight forward lean as he runs down the runway. This position continues and is the key to proper body position as the plant is made.

During the plant, if it were possible to remove the pole, the vaulter would look like a long jumper about to take off from the board. This position is achieved in vaulting the same way as it is in the long jump by approaching the take off with high knee action. The great long jumpers also use the high knee action in their run.

When the plant is made the hands should be above-the-head and out in front. The top hand is not directly over the head but is slightly in front. After impact and the fibre glass pole starts to bend, then the top hand is in position over the head. The vaulter drives his lead leg directly through the box with a high knee lift, and he must keep his elbows in line with his drive. Concentrate on the leg drive. If it is not driving straight ahead it will cause a sideward movement of the body and loss of momentum as the vault is performed.

The vault itself involves many movements. The vaulter must rotate backwards as well as twist. The rotation backwards, known as the rockback, can be accomplished by a high knee lift of the lead leg and rotating the head back as the vaulter goes up. Most vaulters look for the crossbar during the vault and consequently, as they get up closer to it their head rotates forward. This forward rotation of the head will drop the feet, and make it impossible for the vaulter to get his feet above his head. This causes the vaulter to knock off the crossbar. It is also a major mistake of most poor vaulters, once they have gotten the feet above the head, to feel they need not hold this position. As the pole unbends it has a tendency to rotate the partially outstretched body into the crossbar. The problem then is not to rush a vault, but to remain in the rockback, as the pole is unbending. The body if kept in this position will be propelled upwards rather than forward into the crossbar. The higher the crossbar, the longer the time a vaulter has to execute his moves during the vault. Vaulters have a tendency to rush their vaults at greater heights rather than waiting for the pole to help propel them over the crossbar.

Some vaulters take off by keeping the legs straight, doing a pike or jackknife at the waist as they ride the pole. This motion is helpful in getting the pole to bend, but it does not help the rockback. Vaulters who don't believe this may sit on the ground with legs out-stretched and try to raise the feet. Note how it is difficult to rotate backwards. Now repeat the movement, but this time pull the lead leg up and let the head go back. Now it becomes easy.

Crossing the bar in a sidewards action is caused by allowing the elbows to move out of line. If held wide, the elbows will cause the body to drift sideways or rotate sideways as the push is made during the flyaway.

As the vaulter rides the pole he should be familiar with Newton's Law of Acceleration. This law states that the rate of change of momentum of a body is proportional to the force applied, and occurs in the direction in which that force acts. Applying this law to vaulting means that the pull through and the push away at the top of the vault must take place parallel to the direction of the vault. Application of any force that is not parallel to the line of vault will only reduce the amount of momentum available and cause a rotational movement. It is, therefore, very important that the vaulter keeps his arms and legs in line with his vault. Otherwise, unwanted rotational movement and decrease in the height of the vault will result.

It is also easier to apply a force in the direction that an object is moving than in some other direction. A force in the direction of movement of the body will increase its acceleration. It is therefore easier to throw an object which is already moving in the direction you want it to go than to throw it from a standstill. If the vaulter realizes this, then he must start his pull through at the top of his vault before the pole has completely straightened out. This would give an extra impulse to his body, resulting in a good fly-away at the top of his vault. Pulling through too late requires much of the vaulter's strength merely to lift his body weight.

During the fly-away there are two points worthy of attention. Too often vaulters tend to pull the arms in toward the body rather than raise them above the head. During the fly-away the vaulter will often knock the crossbar off with his elbows. Lift the arms to correct this fault. Some vaulters have a tendency to drive the legs down to help them rotate around the crossbar. This causes them to rotate into the bar, knocking it off with the knees or waist. Instead, remain extended and allow the head to to back.

In conclusion, vaulting is an intricate event that requires many hours of practice. However, practice does not automatically produce the desired perfection. A successful coach will make sure that the vaulter does not practice alone, but remain under the constant supervision of someone who will identify his faults. Concentrate on one fault at a time. Start with the larger movements, and then work into the more intricate. In some instances, correcting one fault will correct a series of mistakes.

# FIVE SERIOUS MISCONCEPTIONS ABOUT THE ATTRIBUTES OF FIBERGLASS POLES

By George Moore, U.S.A., President, Pacer-American Division, Santa Fe Springs, California

**Misconception number 1: "Heat and weather affect the performance of a fiberglass pole."** No weather variation encountered by a pole vaulter will affect the performance of his fiberglass pole. There is no appreciable difference between a pole used at 30° F. and the same pole used at 110° F. We have conducted many tests in and out of the laboratory to verify this fact. Heat and sun definitely do affect an athlete. In general, pole vaulters use a slightly different routine to warm-up than most other athletes. The sprinter or distance runner can warm-up before a race, step to the starting line and run his race and be through for the day. A pole vaulter will warm up, take one vault and then sit for times up to 45 minutes or an hour or more before his next vault, so he must warm up thoroughly prior to each vault in competition. The colder the temperature, the longer it takes a vaulter to warm up. The warmer the temperature, the less time it takes a vaulter to warm up. In cold weather, vaulters are generally more tense and not thoroughly warmed up and do not drive as hard, therefore, the pole feels stiffer to them. In hot weather they are generally looser and do not require as much warm-up time and are warmer at each attempt. The pole then feels "softer" to them. The changes that occur, occur in the athlete and not the pole.

It is possible for an exposed pole to lie in the sun and receive a "set". That is, a vaulter may lay the pole down and pick it up and find that it has a slightly different curve than it had originally. This is caused by heat absorption on the side of the pole exposed to the sun, expanding the molecules and making that side of the pole slightly longer than the side of the pole away from the sun. This does not change the flexibility of the pole, though it may have an effect on the vaulter if used in this condition. When this phenomenon occurs, the pole should be put back into its shipping tube or put in the shade. Within a matter of moments it will return to its original configuration. No damage will have taken place and there will be no change in the pole. This can happen with any brand of pole available today but will be more evident in darker poles since dark colors absorb more heat than lighter colors.

**Misconception number 2: "Continued use softens a fiberglass pole—and the pole, therefore, wears out."** This is a misconception among many vaulters though extensive tests have proved that it is not so. We have flexed poles that have been in use three and four years and find no change in flexibility from the time they left the factory. Fiberglass poles do not grow softer by continued flexing nor deteriorate with age. A particular vaulter may find that a pole that was too stiff for him at the start of the year is too soft for him at the end of the year. The change again is in the vaulter and not in the pole. A fiberglass pole will act as a resistance exercisor to the athlete, ane he will find that at the end of the year the pole feels "soft". Any athlete using any type of resistance exercisor finds that a job that is very difficult for him to do when he starts using the exercisor will grow easier as time goes on because his muscles strengthen to the resistance involved. The same thing happens with the pole vaulter. Continued use of the same muscles do the same job, strengthens the athlete to a great degree and, as he becomes stronger, the pole feels softer. Once again the change is in the athlete, not the pole, i.e. increased strength overpowering the pole's resistance.

**Misconception number 3: "Continued flexing or flexing a pole in the box 'warms up' a fiberglass pole."** This probably causes more broken poles than any other misconception concerning fiberglass. Flexing a pole in no way changes the resistance of the pole itself. Flexing a pole in the box or in any other fashion serves no useful purpose. A fiberglass pole cannot be "warmed up" in any way nor can the resistance be changed by continued flexing. Many vaulters see world class vaulters flexing a pole. In an attempt to emulate their idols, they do the same thing. Literally dozens of fiberglass poles are broken every year by this activity. The stresses applied when flexing a pole in this fashion are in no way related to the stresses that the pole was manufactured to accept. The stresses applied to a pole while flexing in a box are totally erratic and only broken poles can result. If the pole does not break, you haven't harmed it but the chances of breaking the pole are very great since the stress is very erratic. This activity should be discouraged.

**Misconception number 4: "The further a pole bends the greater the reaction."** This is not true, though the concept is shared by many coaches and athletes. A fiberglass pole stores energy in relationship to the amount of energy applied to it. Beyond 90° the energy stored is at a decreasing rate. There is little additional thrust stored in the pole by overbending. Any vaulter bending beyond a 90° arc is in the danger area. He is constantly in danger of breaking his pole. There isn't sufficient additional reaction in a bend of 110° to risk breaking an expensive implement and personal injury. Bending excessively, does, however, hinder the vaulter by disrupting the smooth flow of the vault and allowing the vaulter to travel too far into the pit. Vaulters who consistently overbend find themselves coming up under the crossbar no matter how far back the standards are positioned.

**The 5th misconception: "The weight rating on a pole insures that a particular vaulter cannot break a given pole."** Regardless of the origin of manufacture, the weight rating on a pole is at best a compromise. The weight rating assigned to any fiberglass pole is based on two measurables—weight and height of hand grip. There are several unmeasurables that have as great a bearing on the load a particular pole will withstand and, therefore, averages are utilized. Any weight rating system that uses averages in its computations is at best a compromise. One thing every weight rating system has in common is that the weight listed is a maximum and should not be exceeded. Many coaches and athletes assume that because a pole is rated at 150-lbs. a 150-lb. vaulter cannot break it. This is not so. It is possible for a 150-lb. vaulter to break a pole rated at 170-lbs. if his drive is sufficient or if his weight shift is erratic. There are many factors involved during a vault that are immeasurable. Any weight rating system is simply a guide and should be used as such. Any vaulter who can overbend any pole, regardless of his weight or the rating on the pole, should be moved to a stiffer pole or his technique should be thoroughly analyzed to find its deficiencies. Since the weight rating applied to a given pole under the circumstances set forth by the manufacturer is a maximum, no vaulter should be allowed to vault on a pole rated below his body weight.

# A SUMMARY OF PHYSICAL AND TECHNICAL CHARACTERISTICS OF OUTSTANDING VAULTING

By Pete Boudreaux, U.S.A., Catholic High School, Baton Rouge, Louisiana

The purpose of this study was to compare the vaulting techniques and physical characteristics of outstanding vaulters using the fiberglass pole with outstanding vaulters who used the bamboo or metal poles with regard to the following: (1) standing height; (2) body weight; (3) the height of the handgrip on the pole; (4) the effective handgrip; (5) the vaulting height that was attained; (6) push off; and (7) speed as measured by 100 yard dash time. A survey of the literature was utilized to obtain information on twenty-seven pre-fiberglass vaulters; and a questionnaire was used to obtain information from twenty-seven fiberglass vaulters.

The data for the pre-fiberglass pole vaulters were gathered from literature dated from August, 1940, to January, 1963. The data for the fiberglass pole vaulters were gathered during the month of May, 1969. The data collected from the vaulters were recorded and the mean scores for each group were computed for each of the seven selected factors in the study. The mean scores were then compared to determine whether significant differences existed between the two groups in any of the selected factors.

## FINDINGS

The findings of the study were as follows:

1. There was no significant difference in the physical characteristics of height and weight between the fiberglass and pre-fiberglass pole vaulters.

2. The fiberglass vaulters had significantly higher handgrips and effective handgrips than the pre-fiberglass vaulters.

3. The fiberglass vaulters had vaulted significantly higher than the pre-fiberglass vaulters.

4. There was no significant difference in the push-off distance between the fiberglass vaulters and the pre-fiberglass vaulters.

5. There was no significant difference in the speed of the fiberglass vaulters and the pre-fiberglass vaulters, as measured by 100 yard dash time.

## DISCUSSION

No significant differences existed in the physical characteristics of height and weight in the fiberglass vaulters and the pre-fiberglass vaulters. The slight difference in the speed as measured by 100 yard dash time was not significant.

Throughout the review of the literature, statements were made that one of the principal advantages of the fiberglass pole was the higher handgrip allowed on the pole; therefore allowing greater heights to be achieved. This point was borne out conclusively in the study. The fiberglass vaulters had a mean handgrip of 14 feet 10 inches while the pre-fiberglass vaulters had a mean handgrip of 13 feet 2 inches; a difference of 1 foot 8 inches. The mean height achieved by the fiberglass vaulters was 16 feet 9½ inches while the mean height achieved by the pre-fiberglass vaulters was 15 feet 2 inches; a difference of 1 foot 7½ inches. The increased handgrip of the fiberglass vaulters was almost exactly the same distance as the difference in the height achieved between the two groups.

Seven fiberglass vaulters had push-offs of three feet or more, while only four pre-fiberglass vaulters had three foot or more push-offs. However, at the other extreme, five fiberglass vaulters had push-offs of two feet or less while only one pre-fiberglass vaulter had a push-off of two feet or less. In comparing the mean push-offs of the two groups, less than one-half inch difference existed. It was the author's contention that this should prove that the present fiberglass pole vaulter is not being thrown or catapulted high into the air, because, if he were, his push-off as measured by present methods should be much greater than that of the pre-fiberglass vaulter.

It is not hard to imagine an 18 foot 6 inch or 19 foot jump in the not too distant future. The highest handgrip in the study was used by Railsback (15 feet 8 inches, effective handgrip of 15 feet) and the best push-off, by another subject, was 3 feet 7 inches. Conceivably, if an individual could put together the extremely high handgrip with the excellent push-off the resulting jump would be 18 feet 7 inches.

## CONCLUSIONS

Within the limitations of this study the following conclusions were considered justified:

1. There is no difference in the physical characteristics of height, weight, or speed, as measured by 100 yard dash time, between the fiberglass vaulters of today and the pre-fiberglass vaulters of the past.

2. The fiberglass pole offers definite advantages to the vaulter; the principal advantage appears to be the bending of the pole which allows the vaulter to utilize a much higher handgrip, which, in turn, allows for greater heights to be achieved while the push-off remains relatively constant with that observed in the pre-fiberglass era.

### APPENDIX A  Raw Data of Fiberglass Pole Vaulters

| Name | Height | Weight | Handgrip | Height Achieved | 100 Yard Dash Speed |
|---|---|---|---|---|---|
| B. Barrett | 5'10½" | 170 | 14'6" | 16'7" | 10.1 |
| V. Bizarro | 6'3" | 185 | 14'10" | 16'7¾" | 10.1 |
| C. Carrigan | 6' | 170 | 15' | 17' | 9.9 |
| S. Carruthers | 6'2" | 170 | 15'7" | 16'6" | 10.0 |
| R. Carter | 5'10" | 165 | 14'3" | 16'4" | 10.4 |
| P. Chen | 5'7½" | 145 | 14'8" | 17'1" | 9.8 |
| J. Cramer | 6'3" | 190 | 14'4" | 16'7¼" | 10.0 |
| J. Eshleman | 5'11" | 144 | 14'9" | 16'11¼" | 10.2 |
| M. Flanagan | 6'2" | 175 | 15'6" | 16'6" | 10.0 |
| F. Hansen | 6' | 165 | 15' | 17'4" | 10.2 |
| P. Heglar | 6'1" | 180 | 15'2" | 16'6" | 10.1 |
| J. Johnson | 5'11" | 163 | 14'11" | 16'4" | 9.9 |
| E. Mustakari | 6'2" | 170 | 15' | 17'½" | 10.2 |
| P. Nikula | 5'10½" | 154 | 14'7" | 16'8¾" | 9.9 |
| J. Pennel | 5'11" | 170 | 14'10" | 17'6¼" | 9.8 |
| D. Phillips | 6' | 175 | 14'6" | 17'1" | 9.6 |
| D. Railsback | 6'1½" | 168 | 15'4" | 17'6¼" | 9.7 |
| G. Riley | 6' | 165 | 15' | 16'7" | 10.2 |
| S. Schoonover | 5'8" | 152 | 14'8" | 16'4½" | 10.1 |
| R. Sloan | 6'½" | 192 | 15'4" | 16'8" | 9.8 |
| B. Slover | 6' | 180 | 14'7" | 16'6" | 10.2 |
| R. Sprung | 6'1½" | 160 | 15'1" | 16'6¾" | 10.3 |
| A. Steben | 6'1¾" | 180 | 14'3" | 16'8" | 10.5 |
| B. Steinhoff | 6'2" | 165 | 15'4" | 16'6" | 10.1 |
| J. Vaughn | 6'2" | 180 | 14'6" | 17'5" | 10.5 |
| C. Wiley | 5'10" | 175 | 14'3" | 16'4" | 10.3 |
| P. Wilson | 6'1" | 163 | 15'1" | 17'7¾" | 10.3 |
| Late Returns: | | | | | |
| B. Seagren | 6' | 175 | 15' | 17'9" | 9.8 |
| J. Chase | 6'4" | 189 | 15'2" | 17'½" | 10.4 |
| S. Owens | 5'10" | 164 | 15'2" | 16'8" | 10.3 |
| RANGE | (5'7½"-6'3") | (144-192) | (14'4"-15'7") | (16'4"-17'7¾") | (9.6-10.5) |
| MEAN | 6' | 169.3 | 14'10" | 16'9½" | 10.07 |

## APPENDIX B  Raw Data of Pre-Fiberglass Pole Vaulters

| Name | Height | Weight | Handgrip | Height Achieved | 100 Yard Dash Speed |
|---|---|---|---|---|---|
| D. Bragg | 6'2¾" | 198 | 13'10" | 15'9½" | 10.2 |
| D. Clark | 6'2" | 165 | 13' | 15'3" | 9.9 |
| D. Coleman | 5'11" | 163 | 12'10" | 14'5" | 10.2 |
| D. Cooper | 6'1" | 167 | 12'9" | 15'2½" | 9.7 |
| H. Cooper | 5'10" | 150 | 12'8" | 14'8" | 10.5 |
| J. Cramer | 6'2¾" | 180 | 13'10" | 15'8¼" | 10.0 |
| R. Ganslen | 6'1" | 145 | 12'10" | 14'5¾" | 10.5 |
| J. Graham | 6'4½" | 185 | 13'8" | 15'5" | 10.2 |
| B. Gutowski | 6' | 150 | 13'7" | 15'9¾" | 9.7 |
| D. Laz | 6'2" | 178 | 13'7" | 15'3" | 10.0 |
| W. Levack | 5'9" | 140 | 12'11" | 14'9¼" | 10.3 |
| J.D. Martin | 6'4" | 193 | 13'10" | 15'9¾" | 10.4 |
| G. Mattos | 5'10" | 170 | 12'8" | 14'10½" | 10.0 |
| E. Meadows | 6'1" | 160 | 13'2" | 14'11" | 10.6 |
| R. Morcom | 5'10½" | 142 | 13'9" | 14'9" | 9.8 |
| R. Morris | 5'10½" | 147 | 13' | 15'8" | 10.3 |
| J. Pennel | 5'11" | 164 | 12'8" | 15'½" | 10.0 |
| E. Poucher | 5'7" | 142 | 12'11" | 14'10" | 10.6 |
| M. Preusseger | 6' | 165 | 13'5" | 15'5" | 10.5 |
| B. Richards | 5'10" | 163 | 13'7" | 15'6½" | 9.9 |
| J. Rose | 5'9¼" | 163 | 12'7" | 14'10" | 10.0 |
| M. Schwartz | 5'9¾" | 175 | 13'2" | 15'4" | 10.1 |
| B. Sefton | 6'3" | 185 | 12'8" | 14'11" | 10.9 |
| G. Smith | 6'2" | 175 | 12'11" | 14'8" | 9.8 |
| H. Wadsworth | 6' | 185 | 13'5" | 15'4" | 10.1 |
| C. Warmerdam | 6' | 160 | 13'11" | 15'8½" | 10.2 |
| J. Welbourne | 5'10" | 156 | 12'7" | 15'1½" | 10.9 |
| RANGE | (5'7"-6'4½") | (140-198) | (12'7"-13'11") | (14'5"-15'9¾") | 9.7-10.9 |
| MEAN | 6' | 165.4 | 13'2" | 15'2" | 10.2 |

## APPENDIX C  Effective Handgrip and Push-off of Fiberglass Pole Vaulters

| Name | Handgrip (HG) | Effective Handgrip (HG-8 inches) | Height Achieved (HA) | Push-off (HA-EHG) |
|---|---|---|---|---|
| B. Barrett | 14'6" | 13'10" | 16'7" | 2'9" |
| V. Bizarro | 14'10" | 14'2" | 16'7¾" | 2'5¾" |
| C. Carrigan | 15' | 14'4" | 17' | 2'8" |
| S. Carruthers | 15'7" | 14'11" | 16'6" | 1'7" |
| R. Carter | 14'3" | 13'7" | 16'4" | 2'9" |
| P. Chen | 14'8" | 14' | 17'1" | 3'1" |
| J. Cramer | 14'4" | 13'8" | 16'7¼" | 2'11¼" |
| J. Eshleman | 14'9" | 14'1" | 16'11¼" | 2'10¼" |
| M. Flanagan | 15'6" | 14'10" | 16'6" | 1'8" |
| F. Hansen | 15' | 14'4" | 17'4" | 3' |
| P. Heglar | 15'2" | 14'6" | 16'6" | 2' |
| J. Johnson | 14'11" | 14'3" | 16'4" | 2'1" |
| E. Mustakari | 15' | 14'4" | 17'½" | 2'8½" |
| P. Nikula | 14'7" | 13'11" | 16'8¾" | 2'9¾" |
| J. Pennel | 14'10" | 14'2" | 17'6¼" | 3'4½" |
| D. Phillips | 14'6" | 13'10" | 17'1" | 3'3" |
| D. Railsback | 15'4" | 14'8" | 17'6¼" | 2'10¼" |
| G. Riley | 15' | 14'4" | 16'7" | 2'3" |
| S. Schoonover | 14'8" | 14' | 16'4½" | 2'4½" |
| R. Sloan | 15'4" | 14'8" | 16'8" | 2' |
| B. Slover | 14'7" | 13'11" | 16'6" | 2'7" |
| R. Sprung | 15'1" | 14'5" | 16'6¾" | 2'1¾" |
| A. Steben | 14'3" | 13'7" | 16'8" | 3'1" |
| B. Steinhoff | 15'4" | 14'8" | 16'6" | 1'10" |
| J. Vaughn | 14'6" | 13'10" | 17'5" | 3'7" |
| C. Wiley | 14'3" | 13'7" | 16'4" | 2'9" |
| P. Wilson | 15'1" | 14'5" | 17'7¾" | 3'2" |
| Late returns: | | | | |
| B. Seagren | 15' | 14'4" | 17'9" | 3'5" |
| J. Chase | 15'2" | 14'6" | 17'½" | 2'6½" |
| S. Owens | 15'2" | 14'6" | 16'8" | 2'2" |
| RANGE | (14'3"-15'7") | (13'7"-14'11") | (16'4"-17'7¾") | (1'7"-3'7") |
| MEAN | 14'10" | 14'2" | 16'9½" | 31.40" |

## APPENDIX D  Effective Handgrip and Push-off of Pre-Fiberglass Pole Vaulters

| Name | Handgrip (HG) | Effective Handgrip (HG-8 inches) | Height Achieved (HA) | Push-off (HA-EHG) |
|---|---|---|---|---|
| D. Bragg | 13'10" | 13'2" | 15'9½" | 2'7½" |
| D. Clark | 13' | 12'4" | 15'3" | 2'11" |
| D. Coleman | 12'10" | 12'2" | 14'5" | 2'3" |
| D. Cooper | 12'9" | 12'1" | 15'2½" | 3'1½" |
| H. Cooper | 12'8" | 12' | 14'8" | 2'8" |
| J. Cramer | 13'10" | 13'2" | 15'8¼" | 2'6¼" |
| R. Ganslen | 12'10" | 12'2" | 14'5¾" | 2'3¾" |
| J. Graham | 13'8" | 13' | 15'5" | 2'5" |
| B. Gutowski | 13'7" | 12'11" | 15'9¾" | 2'10¾" |
| D. Laz | 13'7" | 12'11" | 15'3" | 2'4" |
| W. Levack | 12'11" | 12'3" | 14'9¼" | 2'6¼" |
| J.D. Martin | 13'10" | 13'2" | 15'9¾" | 2'7¾" |
| G. Mattos | 12'8" | 12' | 14'10½" | 2'10¼" |
| E. Meadows | 13'2" | 12'6" | 14'11" | 2'5" |
| R. Morcom | 13'9" | 13'1" | 14'9" | 1'8" |
| R. Morris | 13' | 12'4" | 15'8" | 3'4" |
| J. Pennel | 12'8" | 12' | 15'½" | 3'½" |
| E. Poucher | 12'11" | 12'3" | 14'10" | 2'7" |
| M. Preusseger | 13'5" | 12'9" | 15'5" | 2'8" |
| B. Richards | 13'7" | 12'11" | 15'6½" | 2'7½" |
| J. Rose | 12'7" | 11'11" | 14'10" | 2'11" |
| M. Schwartz | 13'2" | 12'6" | 15'4" | 2'10" |
| B. Sefton | 12'8" | 12' | 14'11" | 2'11" |
| G. Smith | 12'11" | 12'3" | 14'8" | 2'5" |
| H. Wadsworth | 13'5" | 12'9" | 15'4" | 2'7" |
| C. Warmerdam | 13'11" | 13'3" | 15'8½" | 2'5½" |
| J. Welbourne | 12'7" | 11'11" | 15'1½" | 3'2½" |
| RANGE | (12'7"-13'11") | (11'11"-13'3") | (14'5"-15'9¾") | (1'8"-3'4") |
| MEAN | 13'2" | 12'6" | 15'2" | 31.89" |

LONG JUMP            Credits

*Teaching the Long Jump* by Kenneth O. Bosen. Originally published in *Modern Athlete and Coach*, Vol. 6, No. 4A, August, 1968.

*The Long Jump Take-Off,* by Jess Jarver. Reprinted from *Modern Athlete and Coach,* Vol. 9, No. 1, January, 1971.

*The Long Jump,* published anonymously. First publication.

*The Most Important Phase in the Long Jump,* by Jess Jarver. Reprinted from *Modern Athlete and Coach,* Vol. 7, No. 6, November, 1969.

*The Dropping of the Legs in Long Jumping,* by Bernard J. Hopper. First publication.

*Importance of Swinging Movements at the Take-Off,* by Yuri Verhoshanski. Originally published in *Der Leichtathletik-Trainer,* East Germany. Translated and synthesized by Jeff Jarver.

*The Long Jump and Triple Jump Approach,* Yuri Verhoshanski. Originally published in *Lehkaja Atletika,* U.S.S.R. Translation provided by Don Steen, Simon Fraser University, Burnaby, B.C., Canada.

*The Length of Long Jump Run-Up,* by J. Vacula. Originally published in *Der Leichtathlet,* East Germany. This translation (and condensation) appeared in *Modern Athlete and Coach,* Vol. 8, No. 3, May, 1970.

*Optimum Speed in the Long Jump,* by D.C. Chambers. Reprinted from *Modern Athlete and Coach,* Vol. 8, No. 1, January, 1970.

*Landing in Beamon's Record Jump,* by Toni Nett. Originally published in *Leichtathletik,* Germany. This English translation and condensation appeared in *Modern Athlete and Coach,* Vol. 8, No. 6, November, 1970.

# TEACHING THE LONG JUMP

By Kenneth O. Bosen, Olympic Coach of India, 1964.

The squad first warms up briefly and takes a few jumps at random to get the feel of the event. Now get the boys aside and, after a brief explanation of the procedure. Make sure you keep to fundamentals and don't get involved in technical matters too soon. Take up each stage separately at first but link it to the whole as soon as possible to keep the squad interested.

**Stage 1. The TAKE-OFF:—** Technique in any jumping event is only efficient when the fundamentals of a good take-off and landing have been inculcated at the very beginning. Remember that 90% of any jumping event depends on a well executed take off.

(a) Using a short approach and no take-off board, make the squad go through the take-off actions. To assist in forcing upwards leap, place pole vault uprights and a cross-bar about six feet from the take-off with a string or a light ball suspended from it. While the boys are trying to leap up and head the suspended object, stress the full drive and extension of the take-off leg, the fast high pick-up of the free leg knee, the use of the arms in aiding the lift, the position of trunk and head etc. No mention is made of any particular style of jumping at this stage. Just let the boys jump while you keep an eye on their take-off fundamentals.

(b) You are bound to find a few on the squad who do everything the hard way. Get these boys aside and break down your teaching as follows: line up the squad with take-off leg forward and go through the take-off motions from a stationary position. All the time stress the points mentioned earlier. Next have them go through the motions at a slow walk and later with a slow jog. You will also find that the use of the suspended object gives them an incentive to lift and drive. Move these boys back to join the rest of the squad as soon as possible. Separation does not always speed up the learning process.

Fig 1    Stationary         Walking              Running

**Stage 2. Link TAKE-OFF with proper LANDING position:—** In events like the long and triple jump, valuable distance is usually lost in poor landing at the end of an otherwise excellent jump. It is therefore necessary to link the teaching of the landing position with the take-off as early as possible.

(a) Still maintaining the high suspended object, use a short approach with no take-off board. Go through the actions of the take-off just as before, only this time stress getting the legs up and out fully extended for the landing. To assist in bringing the two legs up and force a full extension before landing, place high jump uprights and a cross bar a few feet from the landing area at a height of about 18". The presence of this low obstacle makes it necessary to get the legs up and out for the landing.

(b) Again it may be necessary in some cases to break down the learning process. Therefore the following may prove useful; line the squad up at the edge of the pit and have them do standing jumps into a soft pit, landing flat on the buttocks with both legs fully extended and arms out for balance. While they do this you may stress the idea of shooting the legs up and out so that the shoe laces come up to about eye level. This gets the legs up and way out. Next, in order to avoid sitting back in the pit, it is necessary to stress the use of the arms, which must swing vigorously up and forward as the two heels hit the pit. This takes time and patience but is well worth the trouble in the long run. Have the squad do the same flat landing on the buttocks but this time using a short approach, with stress on leaping up and out first. As soon as possible move the squad back to the use of the high jump cross bar in front of the landing area as before.

Fig 2

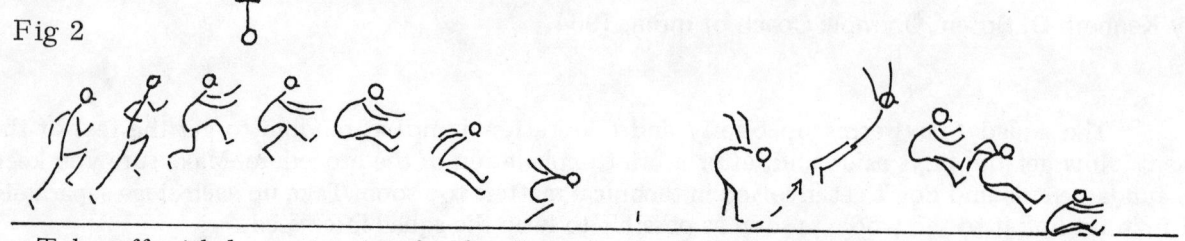

Take off with leg extention for landing       Standing jump landing on buttocks

**Stage 3. JUMPING TECHNIQUE in flight:—** The two basic forms in flight that are widely used in long jumping are the hang and the hitch-kick. The use of a particular jumping form may be considered a matter of individual choice, but from a technical point of view, the use of a particular flight must take into consideration the mechanical aspects of the event in order to assist a full drive at the take-off, balance in flight, and an efficient landing position.

(a) The Hitch-kick. Using a short approach, still maintaining the overhead suspended object to stress lift, have the squad leap up, stressing a high pick-up of the free leg knee. The object is to get the free leg up bent and float in the air and wait for the pit to come up to you. Land in a wide split of the two legs. The take-off leg drives the jumper up and remains at the rear, the lead leg is picked up vigorously in a high knee action and remains bent at right angles in front of the jumper. Float in this position and land in the pit in exactly the same position as in flight. Be sure to hold the trunk erect at all times and use the arms for balance.

Next, add a simple forward-backward split of the lead leg in mid-flight so that you land with the take-off leg forward and lead leg to the rear in exactly the same manner as described for the previous learning stage. Everything remains the same, only the lead leg has performed a backward stepping movement in co-ordination with the forward split of the take-off leg. It will be found that this stage will take a little more time to master than the previous. The co-ordination of the two legs splitting back and forward, yet maintaining an erect body, is often quite a problem with beginners.

To complete the whole action the next stage merely requires the jumper to bring the free leg quickly forward once again in mid-flight to join the take-off leg for a regular two-legged landing. At this stage it will be seen that the jumper feels he does not have enough time to perform the complete hitch-kick action before the landing is made. To give the jumper a feeling of lift and more time in flight it has been found useful to use a built-up take-off or, if available, a gymnastic spring-board.

You are almost certain to find a few in your squad who will have difficulty in adopting the hitch-kick. In such cases it may be wiser to try them out in the simpler, but slightly less efficient, hang technique. This method of flight is still in use by many good long jumpers, but is considered less efficient since it does not encourage the continuity of action that is possible with the hitch-kick, which not only off-sets rotation to some extent but also facilitates a better take-off and leg lift for the landing. There are a few jumpers, however, who have successfully combined the hang with the hitch-kick after having started with the former.

(b) The Hang. Line up the squad on a soft grassy stretch and have them perform repeated squat jumps. In performing the squat jump stress a vigorous two-legged thrust, thus elevating the hips which must be up and forward, chest up and out, head held in proper alignment and not thrown back, with the arms coming up to shoulder height bent at the elbows and slightly backwards, thereby causing an arch of the entire body. It will be found that legs naturally flex slightly and trail to the rear as a direct result of the hip thrust and arch of the body. As the jumper reaches the peak of his leap he must hold this body arch very briefly and then unarch on his descent, to land balanced on both feet in a semi-crouched position from which he is required to repeat the same actions over again. As learning progresses, move the squad to the built-up take-off. Now they will have to leap up and out into the pit. After a few attempts you will be ready to try them out walking in a true long jump fashion. The high take-off will give the boys time to hang, but never fail to stress the drive of the take-off leg and high pick-up of the free leg knee. It is also necessary to stress the form action at the hang only at the peak of the flight and not just after the take-off. Soon the squad will be using a short approach and take-off from the springboard performing the total jump with a hang.

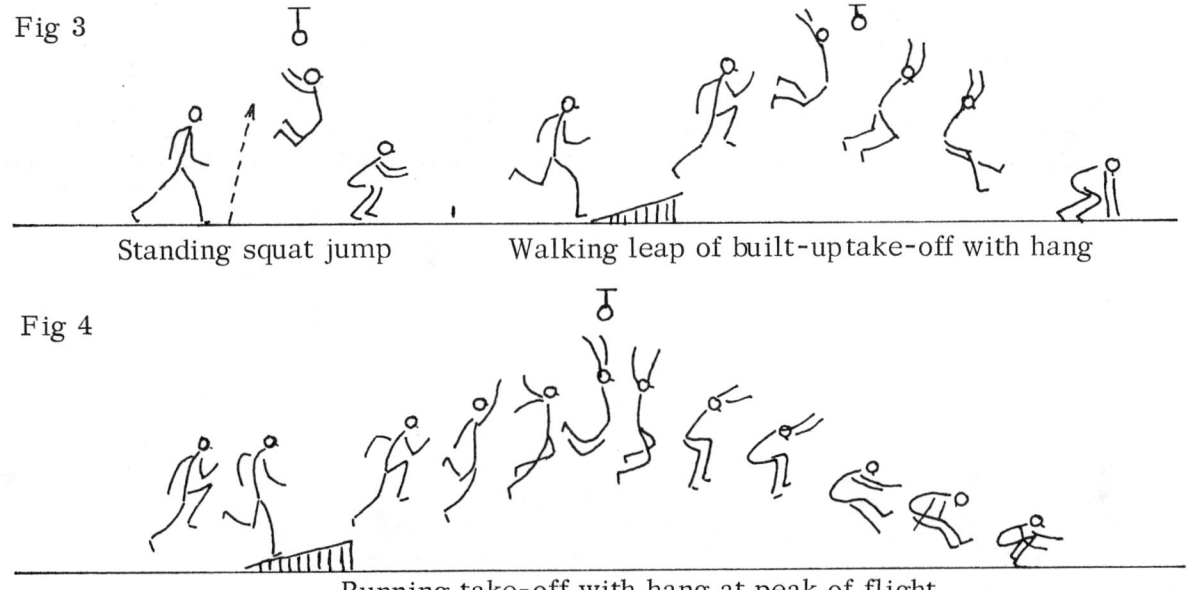

Fig 3

Standing squat jump     Walking leap of built-up take-off with hang

Fig 4

Running take-off with hang at peak of flight

**Stage 4. Locating CHECK MARKS and the RUN UP:—** The presence of the take-off board creates problems with regards to the last strides. To overcome this, simply use a larger take-off area in practice. The presence of the board creates the problem of deciding whether the last stride is shortened or lengthened. Without a board the boys are not conscious of making any adjustments and therefore approach freely. Stress the proper maintenance of speed to the take-off and concentrate on a relaxed 'gather and settle'. It will be found that this way there is a greater fluency in the approach and an automatic adjustment, if any, in the last crucial strides to the take-off. It is not necessary to coach or even mention anything about the last stride except to make sure that the jumper gets his whole body over his take-off foot.

Use the blank take-off area for the purpose of form practice, but use the take-off board when taking all-out or regular trial jumps for distance.

A twenty stride approach is the basic distance to begin with. If necessary, at a later stage the number of strides may be increased or decreased as desired. While speed is important it is also necessary to bear in mind that over-all consistency and smoothness in acceleration is a vital factor to the success. A fast but relaxed and well controlled approach is the answer to the efficient conversion of speed into lift at the take-off. The use of just one check mark placed on the eighth stride from the start of the run up is generally enough. In practice, however, I find it useful to place a second check mark at about three strides before the take-off to indicate the beginning of the gather phase. This is especially useful in case the jumper is not using a board but a blank take-off area.

To establish the run-up brush the track clear of all previous spike marks and mark the starting point with lime. Have two persons located approximately where the eighth and twentieth strides would fall. Make each boy run through on a different part of the track, while the helpers locate the exact spot at which the eighth and twentieth strides have left marks. Repeat this a number of times to assure consistent markings, then measure and record distance. On the next day you can transfer and measurements to the long jump runway and have the squad make their final adjustments. It must be remembered at all times that merely running through to check the run-up is dynamically different from a full approach at optimum jumping. Hence, adjustments are necessary to establish the exact check marks.

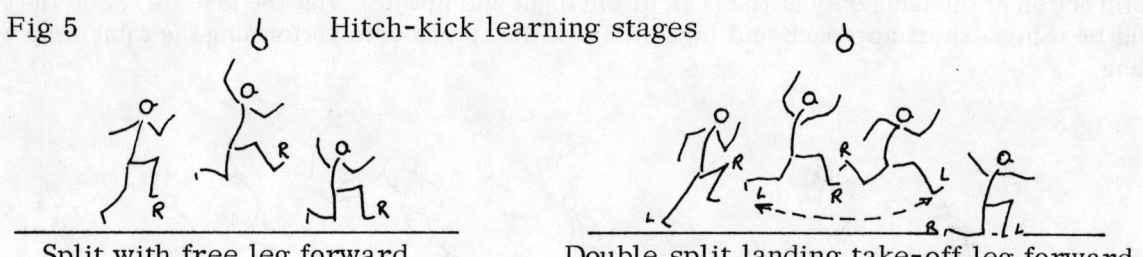

Fig 5     Hitch-kick learning stages

Split with free leg forward     Double split landing take-off leg forward

# THE LONG JUMP TAKE-OFF

By Jess Jarver, Australia, editor, *Modern Athlete and Coach*

*This article attempts to summarize the important aspects of the complicated but deciding action which occur in the split second transfer of horizontal speed into angular velocity during the take-off in the long jump.*

The long jump consists of an action sequence which starts with a run-up, aiming to accumulate maximum horizontal speed. The jumper attempts to approach the take-off board with extreme accuracy before transferring the horizontal speed into angular velocity with a minimum loss of momentum. The take-off action responsible to project the jumper at a best possible angle into the air, takes a little over a tenth of a second. During this short period the take-off foot is actively planted onto the board, the shock is absorbed by a slight flexion of the ankle, knee and hip, and is followed by a vigorous extension of all these joints. The explosive extension which lifts the jumper off the board is assisted by the movements of the free leg and arms. The center of gravity of the jumper leaves the board at an angle in the vicinity of about 20 degrees and, as contact is lost with the ground, the forces developed during the run-up and take-off become effective.

## MAJOR TASKS

At the take-off the jumper is concerned with two important tasks:—
* Obtaining a vertical lift
* Maintaining as much as possible of his horizontal velocity.

Thus, the take-off phase is responsible for attaining the best vertical velocity without drastic reductions in the essential horizontal speed.

The action at the take-off allows only for a fraction of a second to convert the horizontal momentum into vertical. It is achieved by the application of the maximum force from the take-off leg to obtain the required vertical lift. The velocity of the vertical lift depends on the time this force is applied and the impulse. Although the duration in which the force can be applied is important, it is the intensity (maximum power produced in the shortest time) that decides the effectiveness of the take-off.

The take-off is usually divided into three major phases:—
1. The foot plant; 2. The absorption of the impact; and 3. The active lift.

In planting the take-off foot the action is similar to the actual movement in running. The jumper does not wait until the foot has touched the track but places the leg on the board in an active backward and downward movement. The knee is only fractionally bent as it touches the board. As the take-off foot has been placed the forces of the active placement and the transfer of the body weight on to the take-off leg are absorbed by a slight flexion in the ankle, knee and hip joints. The knee starts bending as the jumper's C of G continues to move forward and reaches 145 to 150 degrees at the moment when it is directly over the take-off foot. During the flexing of the knee joint the extensors in the take-off leg are pre-tensed for the following explosive stretching action.

As the C of G moves forward, the take-off leg starts to extend until the toes leave supporting phase, the importance of the second part of the take-off is more emphasized. forming an angle of about 80 degrees with the track. As the jumper's take-off leg changes to the ball of the foot, pre-tension of the foot extensors is created to conclude the lift off the board. Finally, the jumper is projected into the air with the trunk upright, strongly assisted by the upward-forward swinging movements of the free leg and arms.

The whole action, from the moment the take-off foot touches the board until it leaves it, according to Schmolinsky takes only 0.12 seconds. During this short time the theoretical length of the jumps will be determined by the take-off velocity, take-off angle and forces created by the jumper.

## VELOCITY

It is impossible to perform the movements of the take-off without reduction of forward speed as the take-off foot, in order to go through the jumping movements, has to stop on the board longer than it would normally in the supporting phase in sprinting. As the take-off foot contacts the board further losses occur because the thrust checks the jumper's forward speed. Research data from U.S.S.R. indicates that about six per cent of speed is lost when the jumper prepares for the take-off. According to Toomsalu a further 10 to 15 per cent is lost during the actual take-off action itself.

To cut the deceleration to a minumum the jumper is forced to compromise between the run-up speed and the take-off force. As neither speed, nor spring, can be at maximum, Dyson suggests that the proportion should be approximately two to one in favor of horizontal velocity. This means that more explosive power must be developed during the take-off to avoid sacrificing forward momentum in order to obtain a better lift.

The force developed at the take-off in a vertical jump from a squat position has been measured to range from about 180 lb. at the beginning to 1000 lb. at the end of the take-off. This makes it obvious that the deciding force is applied during the last phase of the extension of the knee joint and that over-bending the knee or a reaching stride are sufficient, as both will reduce forward speed without adding much to the lifting force.

## TAKE-OFF ACTION

The take-off action must be executed so that it ensures full continuity of converting the run-up into a jump. The take-off foot must strike the board just in from of the jumper's C of G so that it is directly over the board when the foot has settled. The foot hits with the heel slightly in advance but a full heel to ball to toes roll is not practical in the long jump since it would mean loss of velocity. The flat of the foot is put down fast and firm at right angles to the board with the knee slightly flexed. The body weight passes over the take-off leg, which is extended powerfully, driving the jumper forward-upward with the maximum vertical impulse directed through the jumper's C of G. The C of G has meanwhile been caught on a slight raise as it travels through a distance of approximately three to four feet during the contact of the take-off foot with the board.

Simultaneously the free leg, shoulders and arms are accelerated upwards to add to the impulse of the lift. The proper use of the swinging movements of the free leg and arms is important. Provided the momentum achieved through the swinging movements coincides with the force achieved by the extension of the take-off leg and is correctly directed through the jumper's C of G, they add considerably to the vertical impulse of the jumper. According to Korenberg the swinging movements also lead to an increase in the distance between the jumper's C of G and the point of support. Hence, the instant when the take-off is completed, the body's C of G is more displaced in the direction of the swing.

It is noticeable, according to Verhosanski, that at the start of the take-off the mass of the swinging parts of the body has a negative acceleration compared to the jumper's C of G. As the C of G of the swinging parts shifts forward the vertical acceleration changes to positive. The supporting force is now directed downwards and the load on the supporting leg is increased. At the end of the take-off the vertical acceleration once again changes to negative. This is why in the case of an experienced jumper the maximum force of the swing precedes the straightening action of the supporting leg, as the forces acting on the point of support are reduced with the final effort of the take-off leg.

TAKE-OFF ACTION
Note that the jumpers C of G continually moves upwards
over a distance of about 3ft. 6in.

Because the swinging movements are most effective towards the end of the supporting phase, the importance of the second part of the take-off is more emphasized. It is here that by making full use of the free leg and arm power, a more vigorous action is created without sacrificing speed. Only when all movements at the take-off are coordinated and the jumper's C of G is directly over the line of forces exerted, will the body be driven at the maximum possible speed in the required direction. This is achieved by coordinating the free leg and arm swing to start with the take-off drive. A simultaneous increase of the force and duration of this action leads to an increase in the force impulse.

The importance of developing speed in all take-off movements should be obvious. The faster the body is projected into the air the longer is the pull of gravity counteracted and the greater is the distance the C of G will travel. However, to ensure that the take-off action is allowed to exert its full force, there should be no attempt to introduce other movements before it has been completed.

## TAKE-OFF ANGLE

The optimum angle of 45 for the projection of a missile is not suitable for the long jumper who needs a much lower angle to avoid losses in horizontal velocity. It is further to be considered that 45° is the optimum angle only when the C of G would be at the same level at the take-off and landing points. In the long jump it is higher at the instant of the take-off.

It has been generally been recommended that the take-off angle, the angle between the vertical line and the line from the take-off foot through the jumpers C of G, should be below 30°. In fact, film studies of first-class performers show a wide variety of take-off angles with the majority falling between 15° and 25°. The exact angle of projection apparently depends on the jumper's sprinting and jumping abilities.

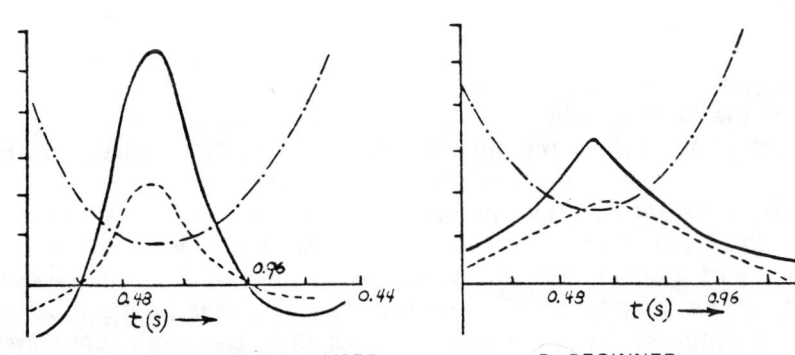

A. ESTABLISHED JUMPER     B. BEGINNER
SWINGING MOVEMENTS AND THE SUPPORTING LEG.
- - - - Vertical acceleration of arms. - - - - Vertical acceleration of the swinging leg.
- - - - Angle of bend of the supporting leg.

# THE LONG JUMP

*(The following article was written by a former student at the DHFK Sports Institute, Leipzig, East Germany. The article is based upon notes from lectures attended, study, and experience gained while attending this world-renowned athletics school in pursuit of the Master's degree. Much of the material included was originally produced by Soviet researchers. The author has requested that his name remain confidential, inasmuch as he is still an active coach at the national level behind the Iron Curtain.)*

The technique of long jumping consists of the approach-run, takeoff, flight in the air, and landing. The jumper is at liberty to execute the motions during the flight phase in different ways. Experts label the technique of long jumping according to the flight phase of the jump, as the sail style, hang (hollow-back) technique, and the walk-in-air (hitch-kick) style.

It would be wrong to overestimate the importance of the flight phase of each long jump technique.

A fast approach-run, especially rhythmical on the last strides, combined with a quick, vigorous and well coordinated take-off, easily guarantees maintenance of balance during the flight phase, and has decisive influence on a good length of jump.

The maximum length of jump is determined by the trajectory of the center of gravity resulting from the take-off speed and angle. After having left the ground, the flight path of the center of gravity cannot be influenced. During the flight, the jumper need only keep balance and prepare for landing in the most efficient manner. During the flight and landing, the jumper must try to keep the loss of distance in landing as insignificant as possible.

As a matter of principle, therefore, the long jump is divided into two main phases:
a) The approach-run and take-off.
b) The flight in the air and landing.

In the first part of the long jump the conditions for the flight phase and the landing are created. Therefore this first phase is the most important part of technique in long jumping. The forces which have been developed in the approach-run and take-off become effective during the flight and landing. So the value of the two main parts is clearly decided in favor of the first. In an analysis of the technique of jumping, it must always be remembered that single actions should only be considered as parts of the complete motion and therefore always in their mutual relation. It is in most cases impossible to improve the landing without correcting the whole jump, including the last part of the approach-run.

1. Loss of landing means the difference between the length of jumping theoretically possible (determined by the take-off speed, the take-off angle and jumping height) and the actual length of jump. There cannot be a gain in theoretical landing distance because the length in jumping which would be theoretically possible for mechanical reasons cannot be increased by farther

advancing the legs.
## Approach
The long jump approach-run is of supreme importance. The higher the speed of the approach-run which the jumper can maintain at take-off without great loss in momentum, the better will be the result.

| Name | | Long Jump | 100-m. time |
|---|---|---|---|
| **men** | | | |
| Ter-Ovanesyan | Soviet Union | 8.31 m. world record | 10.5 sec. |
| Boston | United States | 8.28 m. | 10.4 sec. |
| Owens | United States | 8.13 m. | 10.2 sec. |
| Brown | United States | 8.00 m. | 10.5 sec. |
| Beer | G.D.R. | 7.79 m. | 10.7 sec. |
| **women** | | | |
| Stachelkanova | Soviet Union | 6.62 m. world record | 11.6 sec. |
| Krepkina | Soviet Union | 6.37 m. | 11.3 sec. |
| Popova-Vinogradova | " " | 6.31 m. | 11.5 sec. |
| Krezeainska-Dunska | Poland | 6.35 m. | 11.7 sec. |

It is never by chance that top-class long jumpers also attain good results in 100 m. sprinting and in hurdles.

The 100 m. times, however, cannot be compared directly with the results of jumping, because for the long jumper it is the speed in 40 to 50 m. which is decisive.

The approach must guarantee that the jumper, at highest speed and in the best take-off conditions, can hit the take-off board accurately with his foot.

Those are the basic demands of the approach-run.

## Length of the approach-run and speed
It should be the aim of every long jumper to take-off at maximum speed. But approach acceleration should not cause too much strain, because the run-up represents only one part of the total jump.

In a suitable approach-run, full speed is seldom attained in less than 40 m. This implies that the approach-run should be at least as long as 40 m. The present top-class jumpers have an approach of 40 to 45 m., or about 22 to 24 strides. The three medal winners of the Olympic Games 1960 used an approach-run of 22 strides.

Women averaged 17 to 20 strides at the Olympic Games in Rome. This corresponds to a distance of 30 to 35 m. Children, adolescents and novices take a shorter approach. In any case, the figures given here are only approximate values. The exact distance of the approach-run should be determined individually by the jumper.

## The Start and Acceleration in the Approach
The jumper begins his approach-run from a standing start. The degree of body lean depends on the increase of stride length and cadence of strides. Long jumpers who quickly increase speed have more forward lean than those who increase speed more slowly. In any case, the first strides should always be executed in the same way. The beginning of the approach-run should guarantee concentration without overstraining. In good jumpers, we often observe their first strides are walking, and at a check-mark the approach-run begins with a small hop. The advantage of this is that the jumper can find it easier to get into his running rhythm.

The first strides after the start resemble those of a sprinter using a standing start; but here they are not so forced in order to maintain elasticity of muscles. With increasing speed the upper part of the body straightens up and the run becomes energetic. The strides remain elastic.

The arm action in the approach-run should be executed without too much strain and should also help to increase speed.

Accuracy of the approach-run

It is important for every long jumper to find the form of approach-run that best suits his personal qualities. The high-spirited long jumper will increase his stride cadence more quickly than the more steady jumper who increases his cadence during most of the approach.

As a matter of principle, every long jumper should work out his own rhythm of approach-run. In each approach he must increase the stride cadence in the same way.

The degree of lengthening the approach strides must be stabilized, thus insuring accuracy of the distance of the approach-run. Thus, the long jumper can always strike the take-off board under nearly the same conditions, thereby insuring an efficient take-off.

Therefore, the approach-run should always begin in the same way. The more actual experience a jumper has, the sooner the approach-rhythm will be stabilized.

In important competitions, inexperienced jumpers often get excited by the whole atmosphere, and change their start and approach acceleration. Instead of an increase in speed, a foul will often result. This is caused by the inaccuracy of approach and the resulting negative influence of the taking-off mechanism.

**Check marks**

Check marks are used as means to train and control the approach during training and competition. They help to establish an accurate approach and therefore should be recommended to young jumpers. Check marks have to be placed in such a manner that they can be hit by the take-off foot. Usually one check mark in the middle of the approach-run will be sufficient.

The long jumper must never be influenced by check marks to such a degree that his only aim would be to hit them. That would only disturb his concentration for reaching a high take-off speed.

With the help of check marks as orientation points, the athlete may develop an almost automatic, optimum approach run which tends to become a conditioned reflex.

Experienced athletes who, during a long training, have already acquired an automatic, correct approach—and consequently have good stride consistency, may do without check marks at any time.

**The change of rhythm on the last strides before take-off**

During the last strides, the jumper prepares for the transmission of the approach into the take-off. Contrary to the out-of-date theory that on this part of the approach the jumper coasts or "lets himself drive," the speed until the take-off board should be increased or at least maintained.

During the final strides, the body is kept upright. A forward or backward lean would have negative consequences on the take-off. The change of rhythm can be seen during the last three strides. The second last stride, in comparison to the previous and the last stride, will be 20 to 45 cm. longer.

There are no standards for the change in length of strides, because here the individual difference of each jumper is to be taken into account. Usually with fast jumpers, there are smaller stride length differences than with relatively slow ones. This is because slow jumpers try to jump higher and thus specifically prepare for height during the last three strides.

This change of stride rhythm results from the fact that the last but two and the last stride are performed quicker than the previous strides. The increased cadence makes possible the lowering of the center of gravity during the longer pentultimate stride, in preparation for take-off. At the beginning of the frontal supporting phase of the shorter, quick last stride, the center of gravity does not continue falling, but immediately changes to the upward motion of the take-off. Thus, a further bending of the take-off leg is avoided.

It is advantageous to plant the jumping foot quickly on the take-off board. This planting anticipates the lowering of the center of gravity. However, the last stride must not be too short, because otherwise the take-off foot too quickly passes the vertical line through the jumper's center of gravity, thus leaving insufficient time to execute the take-off movements.

The length proportions on the last three strides in a fast and a relatively slow jumper are as follows:

|                    | BOSTON (USA) | AUGA (E. Germany) |
|--------------------|--------------|-------------------|
|                    | 10.4 sec.    | 11.0 sec.         |
| Last but two stride| 2.10 m.      | 1.95 m.           |
| Pentultimate stride| 2.30 m.      | 2.43 m.           |
| Last stride        | 2.10 m.      | 2.01 m.           |

During the change of cadence, long jumpers must also try to run on the balls of their feet. To prepare for a high take-off (by a stronger planting of the foot against the ground) leads only to an excessively high loss in speed.

According to Dyatchkov, the loss of propulsion may account in the long jump with a height of jump of

60 cm. to 14.4%
42 cm. to  9.5%
36 cm.     6.6%

## Take-off

The take-off is the most important phase in the long jump, but it is also the most difficult one, because in 0.12 sec. all motions of the take-off should be executed in the right sequence.

The take-off is divided into 3 phases:

(a) Planting the take-off foot.
(b) Bending in the knee, hip, and ankle joints (amortization of gathering).
(c) active stretching or extending in the take-off.

The take-off results not only from explosive extension of the hip, knee, and ankle joints of the take-off leg. It also results from the vigorous swing of the free leg and the arms as well as from the lifting of the shoulders. All these movements must be well coordinated.

The take-off speed depends upon the height of the vertical shifting of the center of gravity and the duration of this shifting. Thus the long jump take-off should be executed explosively and the path through which force is applied to the center of gravity should also be optimally long.

Not only must the center of gravity be lowered during the penultimate stride, but more important, all parts of the body must be lifted during take-off.

Furthermore, it is a high takeoff height which gives the center of gravity a longer trajectory.

## PLANTING THE TAKE-OFF FOOT

### Putting down the take-off

The take-off foot is planted on the ground in nearly the same way as the foot in the running stride. Since, however, in the long jump horizontal speed should be transferred into a certain forward and upward speed, the take-off foot must be planted somewhat more forward. But this must not lead to a disadvantageous braking position and consequently to a definite decrease in speed. The foot should be planted actively. The jumper does not wait until the foot has touched ground, but plants the foot actively with a backward and downward "snatching" movement. One should avoid too hard a contact with the ground. When touching the take-off board, the leg is nearly stretched, having an angle of support of 118° to 120° (according to Dyatchkov).

At take-off, the jumper must plant his foot flat if possible, with the whole sole at the same time. This can be obtained by pressing slightly downwards with the front part of the foot a short time before touching the take-off board.

Planting the take-off foot with a pronounced leading of the heel and a following rolling over on the whole foot would result in a considerable loss of speed, in an over-bending of the jumping leg, and consequently in other take-off faults.

### The Preparation Phase

The movements in the preparation phase are not usually given enough consideration. The main function of this part of the take-off is to prepare an effective forward and upward take-off.

In the phase of preparation, the forces created by planting the take-off foot, are prepared by a slight bending in the ankle, knee and hip joints, The knee joint is especially bent. During the preparation phase the take-off leg should be flexed until it has reached an angle of 145° to 150° (according to Dyatchkov). When this angle is too big or too small, two faults may result:

1st fault: Untimely take-off.
Cause: Too slight flexing of the take-off leg.
Consequence: Too strong a braking effect, resulting in over-bending the take-off leg. The athlete can jump relatively high, but not very far.
2nd fault: Delayed take-off.
Cause: Too much bending of the take-off leg.
Consequence: Take-off extension is executed too late. Height of flight and length of jump are too small.

During the preparation phase, there is a pre-tension of the extensor muscles of the take-off leg. This results in a more explosive and efficient muscle action during take-off movements.

At the conclusion of the preparation phase the jumper must rise quickly to the ball. Hence there will be again a short, slight increase of the angle of support, and at the same time an optimal pre-tension of the foot-extensors. The rising to the ball of the take-off foot will take place, when the swinging leg has joined the take-off leg and the trajectory of the center of gravity has not yet surpassed the vertical line.

With the beginning of the rising to the ball of the take-off foot, the take-off motions are directed exclusively upwards.

**The active take-off**

After having created favorable conditions for an active take-off during the preparation phase, it is easy to execute the take-off.

The motion of the swinging leg considerably influences the take-off. With planting of the take-off leg on the take-off board, the swinging leg begins to execute its wide upward-forward swinging motion. Here the following points should be considered:

1. Swinging should begin from the hip, which at the same time is shifted forwards and upwards.

2. Towards the end the free leg swing, it must be braked quickly so that the swinging force may be transferred to the body.

3. During the swing, the leg is very much bent at the knee. At the end of the take-off, the free leg thigh comes to the horizontal position.

4. With the aid of a suitable free leg swing, the effective range of take-off force may be shifted more forward. Thus, if necessary, the possibility arises for creating a backward turning of the body after takeoff. The take-off leg is stretched momentarily, as it is being overtaken by the swinging (free) leg. If the take-off leg is at first stretched slowly, it becomes explosive at the further decrease of the angle of support and the extension of the take-off leg (among other things by the transfer of momentum from the swinging leg and the arms to the trunk). The arms are swung rather high and quickly stopped in their upward motion. The elbows are rotated slightly outwards thus the shoulders may be lifted more easily and it is easier to keep balance. At the moment of breaking contact with the ground, the jumper has created certain conditions and forces for the subsequent airborne flight.

The jumping distance theoretically possible is primarily determined by the take-off speed, the take-off height of the center of gravity and the take-off angle. But it also depends upon the body position at the instant of take-off. From this body position the jumper may derive an advantage as to the theoretical distance possible, or a disadvantage in terms of the loss in landing distance. The take-off speed differs according to age, sex and training level, whereas the take-off angle for all jumpers is between 17° and 24°. At the instant of the take-off the body should be upright. A forward body lean at the instant of take-off would (besides other faults) result in a forward turning of the body in the air and consequently a premature contact of the feet with the ground. There will usually be a forward turning factor in the air because the effective range of take-off force passes behind the center of gravity of the body. There is also a small backward turning impulse generated at take-off (the effective range of the force runs a little in front of the center of gravity). That provides favorable conditions during the first part of the flight phase for an efficient flight with backward body lean.

The decrease of take-off force necessary for the execution of the turning impulse is compensated for by the subsequent better landing position, resulting in optimal utilization of the theoretical maximum possible distance in the flight phase of the jump. An upright trunk position combined with a strong forward-upward swing of the free leg is an essential condition for creating a turning impulse. The popular opinion, that at the instant of take-off the trunk must be in line with the take-off leg, is wrong. The take-off leg makes an angle of 76° to 80° with the ground, whereas the trunk must be kept upright.

**The flight and landing**

Once the jumper has left the ground, he cannot change the trajectory of his center of gravity by executing body movements. His body motions while airborne only maintain his balance in order to achieve the most efficient landing position. The most efficient landing position is that which more nearly approaches the theoretical maximum possible landing distance.

Nowadays the walk-in-air-style is more in vogue, because, among other things, an efficient take-off as well as a timely preparation for landing are best guaranteed. The sail style with all parts of the body drawn toward to the center of gravity, mechanically speaking, provides the worst conditions for an efficient landing. Here small faults in the take-off (forward turning impulse) cause a considerable decrease in distance.

After the take-off, a striding motion is executed and the hip is brought forward. Simultaneously there is a body lean-back characteristic of the first part of the flight. Such a body lean-back must not be confused with a strong back-arching (wrongly designed as "for a hollow back"). Such an exaggerated back-arching cannot cause an improvement of the body position for the landing, because simultaneously with the backward bending of the trunk the legs are also brought backwards. With this, however, the conditions for lifting the legs in order to land are still the same.

When the jumper has reached the highest point of the flight trajectory, he must again come upright with his trunk and start moving his legs forward. Upon reaching the highest point of the flight trajectory, the jumper should start to prepare for landing. First of all he attempts to lift his legs up to the horizontal line, beyond the trajectory of his center of gravity. The trunk must be inclined slightly forward in order to compensate. When the center of gravity has been lowered nearly to the take-off height, the jumper begins to again straighten up slightly. Now the legs (in order to compensate) are lowered to such a degree that the feet are near the trajectory of the center of gravity. The hips are shifted forward. After having prepared for landing in such a way, the feet may be planted very near to the point where maximum landing distance is possible.

This landing in a "sitting position" is more efficient than a landing in which the jumper, a short moment before and at the very moment of touching the ground, is folded up like a jack-knife. This jack-knife style of landing is only possible if, during the last part of the flight, the legs have been lifted up to the horizontal line passing through the jumper's center of gravity. If a jumper, because of incorrect movements during the first part of the flight, is unable to lift his legs, he should strive to land in a crouched position, in order to prevent a still greater loss in landing.

After the feet touch the sand at landing, the pressure of body weight causes the legs to bend. With the help of the forward motion still remaining, the jumper may pass beyond the support of his feet. The arms swinging forward help him to move ahead. In order to land efficiently, the knees and the hips should also be shifted forwards. By experience we know that it is sometimes useful to land with a fall to the side.

**The step method**

The movement known as the sail midair style is the most simple to execute. One can scarcely find a sail style well executed, because here it is very difficult to avoid forward rotation. Those who want to excel in the long jump should use another style. Even beginners should avoid using the sail style (which involves quickly bringing knees to the chest after take-off).

The step method is more suitable than the sail. Contrary to the sail style, in the step method a wide striding position may be held a long time during the take-off phase. Only a short moment before landing the take-off leg is brought forward to the swinging (free) leg. Until then the trunk should be kept erect. The trunk is lowered as a balancing motion in reaction to the lifting of the legs in preparation for landing, but not prior to the lifting of the legs.

**Hollow-back technique (Hang style)**

After the take-off, the jumper drops the swinging leg down near the vertical line and at the same time draws his take-off leg, bent at the knee, to his swinging (free) leg. Both the legs are now close together. Their lower legs point backward, forming nearly a right angle with the thighs. The arms continue the motion started in the take-off and are kept over the head during the first part of the flight.

This position is kept by the jumper up to the half-way point of the flight. Then both bent legs are lifted forward and upward in order to land, and in reaction the trunk bends forward. A short moment before touching ground, the jumper throws his lower legs far ahead. According to his ability, he can land in a "sitting" or a crouched position.

In the hollow-back technique, competitors often attempt to prolong the hang too long. In most cases this results in a poor landing. Furthermore, not all jumpers are successful enough to come into an adequate backward body lean during the first part of the flight.

The combination of the walk-in-air style and the hollow-back techique (hang) would offer a possibility to correct this fault. Here the jumper, in the first part of the jump, executes first a complete leg scissors motion (as in the walk-in-air style) and thus achieves a good backward body lean. After this stride, the bent legs are almost parallel (as in the hollow-back or hang technique), but the take-off leg is a little ahead of the swinging leg. The further sequence of motion corresponds to that of the hollow-back technique (hang).

The advantage of this combination lies mainly in the better use of the swinging leg during the take-off. In addition to a more forceful take-off, in most cases there is also a greater forward inclination of the effective range of force.

**The walk-in-air style**

In this style the jumper merely continues to walk in the air. Usually he does then 1½ strides. Jumpers with very good results (about 8 m.) sometimes use 2½ strides.

After the take-off, the swinging (free) leg, gradually stretching, is actively lowered and moved backwards with knee unbent (1st stride). At the same time, the take-off leg, strongly bent in the knee joint, is brought forward. This action rotates the body backward. As the jumper lifts his take-off leg forward and up to the horizontal line, he leans his trunk forward as a reaction to this motion. The take-off leg must be kept in this position until the swinging leg is brought to the same level. Until this moment the trunk is still inclined forward. The lowering of the legs and bringing forward of the hips causes by reaction the raising of the trunk, thus the jumper is in a "sitting" position in preparation for landing. In this style the landing is made in the "sitting" position only after the legs have been lifted beyond the trajectory of the center of gravity.

The arms help to keep the jumper's balance by a circling motion corresponding to the running rhythm. In order to better prepare for landing the arms move a moment before the beginning of landing to a position slightly behind the body. As the feet touch the ground, the arms swing actively forward.

## SPECIAL PREPARATION

**Technical instruction**

In accordance with the major phases of Long Jumping Technique, the following abilities should be developed.

a) The ability to take-off with one leg at a high speed (strength and agility)
b) The ability to keep one's balance and orientation during the long flight phase.
c) The ability to take-off from the take-off board (development of the sense of distance).

Because each take-off must be executed with one leg, the elementary forms of these exercises are:

**Stalking jump:** From a fast run-up, take-off on one leg. The swinging leg is well-bent. The trunk is upright. Land on the swinging leg.

**Jumping run:** Each stride is a jump. After the take-off, a high swinging leg action is executed and the take-off leg remains behind the body during the flight.

**Springy running steps:** Springy running steps in gymnastics, with emphasized action of the swinging leg and arms.

These three elementary exercises may be executed in many forms of play and thus can be easily adapted to each aspect of preparation. Here are some more examples:

Elementary form: "Stalk Jumping"

1. Execute "stalking jumps" over low but broad obstacles (two bars, two elastic ropes, 2 balls, etc.) with one or three approach steps.
2. Jumping in zones gradually longer distances.
3. Jumping over a ditch. Several teams jump over a marked ditch. The jumper who is able to jump over it without hitting the mark, will score a point for his team.
4. "Stalking jumps" from the spring-board.
5. "Stalking jumps" with a landing target.
6. Relay competition over broad obstacles (upper part of a box horse, mat, etc.).

**Elementary form: jumping run**

1. Competitive jumping from a mark (multiple-jumps) (compare: hop, step and jump)
2. Stairs jumping
3. Jumping run over low obstacles
4. Jumping on marks
5. Zigzag jumping

**Elementary form: springy running steps**

1. Springy running steps with short approach.
2. Competitive hopping (individual competition and team competition)
3. Springy running steps over broad obstacles (chalk marks, etc.)

**Basic exercises of technical instruction**

After a solid preparation in technique of long jumping, the basic instruction in this event does not offer too great difficulties. With respect to the approach-run and take-off there are no differences in the various jumping styles. At first it is not so important which to choose. It is possible to change later from one technique to another, without harming the acquired technique of approach and take-off. Therefore, the beginner should use the easy technique of the step method in the long jump.

In this technique, all elements of a correct take-off are developed, such as a quick taking-off stride, energetic swinging leg action, and upright upper part of the body. In addition, the athlete is not distracted from essential issues by complicated movements during the flight.

Later on, the hollow-back technique or the walk-in-air style can be developed on this base at any time. The advanced long jumper should know all the techniques, in order to choose the one best suited to himself.

When starting the series of exercises, begin with the main phase, "take-off", in connection with the approach-run, and later, after a gradually elongated approach-run, with the movements of flight and landing.

**Basic exercises in order to develop the step method**

Exercise 1—Stalking jump with 3 to 5 strides of approach, over a broad obstacle into the pit.

Use as obstacles such things as two high jump crossbars, elastic bands, etc. It is important to use a soft landing pit. To guarantee a safe landing, it is recommended that the take-off leg should land a short moment after the swinging leg.

Purpose: Training of the take-off and the first parts of the flight.

Essential points: After an active extension in the take-off with a high swinging free leg action, the step position should be kept as long as possible. The upper part of the body is kept erect or slightly bent back, and the take-off leg remains behind the body.

Exercise 2—Using 5 to 7 approach strides, jump over a broad obstacle.

The take-off leg swings forward and upward, over the rear edge of the obstacle, and meets the swinging leg, which now also swings upward with its lower leg. There will be a so-called sitting position in preparation for landing. The jumper will land on both feet.

Purpose: Training the mid-air and landing movements.

Essential points: The step position should be kept as long as possible. The take-off and preparation for landing should be clearly distinguished one from the other.

Exercise 3—Step method jump from a take-off zone of 60 cm. using 5 to 9 approach-strides.

In order to increase the approach-run, take about 2 normal walking strides for one running stride.

Purpose: Introduction of a take-off mark. Execute the total movement without auxiliary apparatus.

Essential points: Quick last take-off stride with upright body, followed by an energetic leg action.

Exercise 4—Step method. Jump over a heap of sand.

In order to utilize the trajectory of the center of gravity as well as possible, the heels should be lifted very high. The heap of sand will demand the best possible performance and force the pupil to prepare for an intensive landing.

Purpose: To learn an economical landing.

Essential points: During the first part of the flight, the upper part of the body should be bent slightly backwards. The legs can only get into a sitting position if a slight backward turn has been started during take-off.

Exercise 5—Step method. Jump with a longer approach-run and a gradually decreasing take-off zone (down to 20 cm.). There is an easy way to fix the distance of the approach-run: from the take-off board one runs until maximum speed is attained. A partner or the instructor marks the foot print of the take-off leg at the place found. The approach-run should always begin with the same leg.

Purpose: Approach-training. Primitive form of the step method.

Essential points: No chopping or lengthening of strides before take-off.

**Basic and auxiliary exercises for developing the walk-in-air style**

Exercise 1—Stalking jump from a higher take-off place with 5 approach-strides, or land in a deeper pit.

Purpose: Increase of the airborne phase, thus providing more time to execute motions during flight. The stalking jump continues motions already acquired, and at the same time the athlete becomes accustomed to the new training conditions.

Essential points: Active landing and an upright upper part of the body. The take-off leg should be behind the body during the flight as too early a forward motion of this leg results mostly from an imperfect stretching action at take-off.

Exercise 2—Jumping from a higher take-off than landing place with a full running stride in the air and immediate running into the pit.

Purpose: Training of the running motions in the air.

Essential points: The novice tends to accomplish the running motions in the air only with his lower legs. As the runner must go on running when landing, he is forced to bring his feet through the full range of motion behind the body. If not executed correctly the jumper cannot continue running into the pit.

Auxiliary exercises: As the beginner does not have at his disposal the ground as a surface of orientation while airborne, a bar has proved to be a good substitute. This bar is held by the teacher at a height of 50 cm. and at a distance of 2 m. beyond the take-off board. By an active downward and backward action of the swinging leg, the jumper should try to kick the bar.

Exercise 3—Walk-in-air jump from a higher take-off than landing place, with 5 to 7 approach strides.

Purpose: Introduction to the total movement.

Essential points: After having taken-off vigorously, a distinct sequence of strides must be visible. Special attention should be paid to the second stride, since this one directly prepares the landing.

Auxiliary exercises:

a) Practice leg motion while hanging from parallel bars or from a high apparatus.

b) Repeated jumping with the help of a partner. Two partners run by the sides of the athlete grasping and supporting him at his upper arms. During each jump he will be lifted somewhat and thus the time of flight will be prolonged. In this way, exercises in stride motions during the flight are facilitated.

Exercise 4—Walk-in-air jump from the take-off board with 7 to 9 approach strides.

Purpose: Application of the skill acquired so far, under normal taking-off conditions.

Essential points: Sufficiently fast approach-run, and fast, energetic take-off stride with vigorous planting of the foot. The hip and knee joints are only slightly bent. Make certain that while striving to jump high, the jumper does not execute any braking action to forward motion in his approach strides.

Exercise 5—Walk-in-air jump with 9 to 15 approach strides; fixing the approach checkmarks (See "step method").

Purpose: Jump under competitive conditions.

Essential points: Cf. exercise 4.

**Basic and auxiliary exercises for developing the hollow-back technique (hang)**

Exercise 1—"Stalking jump" from a higher take-off point (Cf. exercise 1 of walk-in-air style).

Exercise 2—Easy jumps, one after the other. Landing on both feet followed by two or three steps.

Purpose: Introduction to the sequence of motions.

Essential points: Pronounced swinging (free) leg action. In the flight, the swinging leg falls back immediately and the hip is shifted slightly forwards. Both legs are beneath the body.

Exercise 3—Using a 5-stride approach, jump from an elevated take-off point, use the hang mid-air technique, without emphasizing landing motions.

Purpose and essential points: (Cf. exercise 2.)

Exercise 4—Hollow-back technique (hang) from a higher take-off place with emphasized landing motions.

Purpose: Practicing the total movement, especially the preparation for landing.

Essential points: Distinct swinging leg work: The beginner tends to immediately assume the flight position without swinging his free leg forward.

Auxiliary exercise: Cf. exercise 3 of walk-in-air style.

Exercise 5—Hollow-back technique (hang) from the take-off board with 9 to 15 approach strides.

Purpose: Practice the approach-run; mastering the elementary form of hollow-back technique (hang).

Essential points: Cf. exercise 4.

**Supplementary exercises:**

The great difficulty of long jumping lies in the high speed, developed during the approach-run, from which the jumper must take-off efficiently. The quick taking-off motions require excellent co-ordination. The take-off should be executed as accurately as possible from the take-off board, for best results.

Supplementary exercises for the long jump concentrate mainly on improving take-off movements and accuracy of the approach-run. They are executed in closest connection with special strength exercises. It is often difficult to distinguish them from these exercises.

**Supplementary exercises for improving the approach-run:**

1. Improving the accuracy of the approach by repeated approach-running over different approach distances, but using an equal number of strides (Rewson method.)

This method, developed in the Soviet Union, and here slightly altered as to its structure, suggests the following composition of exercises:

(a) Establishing the starting mark (4 to 5 trials). (Based on this established mark, during all the following exercises the approach should be shortened or lengthened.)

(b) Lengthen approach-run by about 2 feet-lengths (2 to 3 approach runs).

(c) Shorten approach by about 2-foot lengths (2 to 3 approach runs).

(d) Lengthen approach by about one-foot length (2 to 3 approach runs).

(e) Alternative approach-run, one-foot length behind the mark, the second time one-foot length in front of the mark and a third time precisely from the mark (two trials).

The jumper should try to hit the take-off board at each approach-run without lengthening or shortening his strides too much before the take-off board.

With the help of this method, attempt to improve the perception for estimating approach distances in connection with the most suitable execution of strides up to the take-off board. Therefore, the following combinations should also be used in a similar way: approach-runs with following wind-head wind-cross wind alternating; approach-runs on a soft track-on the cinder track—on grassy ground, alternating; approach-runs with spikes—with warm-up shoes-barefooted, alternating. An equal distance should always be covered by a constant number of strides.

2. Development of a take-off rhythm with the help of check marks.

Begin with a short approach-run in order to become accustomed to the rhythm, and then gradually increase the distance of approach.

**Supplementary exercises to improve the take-off:**

1. Jump off a spring board and the upper part of a box horse. The last stride must be short. Will quickly correct the main fault of beginners, which is to brake somewhat with the heel.

3. Taking-off from a bench. In order to prevent the bench from tipping over, if the foot has touched it in a wrong way, a teammate or the instructor should sit on it.

4. Jumps from a short approach, where the take-off stride must be executed over a very low obstacle (bar, rubber rope).

5. Jumps from a lower take-off point, using a medium to full approach. Thus, not only speed, but also coordination of the take-off will be improved.

6. Take-off after approaching from a downward sloping runway. The higher approach speed has nearly the same effect as in exercise 5. But at the same time also special strength is developed for the take-off.

7. Jumps with a pronounced swinging leg driving into the hang. Seize a branch of a tree, a horizontal bar or something similar while airborne. By intending to seize the apparatus, the jumper avoids the frequent fault of bending the upper part of the body forward.

**Supplementary exercises for flight in the air:**

1. Long jumps from a spring-board. Here, higher demands are put on the equilibrium on account of the artificially prolonged flight path. (This should not be done too frequently, because the active take-off is neglected!)

2. Long jumps into a low pit.

3. Jumps with an emphasized stride in the air. Landing on the take-off leg.

**Supplementary exercises for training of the landing:**

1. Long jumps over a rubber rope 20 cm. high, held near the limit of the jump.

# THE MOST IMPORTANT PHASE IN THE LONG JUMP

By Jess Jarver, Australia, editor, *Modern Athlete and Coach*

*This article attempts to sum-up the importance of the approach phase in the long jump and some factors about its length, uniformity, last strides and training.*

## INTRODUCTION

Jumping implies the lifting of the athlete's center of gravity so that contact is lost with the ground. Hence the primary objective in all competitive jumping is to project the athlete's center of gravity through the air at the maximum velocity in the required direction. If the direction is upward we get the high jump, if the direction is forward and upward we are dealing with the long jump.

The distance achieved in the long jump depends mainly on the velocity accumulated in the run-up and forces applied at the take-off when horizontal speed is transferred in the desired direction. It is therefore generally accepted that the most important phases in the long jump are the take-off and approach run. The last, responsible for about two thirds of the distance jumped, is the largest contributor and requires special attention. It must be sufficiently long to enable the athlete to reach the board close to his maximum speed; it must be controlled to allow the horizontal speed to be converged into a jump through an effective take-off; and it must be precise to bring the take-off foot square on the board.

## LENGTH

To reach what can be called the "peak-controlled velocity" is perhaps the greatest single problem in long jumping. Available research data, although limited, indicates that regardless of his sprinting ability the human being reaches maximum speed in about six seconds. (Franklin Henry, "Research on Sprint Running"). This means that if a jumper is to reach peak velocity, he would require a run-up of more than 60 yards. However, the same research shows that at about 50 yards the athlete will be within one per cent of his maximum speed. As the additional speed, gained between 50 and 60 yards, is apparently imperceptible, it appears that a run-up close to 150 feet is sufficient for most athletes.

The exact length of approach is obviously individual and depends mainly on the ability to accelerate, age of the jumper and the stage he has reached in his training. The last is perhaps the most important, as to increase the length of the run-up, the jumper must have gained sufficient strength to enable him to have the required control and energy for the lift at the take-off.

It can be generally said that the run-up for experienced long jumpers is somewhere between 120 and 150 feet, involving 16 to 22 running strides. The possibility of a slightly longer approach should not be overlooked when dealing with well conditioned top-rate jumpers.

## UNIFORMITY

Although the approach in the long jump should be an accumulation of speed right from the first stride, it differs from a sprint acceleration because of the pre-requisite to bring the jumper's take-off foot at maximum controlled velocity on the take-off board. It requires precision in the stride pattern and a consistent rate of acceleration.

To achieve uniformity in the stride length and consistency in acceleration, the approach run has to start from the same position with the same rate of acceleration with no variations whatsoever. Here the practical value of check marks, although used by many jumpers, is rather doubtful. Check marks, usually two are used in addition to the starting mark, are only helpful in the stages when the run-up is in process of being established. Once this has been achieved they serve at the most only as a psychological aid. The first check mark can be eliminated immediately after the approach has been standardized. The second, often placed eight strides from the board, is useless right from the start, as it can consciously be hit only at the expense of losing concentration and it is obvious that adjustments during the last few strides will mean loss of forward speed. It is interesting to note that many experienced jumpers, who by habit keep on using check marks, regularly miss them without noticing it.

**LAST STRIDES**

Just before the take-off point all the jumper's movements should be coordinated to allow for an effective take-off to rocket him into the air along a desired path. This can only be achieved if the action is well under control during the last few strides of the speed accumulating approach run. "Controlled" is perhaps the key word here as horizontal velocity should not be sacrificed. The so-called "gather", or coast, is perhaps best described as using the attained sprinting speed while mental and physical preparations are made for the actual take-off. Although the mental concentration to shut everything else from the mind, except the forthcoming leap, has started already with the first stride, it should reach its peak just before the take-off. The physical preparations include some adjustments in adopting a more upright position of the trunk and sometimes also slight alterations in the length of the last two strides. The straightening of the body allows for the take-off foot to reach slightly ahead of the jumper's C of G for a better forward upward drive from the board. A shorter last stride—although different views exist about it—appears helpful to get the take-off leg slightly bent, described as "compressing the spring" by Dyson. It also allows for the jumper's C of G to be directly over the board as the take-off foot strikes and slightly in advance of it when leaving the board.

The pattern of the final strides is by no means consistent and the word "gather" should be interpreted with extreme care. As the loss of horizontal velocity must be kept to a minimum and proper sprinting action requires relaxation anyway, the preparations for the lift are hardly noticeable in good jumpers. Actually, many first-class jumpers apparently ignore the idea of a coast and either sprint to the take-off, maintaining the speed accumulated or, in extreme cases, even attempt to accelerate. The last, however, could be dangerous as an attempt to accelerate when moving at top speed causes tension and can have adverse influence on the actual take-off.

There are great individual differences over the final stride pattern prior to take-off. Jumpers, who are very fast sprinters and usually have less jumping ability prefer to place less emphasis in the take-off by lowering the C of G during the penultimate stride. Smolensky has recorded the following contrasting examples:

|  | Jumper A (Best 100m — 10.4) | Jumper B (Best 100m — 11.0) |
|---|---|---|
| Third last stride | 6.10¾ (2.10m) | 6.4¾ (1.95m) |
| Second last stride | 7. 6½ (2.30m) | 7.11¾ (2.43m) |
| Last stride | 6.10¾ (2.10m) | 6.7¼ (2.01m) |

Although, there are apparently no standard changes in the length of the last strides because they vary according to the type of the jumper and his speed, an obvious change in the rhythm of the stride pattern is noticeable in most top class jumpers. The rhythm changes occur during the last few strides which are performed at a higher frequency than the previous sprinting pattern. The changes are also influenced by the C of G dropping slightly during the last stride before take-off and being caught on the rise when the take-off foot hits the board.

**TRAINING**

Knowing that the run-up speed is the most important single phase in the long jump it becomes obvious that it must take an accordingly important place in training. Simply asking to improve run-up speed by working together with sprinters appears wrong. It must be kept in mind that the long jump run-up has its own peculiar characteristics—it needs to be only sufficiently long to enable the athlete to reach the board close to his maximum, but not necessarily at his maximum speed. It must also allow for an efficient take-off and must be precise.

It may well be that in the early stages of his career the long jumper benefits by working with sprinters but as soon as his basic sprinting skill has been established the speed work must become specific for long jumping. True the jumper is still involved in the development of muscular power, mobility and neuro-muscular coordination in order to improve his speed, but most other aspects of sprinting are to him relatively unimportant. There is no need for reaction speed to the starter's gun, and no demand for local muscular endurance to maintain speed. A certain amount of endurance, measured by the efficiency of the recovery rate, however, is required in an indirect way. Although this quality is of no direct value in competition (there is usually enough time to recover between each jump) it is needed in training to enable the athlete to perform more work in the time available.

The relative value of the general endurance training must always be kept in mind. A long jumper is not interested in becoming a first class cross-country runner, his aim is to jump further than before. Thus his endurance work is designed to improve his cardio-respiratory efficiency to enable him to increase the amount of work in training. Improved general endurance will allow him to perform more sprinting and execute more jumps with shorter recoveries. He can simply produce far more work in a shorter time—an important factor to most athletes in training.

It is usually during the winter that the sprint training of the long jumper becomes separated from the sprinters as soon as sufficient basic speed endurance is achieved. The long jumper, concerned only with explosive acceleration over a relatively short distance, changes his training accordingly. This does not mean that the long jumper is not running distances over the run-up length. He still needs longer sprint distances which are beneficial to develop rhythm and relaxation. But in addition to 100, 150 and 220 yard repetitions all types of accelerations are now becoming increasingly important. The accelerations, including gradually lengthened distances at top speed and varied-pace sprinting are according to the modern approach to speed training a valuable asset in improving neuro-muscular coordination.

Somewhere during the preparation phase actual run-ups are finding a place in the training and, as the competitive season approaches, are employed in increasing quantities in the schedules. After the change to the competitive phase has been completed the training load and intensity are gradually dropped, allowing for longer recoveries before competitions and emphasizing quality rather than quantity. Sprint training in the competitive phase becomes very specific and is dominated by short explosive dashes and repetitions of the actual approach runs. Numerous repetitions of the run-up, aiming to improve speed and accuracy, at this stage of training are a must.

Knowing the relative value of horizontal velocity it is advisable to conduct regular checks to assure that the jumper is moving as close as possible to maximum speed at the take-off. The first guide is a comparison of the run-up speed in actual jumping with the speed achieved by just sprinting over the approach-run distance. This will indicate approximately how much horizontal velocity is lost by the jumper when preparing for the take-off movements. It can be checked by simply timing the athlete from the start of his run-up to the moment the take-off foot contacts the board and comparing it with the time over the same sequence when an actual jump is executed.

Another method of checking velocity losses at the take-off is to time the jumper over the last two five-meter stretches before the take-off. Comparison of the times indicates not only how much speed is lost in preparation for the take-off but is also helpful to decide whether the run-up has been sufficiently long to allow the jumper to reach his maximum speed. Although this timing is best done with proper equipment, two 1/100-second calibration stopwatches can be used satisfactorily, provided the timer stands well back from the run-up to reduce the angle of vision.

Regular timing over the last 10 meters before the take-off is another simple guidance. When the time is taken by the same person, timing mistakes are usually evened out and the figures, when averaged over a number of repetitions, are sufficient to give a fair indication of the jumper's speed just prior to the take-off on a particular day.

The exactness of the run-up requires more than casual attention. After the maximum speed has been established the work should concentrate on the accuracy to assure that the jumper can cope with the direct and indirect factors influencing his run-up in competition. Among the factors to be considered are track and weather conditions, outside disturbances, physical well-being on the day and many others. Wind conditions can change during the competition or even during a single jump with a sudden gust. Concentration can be affected and adjustments made according to the previous effort become valueless. The jumper therefore has to alter his run-up practice to allow for different track and wind conditions. He also needs numerous full speed repetitions of the run-up to develop an extra sense, allowing him to make adjustments even when moving at close to maximum speed.

In order to achieve an uninhibited take-off the jumper must work on his run-up all the time. Hence, constant run-up practice, not only over the set approach, but practice in short sprints and in judgment of distances, takes priority in the competitive training phase. The jumper must have confidence in his approach knowing that when he starts at a set point, he will take off at a set point. The confidence engendered by this knowledge is measured not in inches but in feet because instructive action is always so much faster than conscious movement.

# THE DROPPING OF THE LEGS IN LONG JUMPING

By Prof. Bernard J. Hopper, England

One of the problems heard frequently in long-jump coaching is the tendency of the novice to allow the legs to drop prematurely into the pit even after what appears to have been a good take-off from the board, i.e. with plenty of height gained and little loss of forward speed. This article is an attempt to apply mechanical considerations in suggesting possible causes of this fault, and in pinpointing the essential features of correct technique.

First, it is well-recognized that the muscular effort made by the jumper during his period of contact with the board is one which derives from the board a very short-lived, but nevertheless very big reaction of average value several times body-weight. It is also true that even experts find it impossible, under the given conditions, to achieve a reaction which has no checking effect on forward speed—indeed, better performance in terms of height gained may result when some loss of run-up speed is accepted. Furthermore, the general direction of this reaction is one which usually gives the body a tendency to rotate forwards about the transverse axis through its center of mass: that is, the body has some angular momentum about this axis in the forward sense while it is in the air, and so has no means of shedding it until it lands. However, there are well-known techniques whereby this unwanted angular momentum is confined to the rotary motion of extended arms and striding legs—the so-called "hitch-kick" method; or, alternatively, the inevitable forward rotation of the trunk can be slowed down to a negligible rate by maintaining the whole body in a fully extended posture longitudinally (with a suspicion of a striding action), as in the "hang" style. The very slow change of body-attitude in the latter method is a result of the big moment of inertia when so much of the mass is far from the body's center of mass, G.

Now it is evident that the tendency of the trunk to rotate forwards from its near-erect attitude is one which would make the final forwardly-directed leg posture difficult to achieve; so if the body's angular momentum is so great that it cannot be controlled, then the legs will be forced down to make too early a landing, and the cause would be the unsatisfactory take-off from the board. Again, if control is effective in keeping the trunk erect, but the "hitch" or "hang" action is stopped too soon in favor of the final forward pike about the hips, then the piking action will be one in which the trunk and arms rotate fast into the piked posture while the legs come up slowly—if at all—and then drop prematurely as the whole body rotates forward over them. The fault here lies in too long a period being given to the adoption of the piked posture.

These are obvious reasons for the involuntary dropping of the feet before landing, but a further one can be found in the very technique used in the final forward-piking action: a technique which, if faulty, can spoil an otherwise sound jump. What we do not often realize is that the forward rotation of the upper part of the body about the hips, and the simultaneous forward and upward movement of the legs, is much more complex, mechanically, than, say, the closing of the jaws of a crocodile or of a pair of wire-cutters: these latter have *fixed* axes of rotation. In general, what happens is that the transverse axis through the line of the hips move either upwards or downwards with respect to the body's center of mass, and its direction of motion depends on more than one factor.

To explain this, suppose the body to be of a much simpler form than it really is: let its upper part be represented by a point mass located at the center of mass of this part, $G_1$; and the legs by their mass at $G_2$. (Fig 1a.) Then before the motion starts, $G_1$ and $G_2$ will be disposed on opposite sides of G, the center of mass of the whole body, and they must, of course, always be so placed that $G_1$, G, and $G_2$ form a straight line. Now if for simplicity, we assume that the system has no angular momentum, then this line will remain in the same direction as the point masses at $G_1$ and $G_2$ move towards G in the piking movement. We also note that the path of G in the air will not be affected in any way by the purely internal impulses causing the posture-change; only the lines $G_1H$ and $G_2H$ will be affected, where H is the hip-joint about which the piking is taking place, and if $G_1H$ is longer than $G_2H$ then the changes in their direction will be as shown in the sequence (Fig 1), with the hips dropping and the feet tending to rise with respect to G. This suggests that correct technique in long jumping requires the maximum distance between the center of mass of the upper body and the axis about which the piking is taking place, i.e. the hip-joint; and this can be done by keeping the back as flat as possible and the arms extended in line with it—the "hang" method provides this admirably, but it has to be held throughout the movement. Effective and ineffective forms are shown in Fig 2.

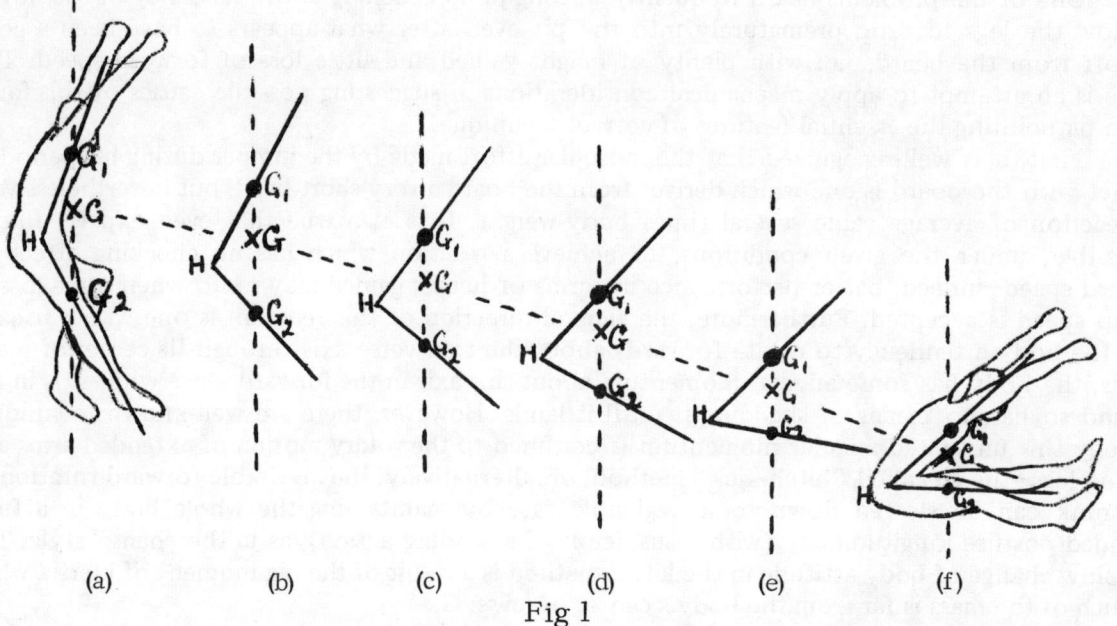

Fig 1

The body as a two-mass system at $G_1$ and $G_2$. The line $G_1G_2$ keeps a constant direction throughout.

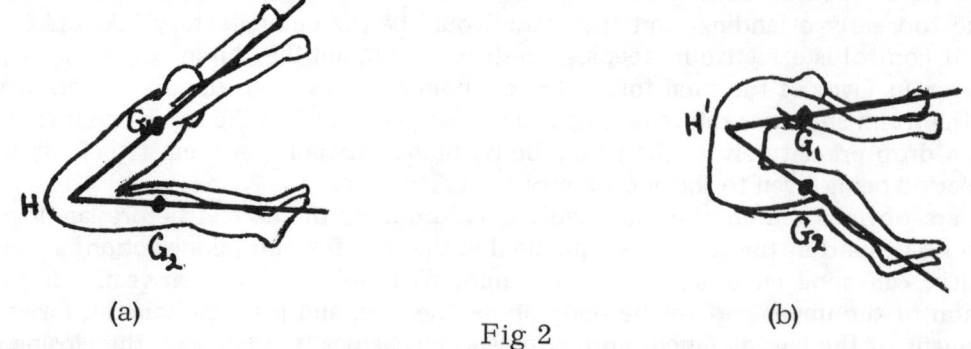

Fig 2

Posture (a) makes $G_1H$ greater than $G_2H$, as required, but in (b) the indefinite "hinge" position H' is closer to $G_1$ than to $G_2$, so the legs rise very little.

However, the human body as a two-part system of point masses at $G_1$ and $G_2$ is a concept of only limited value. A much more accurate picture is obtained when we realize that the masses are not points but distributed masses spread over the configuration of the upper body and the legs respectively, and that each has a moment of inertia about its own center of mass, just as a fly-wheel has about its axle. This means that to start the piking action from the position of Fig 1a, not only has each mass to be brought nearer to G, but each part has to be set rotating about its own center of mass as the lines $G_1H$ and $G_2H$ change direction. If, as before, we start with the simple assumption that the system initially has no angular momentum, then again we remind ourselves that the internal mutual impulses which set the distributed masses rotating as the upper body and the legs are brought together, will not alter this condition, i.e. the turning impulse which starts the upper body rotating in the clockwise sense in Fig 3 is equal and opposite to that sending the legs up towards it. Both impulses are the result of the same muscular action at the hip..

Now if this action caused both parts to move *directly* towards G, as in the much simplified model of Fig 1, then the result would be the same as that of Fig 1, and the angular momenta of both upper body and legs about their own centers of mass would be equal and opposite; but, in general, this is not what happens because the moment of inertia of the legs about $G_2$ is much smaller than that of the upper body about $G_1$, and so the legs start to rotate faster about $G_2$ when the piking movement begins. Looking at the matter in a very popular way, we see that if the two parts were not connected at the hip, they would start to separate there, the head of each femur probably (unless the distance $G_2H$ were very short) moving *back* with respect to the pelvis; but, as things are, each femur would exert a *backward force* on each side of the pelvis and be forced forward itself. This means that instead of $G_1$ moving directly towards G, as it does in Fig 1, it moves to the left of it, with $G_2$ moving to the right. This mutual action at the hip-joints therefore causes the line $G_1G\ G_2$ to start changing its direction as shown in Fig 3a and 3b instead of maintaining a constant one as in the much simplified model of Fig 1; and it is seen that if this change in direction continued as the movement went on, there would be a "rocking back" of the body around G, and an even greater tendency of the feet to rise above the hips.

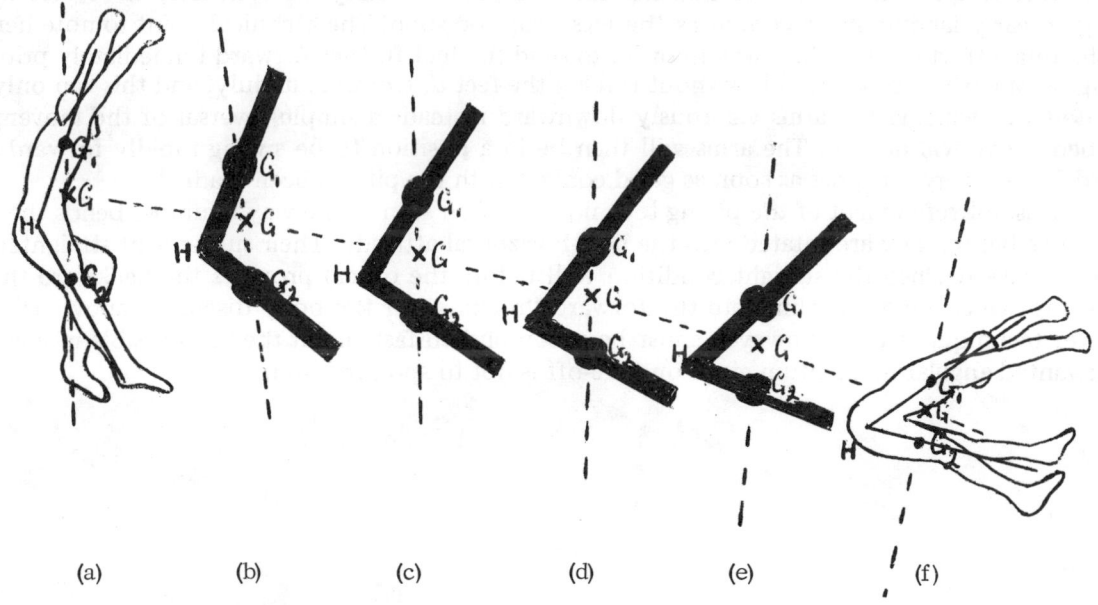

(a)  (b)  (c)  (d)  (e)  (f)

Fig 3

The body more nearly as it is: a two-part system of distributed masses with centers of mass $G_1$ and $G_2$. The line through the G's is almost certain to change direction in the way indicated, so that the upper part of the body rocks forwards over G.

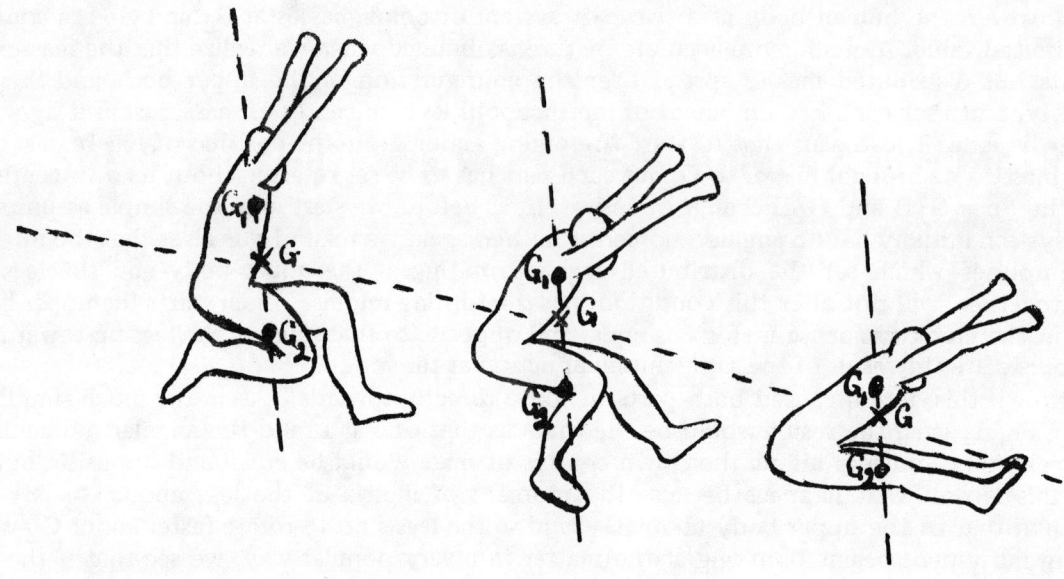

Fig 4

If the piking action starts from a bent-leg posture, then the subsequent straightening of the legs will tend to maintain the direction of the line through the G's.

Unfortunately, this backward rock is very slight and is soon reversed as the legs swing into the attitude of Fig 3c, d, e, and f. This is because the upper part of the femur, as the leg approaches the horizontal, is no longer moving backward faster than the pelvis would be going, and is now pulled *backward by it*, the upper part of the body being forced forward at the same time. This effect is not a particularly big one but it sends the whole body rocking *forward* around G in a way which tends to hinder the uprising of the feet (Fig 3f), and to have a disconcerting effect on the jumper. One result of this could be that he stops his pike too early, or even tries to reverse it, so making an early landing more certain as the legs drop too soon. The technical point to note here is that the final effort to raise the trunk in order to send the feet further forward immediately prior to landing, is one which must do this without forcing the feet *downwards* unduly, and this can only be prevented by swinging the arms vigorously downward instead—a simple reversal of the movement described above will not do. The arms will then be in a position to be swung rapidly forward and upward for recovery purposes as soon as good contact with the pit has been made.

A useful refinement of the piking technique is often seen in the way a jumper bends the legs at the knee before they are rotated into the near-horizontal attitude. Their subsequent straightening (one may have reached the straight condition well before the other) provides the backward thrust on the hip which tends to eliminate the forward "rocking" of the body discussed above. (Fig 4) Whatever technique is used, however, must be accomplished fast and at the last possible moment if the unwanted angular momentum given on take-off is not to spoil the jump.

# IMPORTANCE OF SWINGING MOVEMENTS AT THE TAKE-OFF

By Yuri Verhoshanski, U.S.S.R.

The take-off in jumping events is closely related to the swinging motions of the free leg and arms. Practical experience has shown that these swinging movements improve the efficiency of the take-off.

The importance of swinging movements at the take-off is in the athletic literature usually approached from the mechanical point of view (increased amplitude in raising the C of G vertically and the transfer of certain movements developed during the swing). However the most important aspect of this motion, the biomechanics, have so far been overlooked. For this reason we have for several years conducted a biomechanical study of certain movements in track and field events concentrating on this particular problem.

For example, in the high and triple jumps we attempted to improve the take-off by studying the dynamic structure of swinging movements and their relationship to the supporting leg. Cinecyclographic analyses were used under competitive conditions in addition to complex physiological laboratory methods.

The force applied at the supporting point by the take-off foot during the supporting phase was measured in detail under laboratory conditions, electrical activity in the involved muscle groups was registered and the degree of angle in the hip, knee and ankle joints of the supporting leg established. A Schlepposzillograph registered through a light beam the precise bend in the joints electrically during all stages of the take-off action.

The cinecyclographic analysis was prepared by special methods by composing a cyclogramme from the cine material of the movement without a pre-arranged point of orientation on the person tested. To provide a most accurate kinesiological and dynamical analyses of the swinging movement of the leg in its rotation center the upper part of the supporting leg was also filmed.

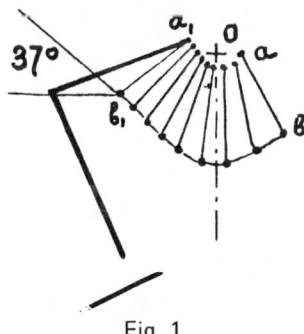

Fig. 1

(Fig. 1. a, -a = the curve of the upper part of the swinging leg. b, -b = the curve of the C of G of the swinging leg; O = the upper part of the supporting leg.)

As can be seen the C of G of the swinging elements shifts at the take-off according to the curve with changing speeds downwards. The acceleration developed during this movement characterizes the strength and the direction of the reaction forces forming the total up-thrust force during the supporting phase of the take-off. Because these forces are transferred through the supporting leg (which has the function of absorbing the shock and the active take-off) to the point of support, it is possible to study the dynamics of the swinging movements and the changes of the degree of bend in the supporting leg to establish their biomechanical relationship.

In order to simplify such an analysis we have concentrated mainly on the changing relationship between the swinging movements and the work of the supporting leg, and the vertical acceleration of the C of G of the leading leg and the arms.

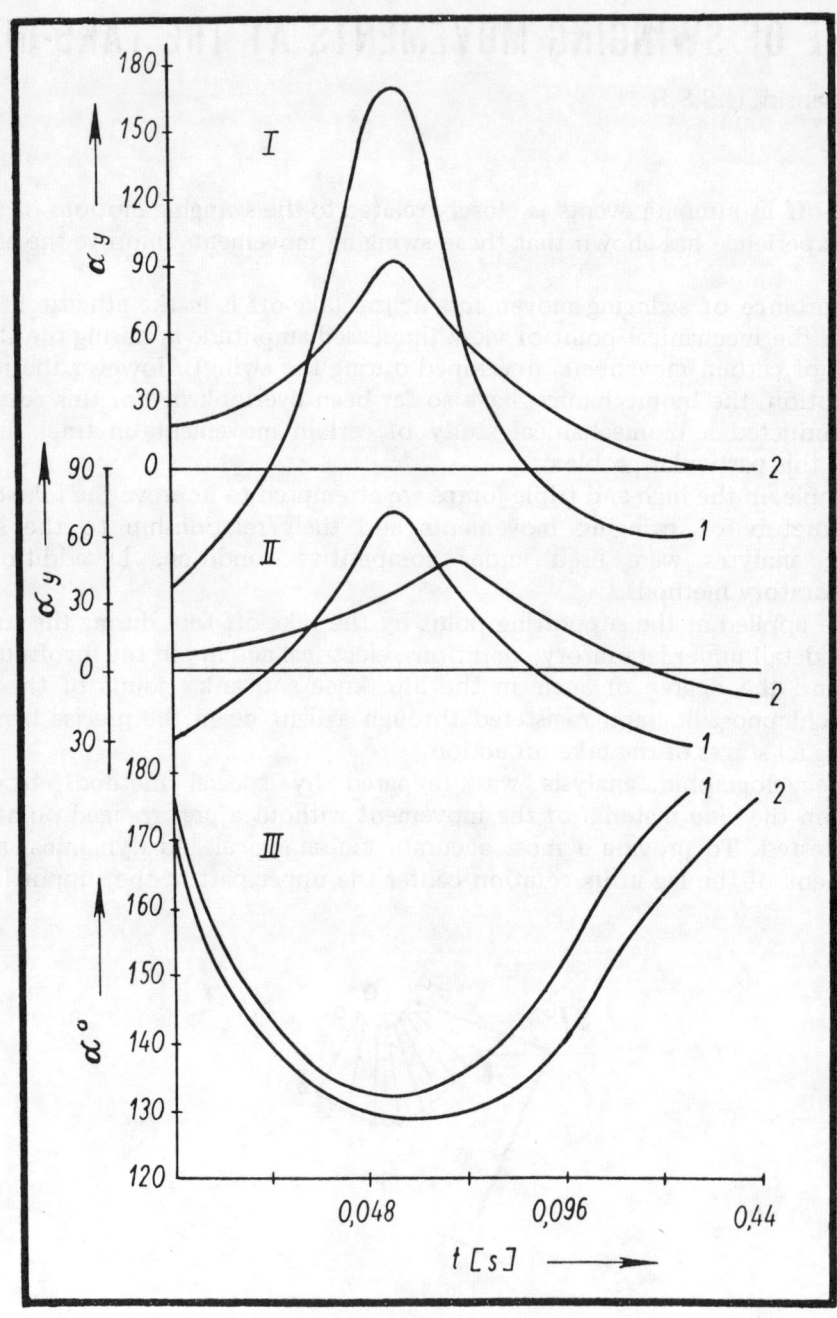

Fig. 2

Fig. 2 shows a typical example of how the swinging movements and the work of the supporting leg are related during the second take-off in a triple jump by (1) an established jumper and (2) a junior. (I—vertical acceleration of the C of G of the arms, II—vertical acceleration of the C of G of the swinging leg, III—angle of the bend of the supporting leg.)

It is evident from the graphs that with the start of the take-off the mass of the swinging parts of the body has a negative vertical acceleration compared to the jumper's C of G, i.e. it shifts rapidly downwards. Consequently, at this moment its inertia operates in the opposite direction and produces in the joints a dynamic reaction which reduces the extent of the pressure on the supporting point.

As the C of G of the swinging leg shifts forward the vertical acceleration changes to positive. The force of inertia is now directed downwards and the load on the supporting leg is increased and reaches its maximum when the C of G of the swinging movement has arrived at the lowest point of the curve. At the end of the take-off phase the vertical acceleration again changes to negative. The pressure on the point of support is reduced which makes the final push-off of the foot easier.

It is characteristic for beginners to have the greatest positive acceleration of the swinging movement at the beginning of the take-off phase. This means an increased force at the point of support at a most unsuitable moment because the reaction forces of the swing act at a sharp angle in the opposite direction of the jumper.

The study to discover the reasons for differences in the vertical acceleration has shown that an established jumper starts swinging movements towards the end of the supporting phase whereas a novice at the beginning of it. In this detail lies the essential differences in the technique of a qualified jumper and a beginner.

It is further to be noticed that the maximum vertical accelerations of the arm and leg of an established jumper are timed together indicating a coordination of all swinging movements. In case of a beginner the swinging action lacks coordination and the emphasis of their force lacks timing. This causes basic differences in the dynamics of the take-off.

The composition of graphs of the vertical acceleration of all swinging movements and the degree of bend in the supporting leg in case of an established jumper shows that the maximum force of the swing precedes the straightening action of the supporting leg, i.e. it takes place at the end of the shock absorbing phase.

Special studies have indicated that this is not a coincidence. The force of the swinging motion is related to the straightening action and the latter depends on the former.

An examination of this relationship in the light of Pavlov's law of intensity of stimulus shows that the concentrated load of the swinging movements on the muscles of the supporting leg in the stage of tetanic contraction forms an additional stimulus to release the reaction that follows.

In practice the forces at the take-off combine and work together as follows:—At the end of the shock absorbing phase the passive contraction of the muscles has reached its maximum. The following short but concentrated increase in the load caused by the swing ("ignition") results in an "explosion." The energetic straightening action of the supporting leg begins and towards the end of the phase of the active take-off the load on the leg is again reduced.

Our observations were proved to be correct by the data collected during the analysis of the take-off movements of a beginner. As can be seen from the graphs in Fig. 2 his maximum additional forces from the swinging movements are not coordinated. Although the total force is less than that exerted by the trained or skilled jumper, the effect lasts longer. For this reason the extension of the supporting leg is accomplished only after a hesitation so that the inertia of the body mass is overcome only with great difficulty. The efficiency of the take-off suffers and the jumper feels as if the swing is "pressing him back towards the ground."

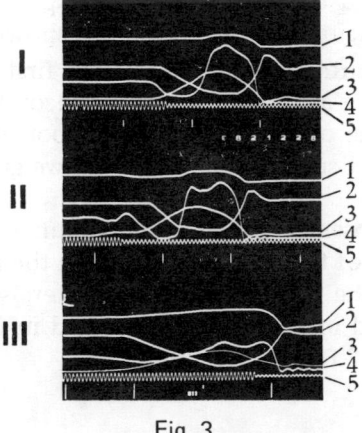

Fig. 3

Fig. 3 shows Oszillogramme registrations of the bend in the upper leg (3), knee (2) and ankle (1), and the dynamogramme of the force at the supporting point (4) during a double leg take-off in a standing high jump. (Read from left to right the time (5) is 0.02 seconds.) The first two were performed (I—without swinging movements, II—using arms). The visual analysis indicates an increased force at the take-off spot through the reaction force of the double arm swing. (2-Rise of the curve on the dynamogramme). Here the active straightening of the legs starts only after the maximum additional load has been applied.

The interaction of the swinging movements with the action of the supporting leg can be most clearly illustrated by another junior test-subject (III). Here the late swinging movements lack coordination and the thrust at the take-off suffers. The additional reaction force of the swing acts unfavorably on the straightening of the leg. As can be seen from the Oszillogramme the straightening starts slowly and only after the maximum additional force is applied is the take-off accelerated.

The results of our research indicate that the technical development of a jumper in training is closely connected with a certain ability to coordinate the forces at the take-off. This applies primarily to the swinging movements and the action of the supporting leg, and the leading part of this combination is played by the swinging movements.

This shows the necessity to develop the strength in the muscle groups used in the swinging movements.

It is usually accepted in practice that special exercises for strength should have the same structure and effect as the main strength exercises. This is a correct but by no means final evaluation of special exercises.

The important factor is that in overcoming outside resistance the dynamic strength in human movement has a ballistic character. In other words, through a concentrated effort the acceleration is transferred by the muscles to the translocalized mass of the body. After that the movement proceeds according to the law of inertia and the application of the force of the muscles only maintains its speed while acceleration is no longer transferred to the body.

Special research has indicated that in such cases the maximum power developed by the muscle action is limited to 0.1 second. Because of this, the end and middle speeds of the translocalization depend on the size and not duration of the maximum development of power. Obviously the most suitable special strength exercises are those where maximum contraction can be developed in the position similar to the angles between the limbs during the important range of the angle amplitude in the actual jump.

From this it follows that the important range of the angle amplitude of the movement is the deciding criterion in evaluating special strength exercises.

Cine analyses of swinging movements in track and field have shown that the angle amplitude in the upper leg in relation to the body is 210 to 90 degrees in long jump, triple jump and sprinting, and 200 to 60 degrees in the high jump. The important range of the angle amplitude is at the beginning of the movement.

Based on this we developed a complex series of special strength exercises for the muscle groups used in the swinging movements. A few samples are shown in Fig. 4.

The exercises are divided into two groups. To the first group belong the exercises for the isolated bending of the swinging leg at the hip joint. The second group includes exercises combined to develop the swinging leg and the upper part of the supporting leg. The exercises are performed with each leg with a maximum and submaximum load of weights and also as an isometric type of partner exercise.

The starting position is chosen to provide a maximum contraction with the angle of the hip joint corresponding with the range of the angle amplitude in the actual jumping.

Experiments have proved the high value of these exercises. The noticeable improvements in performances of our training squad in a short time resulted in 10.5 and 21.1 in sprinting, 7.57 and 15.55 in long and triple jumps and 2.06 in high jump.

Fig. 4

# THE LONG JUMP AND TRIPLE JUMP APPROACH

By Yuri Verhoshanski, U.S.S.R.

There is still no definite answer as to how the long jump and triple jump approach should be carried out.

Should the speed at the end of the approach be maximum or optimum?

Many jumpers support the maximum speed theory and observations of competitive jumps seem to indicate that a great jump requires a very fast approach speed. However, this may not always be so. Even experienced competitors have a critical speed margin, which, when exceeded, reduces the probability of successfully carrying out the jump. These jumpers when using a controlled approach, without jumping, were able to attain a speed which was 6—8 inches per second faster than they were able to attain during competitive jumps. Naturally, many jumpers noticed this fact and therefore prefer an optimum approach speed, somewhat less than the maximum speed they can develop. More than half of the 64 Soviet and foreign competitors questioned favored an optimum speed approach.

The following experiment was carried out (with the Master of Sport, Jurij Jeremin) to answer the question of whether to use maximum or optimum approach speed. During the preparation period, before the jumpers had practiced jumping technique using a full approach, two long jumpers (A Master of Sport and a Jumper of the First Performance Class) were asked to carry out a series of jumps for distance. They were to make three jumps using ¾ effort in their approach, and then three jumps using maximum effort. The performances made using ¾ effort were significantly better. The Master of Sport jumped 22'9 5/8" using ¾ effort and 21'5½" using maximum effort; the First Performance Class jumper was able to jump 22'7 5/8" with ¾ effort and 21'9" using maximum effort. The jumpers were then asked to use a ¾ effort approach in a competition the following week. However, their concentration was disturbed by the competitive conditions; their speed as a result was faster than recommended and their performances worse than in the training session. A repeat series of control jumps, one week later, reconfirmed the results of the first series of jumps.

These results would apparently indicate that the long jump approach should be made using optimum speed. During the continuation of the experiment, the jumpers concentrated on a special program designed to perfect the approach technique, with an emphasis on the transition from the run-up to take-off. As a result, the jumpers were able to confidently jump using the maximum speed possible, without any decrease in speed before the take-off. Their performances improved significantly. The experiment indicated, a jumper should use an optimum approach speed *only* if he is unable to jump using a maximum approach speed. If, however, the athlete wishes to attain the best possible results, he should concentrate on developing a maximum speed approach. In order to prepare a rational training program aimed at developing a maximum speed approach, one must first discover why an athlete cannot jump using a maximum speed approach.

One would normally expect the cause to be a defect in the approach, a lack of strength or a flaw in the transition from the approach to take-off. However, something else must also be involved. The main cause must be irrational technique training. The development of a polished technique, which is basically the ability to carry out the jump using maximum speed, is greatly hindered through the misuse of jumps using short approaches. These jumps are the main means of practice and make up 75% of the total training program. The jumper's concentration is focused predominantly on the take-off and flight movements when a short approach is used. The jumper then believes he can use a long approach and his technique will remain the same and that his distance will improve. But the long approach causes everything to happen differently.

By conscientiously practicing the take-off using a short approach the jumper sets himself very hard during the last step and comes forward flat over a bent take-off leg. The take-off acquires a pushing character and the entire jump becomes completely different from a fast and dynamic jump using a full approach. The movements of the jump using a short approach are quickly consolidated and are observable when the jumper uses a long approach. A very serious methodical mistake is made in that a strong take-off is taught using a slower approach speed than under competitive conditions, rather than teaching a quick take-off using the maximum speed possible. The coaches of young jumpers must consider their jumping background and try to make them realize the advantages of practicing their jumping using a maximum approach speed. Even athletes with extensive jumping experience who cannot yet jump using maximum speed should consider working to improve their technique as they may be able to jump using the maximum speed they can develop. The following technique training is recommended for them:

**November-December**

The first part of the preparation period is spent developing the approach rhythm, practicing sprinting technique and learning to accelerate the approach speed from the start onwards. To accomplish this the approach using ¾ effort should be repeated again and again without jumping. The jumper should concentrate on attaining a fluid acceleration and on gradually lengthening the steps and the tempo. The take-off must, however, not be forgotten. The jumper must practice the transition from the approach to take-off by sharpening the tempo of the steps before take-off and at the same time shorten the length of the steps. Towards the end of this period the approach may be made with an easy take-off and then running on through the pit. The approach must be practiced at least 8-10 times during each session. At the same time special technique exercises may be practiced to help develop the other parts of the jump.

**January-February**

The main objective of this training period is the development of a fast take-off on the basis of a maximum intensity of exertion which is caused by an increase of speed during the final approach steps. The first 2/3 of the approach is made using a ¾ effort and the last 5 to 6 steps are made using the maximum speed possible (under these conditions). Full strength is not yet used to carry out the take-off, but this exercise does allow enough time to complete the take-off and perform the necessary movements in the air without losing one's balance. This exercise is completed with a two-foot landing in the long jump or a one-foot landing followed by a run through as in the triple jump.

As one nears the take-off board, the tempo of the steps must increase but without a significant decrease in stride length. One must actively drive during the last steps to maintain the sweeping forward movement. The power of the take-off will gradually increase as one masters the transition from the approach to the take-off at a high speed. The flight curve will be higher and the jump longer. In order not to lose any speed or rhythm during the last few steps, the jumper must concentrate on using a strong, fast, push-off in each of the last steps. This naturally requires the capacity to produce a maximum expenditure of energy over a very short period of time. Developing a fast take-off during this period is a very important part of perfecting the entire jumping technique. This training period's main emphasis is a very important part of perfecting the entire jumping technique. This training period's main emphasis is on the most difficult part of the jump—the transition from approach to take-off.

**March-April**

During the training period the emphasis is on acquiring a strong take-off using the maximum speed possible. This may be accomplished by strengthening the take-off. Therefore the speed at the end of the approach is increased mainly through an increased acceleration during the initial part of the jump. A fast carry-through of the jump accomplishes the important issue of not reducing speed prior to the point of take-off, otherwise the previous actions of the jumper become useless.

**May-September**

The last period of the training year, the competitive season, necessitates work to perfect individual details of the jump. However, the main attention of the jumper should be directed as before to the transition from the approach to the take-off.

The ability to jump using the maximum speed possible necessitates, first, practicing the approach and take-off as one unit and, secondly, practicing the jump using the maximum speed possible. From a technical standpoint the approach is the most important part of the jump, and not merely the take-off as it was believed to have been until now. To summarize: **What advantages does the recommended training method offer?**

1. The improvement of the jumping technique at a high intensity of nerve-muscle strain causing the training jumps to be made under conditions similar to competition. The transition from approach to take-off is also made at a high speed.

2. Practicing technique using the maximum speed possible rather than the short approach method helps to avoid mistakes during the preparation for take-off and the take-off itself. However, this does not mean that short approach jumps will be totally excluded from the practices. They are often used to help perfect technique. However, as the season progresses, they are used less and less.

3. The take-offs made at high speed during practice guarantees the best conditions for the development of a rational technique and its stabilization.

4. With this program the jumper may compete indoors without changing his training routine.

# THE LENGTH OF LONG JUMP RUN-UP

By J. Vacula

The improvements in long jump distances from 6.80 to 8.30 meters are closely connected with the following factors:
    a) A reduction in take-off time from 0.13 sec. to 0.11 sec.
    b) An increase in the run-up speed before the take-off from 9.0 m/sec. to 10.5 m/sec.
    c) An improvement in the initial flight velocity of the body's center of gravity from 8.5 m/sec to 9.5 m/sec.

The length of the run-up itself is somewhere between 30 to 45 meters for men and between 25 to 35 meters for women. (9 to 11 double strides for men, 8 to 10 for women).

It is important that the speed of the run-up reaches its maximum at the moment of the take-off. This requires the jumper to adjust his approach length according to his acceleration ability. For example, a jumper, who clocks from a crouch start 4.2 to 4.1 sec over 30 meters, equivalent to 11.6 to 11.3 sec. 100 meters time, should choose a run-up of 17 to 18 strides, or about 32 to 36 meters. A jumper who can cover 30 meters in 3.7 sec., equivalent to 10.4 to 10.2 100 meters, should use 22 to 23 strides or 44 to 46 meters for his approach.

The following table gives a guidance to the relationship of sprint times in comparison to the approximately right number of strides in the run-up:

| 30 m Crouch Start | 100 m Crouch Start | Number of Strides in long jump |
|---|---|---|
| 3.7 | 10.2 | 24 |
| 3.8 | 10.5 | 22 |
| 3.9 | 10.8 | 20 |
| 4.0 | 11.1 | 18 |
| 4.1 | 11.5 | 17 |
| 4.2 | 11.8 | 16 |
| 4.3 | 12.1 | 15 |
| 4.4 | 12.5 | |
| 4.5 | 12.9 | 14 |
| 4.6 | 13.2 | |
| 4.7 | 13.8 | 13 |
| 4.8 | 14.0 | |
| 4.9 | 14.3 | |
| 5.0 | 14.7 | 12 |

# OPTIMUM SPEED IN THE LONG JUMP

By D.C. Chambers, Australia

*This article is condensed from a paper presented by D.C. Chambers to the Track and Field Coaches Association of South Australia as part of Grade I Coaches' examination. The author is a teacher at the Immanuel College in Adelaide and has successfully been involved in coaching of school athletes for many years.*

Most coaches concede that the three major maxims to be considered in long jumping are speed of approach, angle of the take-off and landing technique.

I decided that the key to the long jump problem lay somewhere between the start of the approach distance and the instant of post take-off. But what is the approach distance and does it vary for each individual athlete? Kenneth O. Bosen, Chief Coach of the 1964 Indian Olympic Team, suggests that a twenty-stride approach is the basic distance with which to begin. He supplements this statement by adding that at a later date, if necessary, the number of strides may be increased or decreased as desired. He does not, however, give any formula for arriving at this change and thus emerges as the first problem, the solution of how to determine individual approach distance.

Assuming that this distance could be accurately calculated, the second problem is how the athlete should traverse that distance, that is, should his speed at the board be maximal or maximum? John P. Jesse, well known California authority on weight training for athletes, has suggested that the run-up for the long jump should consist of a sprint at maximum speed with a slight gathering of forces during the final three or four strides. Russian athletics writer Yuri Verhoshanski has advocated that athletes, who are determined to achieve top performances, should be advised to work towards a maximum speed at the take-off.

It was while considering this problem that the word 'speed' appeared to become more and more out of context with each succeeding statement. Mechanically speaking, speed is defined as the distance travelled per unit time. In view of the fact that a long jumper starts at the beginning of his run-up and runs up to the take-off board, the more correct term would be velocity. However, as the initial velocity is zero (the athlete starts from rest) then his velocity will be continually increasing, provided his approach distance is not abnormally long. But an increase in velocity is acceleration! Hence I began to consider the approach distance in terms of acceleration. The concept of a complete acceleration over the approach distance was both stimulated and enhanced by watching water-ski jumping in which the competitors strove for increasing velocity (that is, maximum acceleration) in their approach to the inclined surface of the jump itself.

The inherent possibilities of this concept became even more intriguing when I read that Igor Ter-Ovanesyan, who represented the U.S.S.R. in the long jump at the 1956 Olympics in Melbourne, spent the next year in improving what he termed his "run-up speed." Not only did he improve his 100 meters sprint time from 11.1 seconds to 10.5 seconds, but in 1958 set a new U.S.S.R. long jump record of 7.81 meters (25 ft. 7¼ in.). The fact that he apparently did increase his "run-up speed" indicates that he increased his acceleration, because without an increase in acceleration there would not be an increase in velocity. But what of the approach distance itself? Was it proportionately reduced to compensate for the improved acceleration or was the same distance retained? If the latter was the case then, either he required this distance to generate the increased acceleration, or most likely accelerated until he attained maximum velocity which he then maintained until reaching the take-off board. The calculation of the ratio of the distance traversed to the time taken would yield his average velocity. Hence, a comparison of his average velocities recorded in 1956 and 1958 would, without doubt, reveal an increase in his "run-up speed." Consequently the latter alternative would tend to support Jesse's theory at reaching maximum velocity and maintaining it for a short unspecified distance, applicable to, or even advisable for, the less physically developed junior athlete?

The concept of the dual factors of approach distance and acceleration promised to merge into a single problem, as the solution of one component could lead to the solution of the other, in particular, if the distance required by an athlete to complete his acceleration could be determined with reasonable accuracy. It was at this point in the theoretical examination of the problem that three alternatives of maximum acceleration, complete acceleration, and maximum velocity emerged. Consideration of these alternatives revealed certain possible commutative qualities:

1) that maximum and complete accelerations are synonymous.
2) that maximum acceleration and maximum velocity are synonymous.
3) that, if (1) is invalid, complete acceleration is synonymous with maximum velocity.

These three alternatives, of course, could be completely unrelated and could affect the original hypothesis of a correlation between approach distance and acceleration.

The next step was to conduct tests and collect data, to determine the change in acceleration of the individual athlete. This was calculated by dissecting the 100 meters distance into five-meter intervals and recording sprint times at each five-meter multiple. By knowing the distance transversed and the time taken, the acceleration at the end of each five meters could be calculated by the formula $s=½at^2$. The other two formula $v=u+at$ and $v^2=u^2+2$, as both incorporate initial and final velocities, would be approximate only.

For the purposes of these experiments I made use of the fact that Immanuel College is co-educational and co-opted eight students, four boys and four girls, ranging in ages from 13 to 18 years. Bearing in mind that numerous factors can lead to a slight variation in sprint times (such as the velocity and direction of the wind, the state of the College's turf track due to climatic conditions, and so on) I decided to take the average of three 100-meter times for each athlete, recorded on different days.

It was assumed that the athlete's true acceleration ability would only be satisfactorily revealed under race conditions and each athlete was instructed that time trials were to be conducted and that the numerous timekeepers were gathering data for a statistical analysis.

Following the time trials and the recording of the relevant times at each five-meter interval, the results were tabulated and the accelerations, together with their respective changes, calculated and analyzed.

At the next sessions the athletes were informed that long jump trials were to be conducted and that, in preparation for this, they were to assume their normal long jump approach distances. The length of each one was then recorded. Next the athletes were moved to the approach distances calculated according to the greatest acceleration change in the sprint lists and directed to make several runs-through until they were satisfied that their take-off foot was landing consistently on the take-off board. All adjustments have been noted in the third column of the table below, in terms of the corrected distance.

| Athlete | Old Distance (m) | Calculated Distance (m) | Corrected Distance (m) |
| --- | --- | --- | --- |
| A | 23.00 | 30.00 | 29.70 |
| B | 25.00 | 30.00 | 30.00 |
| C | 18.50 | 20.00 | 21.00 |
| D | 18.00 | 20.00 | 21.20 |

| | | | |
|---|---|---|---|
| E | 25.00 | 30.00 | 32.00 |
| F | 31.00 | 30.00 | 29.00 |
| G | 14.00 | 20.00 | 20.30 |
| H | 23.50 | 25.00 | 25.00 |

The athletes were next instructed to try to approach the long jump take-off board with the same acceleration that they would endeavour to generate at the start of a 100 meters sprint. They were each given several trial jumps before being informed that each succeeding jump would be measured and recorded. The results were most encouraging. Jumpers B, D and G enjoyed the increased distances which gave them slightly longer time to generate more acceleration, yet permitted control and relaxation for an efficient take-off. Jumpers A and H admitted that they were finding it a little difficult to adjust to the increased distances but agreed to persevere with it. Only jumpers F and H failed to improve their previous performances but both "happened" to be close to the correct distance anyhow. In case of jumpers B, D and G, the distance jumped exceeded the existing college record for the appropriate age group. I must add that I had decided quite spontaneously, to record the time of each athlete over the approach distance on each jump as one of those rare unpremeditated actions that bore fruit. On comparing times with distances recorded I found that in most cases the slower the time the shorter the distance. From these results I believe that the hypothesis of maximum acceleration over a calculated approach distance has been strongly supported.

The theory of a long jump run-up at maximum speed (velocity) is, I believe, unfounded at least with the age groups with which I am dealing. Calculation of the approximate velocities of each athlete at each 10 meter mark (using $v=at$) make it evident that although athletes reach a maximum acceleration, this does not suddenly cease but merely reduces. As maximum velocity is not reached while there is still an increase in that velocity (that is, acceleration), it is obvious that, if a maximum speed run-up theory is adopted, the youngeters in this experimental group would all have approach distances of well in excess of 40 meters.

# LANDING IN BEAMON'S RECORD JUMP

By Toni Nett, Germany

Comments that Bob Beamon had employed a perfect or unique technique in his world record jump in Mexico City were common after the 1968 Games. His high leg lift before landing attracted attention and was by many poorly informed described as a "special trick".

Actually it was just the opposite. Beamon's leg lift to a near horizontal position occurs too early. He is unable to keep this position and to avoid falling back at the landing is forced to drop his legs. The action represents not an excellent but a poor technique, because movements in the air, as they can't change the path of the jumper's center of gravity, have no value unless they lead to a best possible landing position.

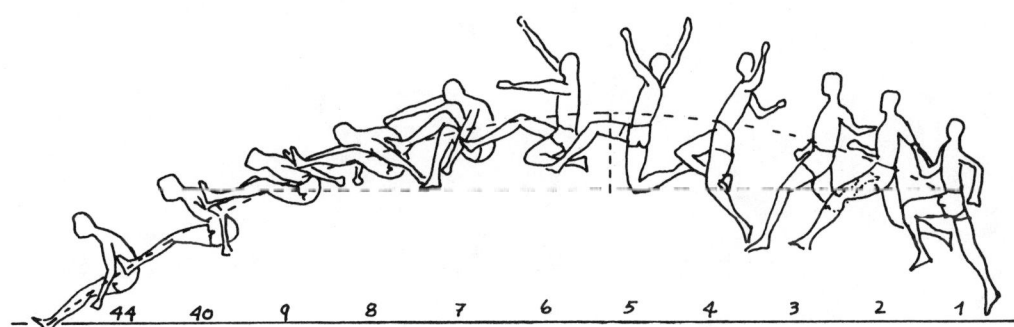

The drawings, taken from a film of Beamon's actual world record jump, indicate that he is not a brilliant technician and his landing, as is the case with many world-class jumpers, is rather average. It is certainly not Beamon's landing position that was responsible for the world record. Distances in the long jump depend on a maximum approach speed, minimum losses of velocity at the take-off, an optimal take-off angle and a ground covering landing action. The first three requirements, assisted by exceptionally favorable conditions (Tartan track, 2m/sec. following wind and high altitude) were employed by Beamon. The last, the landing had nothing to do with the phenomenal jump.

# Triple Jump

TRIPLE JUMP                    *Credits*

*Coaching the High School Triple Jumper,* by Robert Chappell. Reprinted from *Athletics Arena,* Vol. 8, No. 10.

*Triple Jump Technique and Method of Teaching,* by Gabor Simonyi. First publication.

*Triple Jump Training,* by Tadeusz Starzynski. Originally published in *Lekka Atletyka,* Warsaw, Poland. This English translation by Robert Z. Opiola appeared in *Track Technique* No. 45, September, 1971.

*Training of Soviet Triple Jumpers,* by Z. Chrominski. Originally published in *Lekka Atletyka,* Warsaw, Poland. This English translation appeared in *Modern Athlete and Coach,* Vol. 8, No. 5, September, 1970.

*Training a Modern Top-Class Triple Jumper,* by C.M. Muthiah. First publication.

*Practical Ratios for Triple Jumpers,* by Toni Nett. Originally published in *Die Lehre der Leichtathletik,* No. 23, June, 1961. Translated and extracted by Jess Jarver, reprinted from *Track Technique* No. 6, December, 1961.

*Distribution of Triple Jump Phases,* by Vitold Kreer. Originally published in *Lehkaja Atletika,* USSR. This English translation (in condensed form) appeared in *Modern Athlete and Coach,* Vol. 8, No. 6, November, 1970.

*Shallow or Steep?* by L. Prihoda. Originally published in *Lehka Athletika,* Prague, Czechoslovakia, No. 3, 1965. Translated into German by Ernst Wurfer, edited by Toni Nett. This English translation appeared in *Coaching Review,* Vol. 4, No. 1, June, 1966.

*Deviations in the Triple Jump,* by Tadeusz Starzynski. Originally published in *Atletika,* Czechoslovakia. This English translation appeared in *Modern Athlete and Coach,* Vol. 8, No. 6, November, 1970.

# COACHING THE HIGH SCHOOL TRIPLE JUMPER
By Robert Chappell, Great Britain

Since the 1968 Olympic Games in Mexico when six of the finalists in the triple jump bettered the existing world record, there has been a rapid upsurge both in the popularity of the event and in the standard of the performances in the high schools. This in part may be attributed to the better understanding of the fundamental principles of the event by high school coaches and better track surfaces such as Tartan, but it may also be attributed to the fact that both the coach and the athlete are beginning to realize that a boy possessing a certain amount of natural ability and who is prepared to train consistently hard at the event can meet with a great amount of success at the school and state level. A mature international athlete is the result of years of conditioning so that the legs are able to withstand the stress that is forced upon them during each jump and it is on the basis of the training of an international jumper that the high school coach must base his coaching and training of the schoolboy athlete. It must be stressed however that this will only be undertaken in a modified form and that the training will obviously vary according to the age, ability, etc. of the individual athlete.

The main factors to be considered in determining the training program of the athlete are:

1. A general background of fitness upon which can be built the specific skills that are required in the event.

2. Leg strength and power. This is the ability to absorb the shock and the weight that is sustained on landing at the end of each phase of the jump and the ability to drive forward at the end of each phase.

3. Running speed. This means attaining the necessary skill and flexibility in the hips that is required in running at full speed.

4. Rhythm and cadence. This is the area in which the coach will be of the greatest assistance as most high school athletes lack these assets especially in the step phase of the jump.

Dealing with each item individually it can be seen that the greatest difficulty the coach is going to have is organizing the athlete so that he will undertake the specific activities under the headings of 'leg strength and power' and 'running speed.' For the average American high school student who shows any potential in the event there will be little or no need to organize a series of activities that will ensure a general background of fitness as he will probably be undertaking a great amount of exercise by playing basketball, etc. (the outstanding high school triple jumper may well be on the basketball squad).

The training program must be prepared in relation to the individual athlete. For example, the athlete who is participating in some form of sport in the winter will obviously not require as much conditioning as the athlete who is not participating in any form of activity. But even if the athlete is participating in either basketball or football it is necessary to organize his winter track program so that it may be included in his training schedule.

consider as many as possible when constructing a program so that it is varied and interesting to the athlete. Weight training and multiple hopping and stepping are the main forms of attaining strength and power and the latter especially is of the greatest importance. The weight training program will again depend on the amount of sports that the athlete is participating in but in most cases it will be necessary for the athlete to undertake weight training twice a week during the winter, reducing this to once a week in the pre-season months. In organizing the program it is necessary to include approximately three exercises that strengthen the legs specifically, and possibly the best ones are: one quarter squats, split jump squats, and two footed jump squats. (Fig. 1)

It can be seen from the figure that these exercises require differing ranges of movement and work. They can be supplemented or varied by introducing cleans, and work on a leg press machine when one is available. The rest of the program should include exercises that necessitate using the other main muscles in the body, i.e. bench presses, arm curls, stomach curls, etc.

**Figure 1**
(in all relevant cases the right foot is blackened)

Multiple hops and steps are extremely important as they stimulate the actual jumping action. These can be performed either inside (preferably on rubber mats) or on the track and should be performed throughout the winter twice a week if time permits, if they are to prove beneficial. The jumps should be related as closely as possible to the actual event with good form being stressed, and consequently jumps such as hop, hop, step and jump; hop, step, step and jump; hop, hop, hop and jump; four steps and jump (Fig. 2) and of course the actual triple jump from a short approach run are very valuable preparation. By performing these jumps under the guidance of a coach, the athlete will soon acquire the rhythm and cadence that is required in all phases of the triple jump event.

**Figure 2**
(in all relevant cases the right foot is blackened)

The performance of these jumps can be made extremely interesting by the use of personal records which can be posted on the bulletin board and in doing the jumps with a partner of about the same ability so that each training session becomes a competition. As the athlete becomes more efficient at performing these multiple jumps, then the approach speed should be increased so that the jumps closely resemble the actual triple jump. In any one jumping session it is possible to complete approximately thirty jumps in thirty minutes as long as the athlete does not waste an excessive amount of time between each jump, although a short rest is desirable.

The last important aspect to be considered when devising a program for the high school triple jumper is running speed. This can be increased by repetition sprints especially over the distance of the athlete's personal approach run, as the most important aspect of speed is speed off the board and the ability to be able to handle the greatest amount of speed but it is of vital importance especially in those athletes who are not flexible in the hip region. Flexibility is best secured by attaining the "end position" and then attempting to squeeze the muscles further. The hip flexibility exercises need to be performed in the pre-season period, although it would be of greater benefit if they were performed throughout the winter. In doing either speed or flexibility work it is again essential to work in groups so that the athletes enjoy the strenuous training.

In most training sessions it is usually possible to combine two activities so that again the athlete finds his training program more interesting and varied. Therefore in a training session that is to be of one hour duration the athlete could do forty minutes weight training and twenty minutes running practices, or forty minutes of related jumping activities followed by twenty minutes of running practices. It is of little value to combine a weight training session and a jumping session because whichever activity is done last will be unduly affected by the first activity and therefore will be of little value.

Therefore it can be seen that the good triple jumper will consist of an athlete who has a certain amount of natural ability but also the determination to succeed by increasing his strength, power and speed in undertaking a hard but not unduly strenuous training program under the guidance of his coach.

# TRIPLE JUMP TECHNIQUE AND METHOD OF TEACHING

By Gabor Simonyi, North Battleford, Sask., Canada, former National Coach of Hungary and Iceland

Today's triple-jumpers must possess better than average sprinting ability, and they also must be better than average long jumpers. In addition to these attributes, they have to possess extraordinarily strong ankles and knees and a fine sense of rhythm and balance. The nature of the event is such that it demands a very special training for the athlete. To be able to reach a respectable distance, years have to be devoted to special preparations.

The technique is seemingly simple, however, its execution is far from simple; The manner in which the athlete regards his event makes a great difference in his execution of it. A special theoretical approach to it is a necessity, otherwise great performances are almost impossible for the jumper. My special approach to the triple-jump is that the first jump (the "hop") should be regarded and imagined as belonging to the run.

The athlete should imagine and act as if the real jumps begin as the first landing ends. This first "hop" should be imagined as the last stride, but a rather special one, of the run. I instruct athletes to prepare for the first landing both mentally and physically while in the air after this first low "hop" and try to execute a special long-jump action as landing. (In the jumper's mind this is the first real jump; the hop being only a special last stride of the run.) If the hop is regarded in this way, the possibility of being able to perform a good second and a third jump increases considerably. This first hop could also be referred to as an unemphasized take-off.

### I. Run and first jump ("hop")

An ideal run is one by which an optimum speed can be attained without wasting any energy and from which the transition into the jumps is the most natural. The length and acceleration of the run should depend on the ability and characteristics of the athlete. A jumper with a quick and easy acceleration will use a relatively short run, whereas one who is rather slow in accelerating should, of course, use a proportionally longer approach. Whether a jumper is able to utilize the full speed of which he is capable depends on both his technique and his physical strength. Naturally the slower the jumper in his run, the easier the execution of the technique. This is why many athletes dare not run at full speed in their run, feeling they are not strong enough and that their technique is not good enough at a higher speed.

The triple-jumper makes no special preparation for take-off during his last few strides since he does not lift his body high in the air, he simply tries to maintain the body-angle he has had during his earlier run. A long-jumper, on the other hand, makes special preparation for his take-off, lowering his center of gravity slightly and leaning back slightly with his upper trunk seeking a good lift. Due to his unchanged body-angle at his take-off, the triple-jumper will not hit the ground first with his heel, but will keep on landing on the ball of his foot also at the take-off, just as he landed during all his runs. Another difference between the take-off of a triple jumper and a long jumper during the last strides is that a triple-jumper does not break his rhythm of running at take off, while the long-jumper changes rhythm for the sake of a good lift.

A, Body-angles of a broad jumper before and at take-off

B, Body-angles of a triple jumper before and at take-off (unchanged)

The triple-jumper's first take-off will carry his body along a long, low trajectory, because no preparation was made which could result in a lift. Due to this lack of preparation, as little speed as possible is lost here. The arch of the first jump (hop) must not be high to avoid a considerable loss in forward momentum due to the greater impact at landing.

While floating in mid-air during the first jump, the jumper must do two things: 1. preserve his balance and body-angle; and, 2. make mental and physical preparation for an "active" landing. Preservation of balance and body-angle is dependent on the execution of the take-off. The correct placement of the take-off foot on the take-off board is important. The longitudinal axis of this foot should be in line with the direction of the jump. Under mental preparation, I mean that the jumper should be ready in his mind also for what is to be done at landing. Under physical preparedness, I mean that the jumper must pre-tense his muscles to be able to avoid "sinking" at hitting the ground when landing, and to be able to execute an active jump. Thus, the jumper should not drop down passively to the ground at his landing.

However, there is another important action the athlete must perform. To be able to use a parallel double-arm swing immediately at his first landing, he must swing both his arms backwards, behind his body, *before* he hits the ground.

This swinging of the arms backwards is to be performed early enough while in the air so that the arms aid in the second jump immediately on landing from the first. While the arms are swinging backwards, they should be flexed in the elbows, moderately bent, and the palms should face the direction of the jump. Fists should be more or less clenched. Due to the bent state of the elbows, the arms swing not only backwards but also upwards, thus making the shoulders lean forward. This position of the shoulders helps the upper trunk maintain its desired angle.

Both the arms and the legs must be kept relatively close to the center of the body-weight to facilitate a better flight and a more advantageous landing. Thus the knees must also be kept bent. No stamping of the take-off foot should be allowed, for this only decreases the momentum of the jumper.

I personally think that a parallel double-arm swing can be begun at the first take-off. I have tried it myself and have had it tried by some of my athletes. We thought it was not difficult at all, and it certainly made the whole action of triple-jump more uniform. In case this early parallel double-arm swing is tried, the jumper has to carry both his arms backwards during his last two strides. In doing this, he simply swings his arms behind his hips, half extending them.

A triple-jumper with a left take-off foot will naturally swing his right knee forwards and upwards at the take-off, however he will change legs in mid-air, and land on his left foot. During this arch-turn the current rear leg must not trail far behind the body.

## II. Second jump ("step")

As soon as the jumper's take-off foot hits the ground at the completion of the first jump, he simultaneously begins to swing both his arms (parallel double-arm action) and his other knee upwards and forwards, trying to lift his body higher in the air. By these vigorous swinging actions he forces his take-off leg to be burdened momentarily with a greater strain, thus delaying somewhat its jumping action. If the jumper's legs are well-trained and strong enough, this can be an advantage, because when the take-off leg is released from this pressure, due to the greater tension of the muscles, it will execute a proportionally greater bounce.

To make this second jump sufficiently long, another special trick can be carried out by the athlete: he can act as if he wanted to land on his original take-off foot once more. However, in due time, he will change feet in the air again, shortly before his second landing, hitting the ground with the correct leg all the same.

In case of a jumper with a left take-off leg, this action would resemble as follows: in hitting the ground with his left foot, the athlete swings his right knee forward, immediately bringing it backwards, simultaneously swinging the up one forward just as if the jumper wanted to land on the left leg. Another quick, scissor-like changing of the legs, however, would bring the right knee forward once more shortly before landing. To carry out this action, the jumper must flex his knees and keep them fairly close together while executing this change of his legs.

This trick seems to have two main advantages: 1. the flexing of the knees helps the jumper keep his legs closer to the center of gravity thus maintaining a better posture for his flight in the air and at the same time giving him a better balance; and 2. his take-off leg is activated by this action, becoming well prepared for its work upon hitting the ground due to the tension in the muscles.

**Beginning of the second jump**
R = right leg

**End of the second jump**
L = left leg

From the very beginning of the second jump, a quick parallel double-arm swing is to be executed, timed so the arms are swung behind the body before landing on the right foot. Thus, during the first phase of this jump the arms are swung forwards, while during the second phase they are swung backwards. Undoubtedly this rather complicated action requires strong shoulder muscles and a great deal of practice.

Each landing must be an "action" one, meaning the athlete must be both physically and mentally prepared. The athlete should try to contact the ground first with the ball of his foot then let the heel come down too. A direct landing on the heel is likely to result in the slackening of the athlete's forward momentum, and can also cause injury. A direct landing on the heel is usually the consequence of a backward lean of the upper trunk. The jumper is likely to reach forward with his landing leg, and consequently lands on the heel of his foot. In such a case, the center of gravity is too far behind the landing-point, and instead of being able to push away from the landing-point forward immediately upon landing, the jumper is forced to more or less pull his body forward to the point where a push is possible. Furthermore, a landing on the heel will either result in a too high second jump, provided that the athlete's leg is strong enough, or in his knee sinking under the strain. Both are disadvantages for the jumper.

### III. The third jump ("jump")

Upon landing after the second jump, the athlete begins his final effort which is very similar to an ordinary long jump. Simultaneously swinging his arms and his left knee vigorously forwards and upwards, the triple-jumper tries to get a little higher in the air. During the first half of the jump the arms swing forward, then are swiftly brought backwards. In about the middle of the trajectory of this jump the right leg will catch up with the left one. From then on the legs are extended, and a stressed forward lean of the upper trunk will be carried out by the athlete as he approaches the pit when he hits the sand, he quickly bends his knees and swings his arms forward once more.

### Method of teaching the technique

A basic knowledge of the long-jump, both practically and theoretically, is a necessity before anyone can be taught the technique of the triple-jump with good results. The triple-jump prospect must have past experience both as a long-jumper and as a sprinter.

The first thing a beginner should learn is the standing triple jump. He should practice this for quite a long period. When he has become fairly good at it, I set about the task of teaching him a series of exercises gradually leading to the complete technique of the running triple-jump. I found the following order of exercises advantageous: 1. *Standing jumps on the spot off both legs, using parallel double-arm swings* in such a manner that the arms swing forward and upward at the take-off. However, they are quickly swung backwards before landing. Knees should be kept still, the spring coming from the ankles. The body should be rigid and vertical all the time. To be repeated 10-15 times without a break. This exercise strengthens the ankles, the Achilles Tendon, the muscles of the shin, and shoulders. 2. The same exercise, but *with high parallel knee-lifts* in the air. 3. Standing bouncing on both legs, *lifting the knees interchangibly in front.* (Always landing on both

feet). 4. Same exercise as No. 1, moving or progressing forward this time, executing short bounces. (6-10 jumps). 5. Same exercise as No. 4, only with high parallel knee lifts. (10-12 jumps). 6. Same exercise as No. 3, moving forward over the ground. 7. Standing, bouncing jumps on one foot on the spot, without gaining ground. 8. The same, gaining ground, gradually lengthening the jumps. 9. Continuous jumps, bouncing on the same spot using the legs alternately. 10. Same exercise, gaining ground forward. 11. Two bounces (jumps) on the same foot, continually switching over to the other one (twice on left, twice on right, making the switching hop agree with the previous bounces both in rhythm and in length). 12. Standing, regular triple-jump. 13. Regular triple-jump with a very short run. 14. The same with short run. 15. The same with half a run.

Each exercise must be repeated for a sufficiently long period both to learn it well and to strengthen the legs. In all the exercises, parallel double-arm swings should be executed.

When the pupil has mastered the art of the parallel double arm swings, it is time to teach him the trick of changing legs in the air during the second jump ("step"). The demonstration of this exercise must come first. Since the execution of this trick is far from simple, and usually very few are able to imitate it at first sight, one has to teach it using the step by step method.

**First exercise,** the athlete, lifting and bending his right leg with both his arms behind his body, assumes a standing position. He then simultaneously swings both his arms and his right knee forward, executes a jump, landing on his left foot, having once changed knees in the air.

**For the second exercise,** the athlete assumes the same starting position, the athlete will execute a jump as if wanting to land on his left leg, then will quickly change his legs in the air, swinging simultaneously his left leg backwards and the right one forward, thus landing on his right leg. This exercise is very much like a standing long-jump while using the hitch technique.

At first no special attention should be paid to the arms during the hop. Later, however, a parallel double-arm swing should be executed during the exercise.

**The third exercise** consists of a standing double-jump, meaning the first ("hop") and the second ("step") jump of a regular triple-jump from a standing position (standing on one leg only at the beginning of the jump). Draw a line which represents the take-off board. The pupil stands behind this on, say, his left leg. He executes a jump on the same leg, then without stopping, he goes on doing his second jump with the tricky change of legs in the air. The arm-work is exactly the same as in the case of a running triple-jump, i.e., regular arm-work at the first take-off, then swinging the arms behind the body before the landing foot contacts the ground. (Preparation for the double-arm swing.)

**The fourth exercise** is the same exercise as the previous one, only here the pupil takes a few running steps before his take-off.

**The fifth exercise** is same exercise, but with a short run.

During the learning period, the landing after the second jump can be made in the sand to save strain to the landing leg.

To develop the jumper's skill the above-mentioned exercises have to be repeated with the right leg too. Triple-jump with full run must be postponed until the athlete has practiced these exercises for a sufficiently long period, and his technique is becoming good enough. Even then, the run must be made only gradually longer.

When the time for regular triple jumps has come, I use lines on the ground for marking the landing spots, the length between the lines depending on the length of run and on the pupil's abilities. I make the first line on the ground (representing the first take-off spot) thin, suggesting an unemphasized take-off action there. The second line is a double one, meaning that the athlete should emphasize his take-off action landing on it. The third line is also a double one for the same purpose.

For jumpers in the habit of a lateral deviation in their jumps, I use a corridor made of two parallel lines along the jumping track. The width between these lines is made gradually narrower. Using calcium powder I also make short white lines at the landing spots, for the purpose of calling the athlete's attention to a landing exactly in line with the jump.

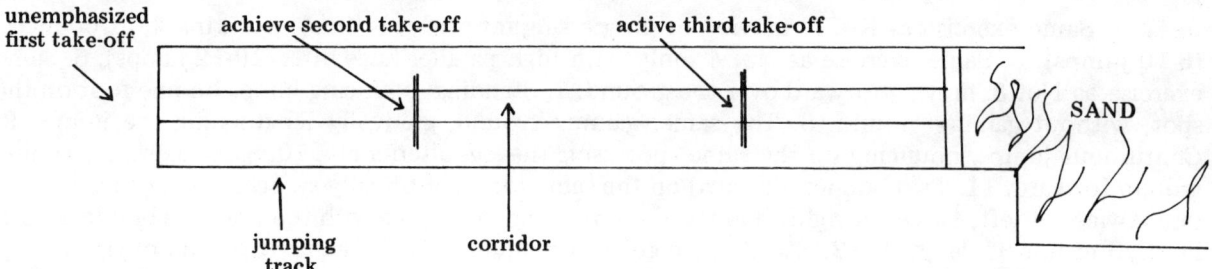

It is a good idea to make the athlete aware of the special rhythm of the triple-jump. The prospective jumpers should know that during a well-executed triple-jump there are only two loud sounds to be heard, both at the beginning of the second and the third jumps. The sound one hears at the first take-off should not be much stronger than those heard during the running steps of the jumper.

The rhythm of the action can be given to the jumper either by clapping the hands or indicating it vocally. Taking the rhythm of the jumper's running, the coach begins to clap his hands synchronizing the two sounds, and making the clapping even in its volume. At the first take-off the rhythm and the volume of clapping do not change, however, there is a loud clap to be made between the first and second landing. The rhythm can be given to the jumper before he begins his action and also in doing it.

It can be both amusing and useful for the jumper to have small circles drawn at the take-off spots, instead of using straight lines.

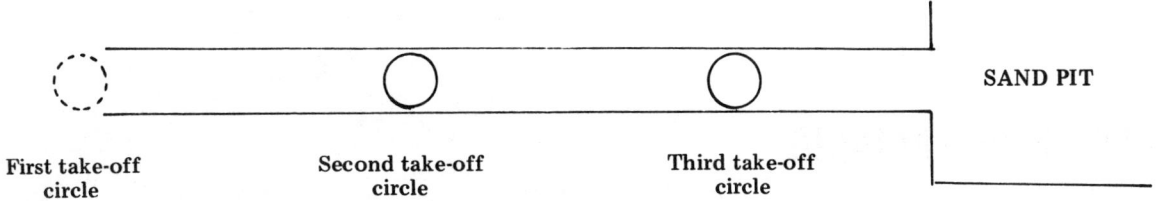

First take-off circle      Second take-off circle      Third take-off circle

I lay great stress on the maintenance of a correct body angle, both during the landings and the flight periods, often calling the pupils' attention to the importance of it.

If circumstances permit, I let my pupils practice on grass, barefooted, quite often.

# TRIPLE JUMP TRAINING

By Tadeusz Starzynski, Polish National Triple Jump Coach

The general use of the strength training, as well as its effects, points to the fact that the development of strength should institute the integral part of the training program, especially in the strength-speed disciplines, among which we number the triple jump. In spite of many experiments and many ways of the development of strength used by many coaches, and in spite of the scientific examinations, strength training even at the same disciplines still is based on different methods and various means.

The experience of many years and the results of the strength training by Polish triple jumpers made possible the systemization and channeling of effort to develop this feature (characteristic or quality) from the point of view of the needs of the triple jumper in the preparatory period (see Diagram I) of the yearly cycle (see Diagram II), as well as in the multi-year plan (see Diagram III). In the systematization of work in the development of strength in a triple jumper, we are using nomenclature of Gundlach (East Germany).

The following nomenclature is provided for those who wish to examine the Plates and Diagrams carefully: Caption, Plate I, "Scheme of the strength training for a triple jumper". In the graph, below the circles in Plate I, the thicker line indicates strength and the thinner line indicates special strength and spring-technique training during the 12-month period: (A) Maximal (and sub-maximal) strength; (B) Fast (rapid) strength (dynamic); and, (C) Endurance-strength.

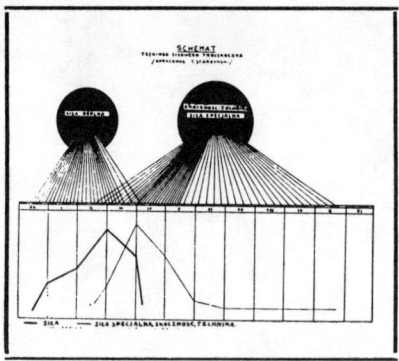

PLATE I

We based our experiments upon *isotonic* methods. We applied three sets of exercises, constantly trying to enrich them and adapt them to the new (changing) requirements of the improving training structures. This leads to the growing individualization and specialization of the methods of training. As a rule, up to now, we did not apply any *isometric* exercises in triple jump training. In some individual cases, however, we did recommend isometric exercises concurrently with basic or fundamental training. It was used in the cases of athletes with specific physical weaknesses. Selection and character of the exercises help and foster the shaping and development of the triple jumper's strength. These exercises dove-tail with each other and are applied chain-like. They should be tightly bound to the requirements of the technique and coordination of the triple jump event. They should also facilitate the development of speed.

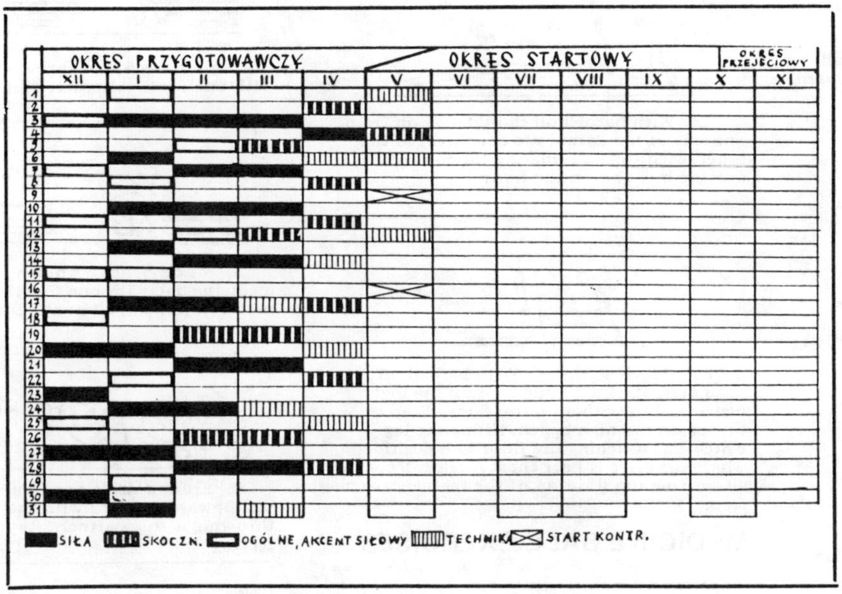

**DIAGRAM 1**

Trening siłowy skoczka (okres przygotowawczy)

Diagram 1 shows the various periods of training. *Okres Prezygotowawczy* means preparatory period. The Roman Numerals XII, I, II, III, IV beneath *Okres Przygotowawczy* indicate the months December, January, February, March, and April. *Okres Startowy* means competitive period, and the Roman Numerals V through XI indicate the months May through November. *Okres Prezejeciowy* means the period of transition. The left vertical column of numbers 1 through 31 indicate the days of the month. *Sila* means strength, *Skoczn* spring, *Ogolne*, *Akcent Silowy* general exercises, accent on strength, *Technik* technique, and *Start Kontr* means controlled competition.

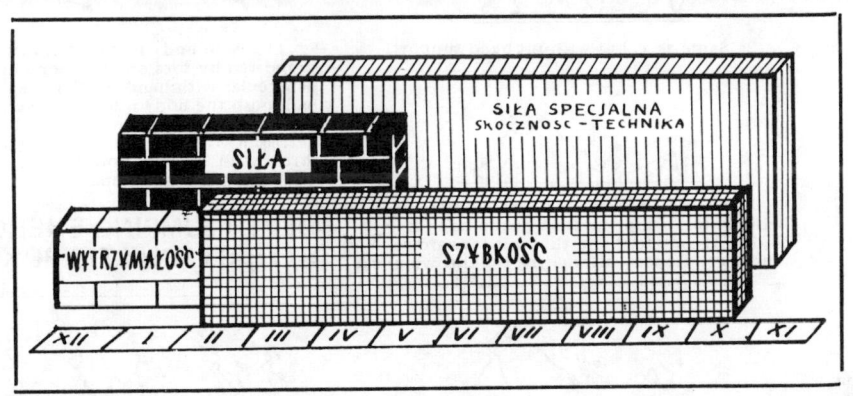

**DIAGRAM 2**

Elementy całorocznego treningu trójskoczka

Diagram 2 graphically portrays the elements of the entire year's triple jump training. *Wytrzymalosc* means endurance. *Sila* means strength. *Szybkosc* means speed. *Sila specjalna* means special strength. The blocks in the diagram indicate the types of training and their relative amounts in relation to the 12 months of the year, starting with the 12th month on the left, and ending with the 11th month on the right.

1. While hanging from bar with feet held by a partner at his chest height, swing the hips upward and downward. (1A.) While hanging from rings with feet held at hip-height by a partner and weight fastened around the hips, swing the hips upward and downward. (1B.) The same exercise as 1A may be executed while hanging from wallbars, with the feet on the floor but one meter forward of the wallbars. (1C.) Hang from wallbars. Place the feet on a one-meter/3'3½" high box placed one-meter in front of the wallbars. Swing the hips upward and downward.

2. Clean and jerk barbell. Keep the knees straight.
3. One-fourth squat-jumps with barbell on shoulders.

4. Full squats with barbell on shoulders.
5. One-half squat-jumps with barbell on shoulders.

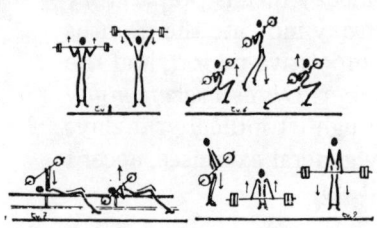

6. With barbell on shoulders, alternate stride jumping, landing with first one foot forward and then the other.
7. Bench press with barbell.
8. Standing military press with barbell.
9. Dead-lift with barbell, starting with knees bent.

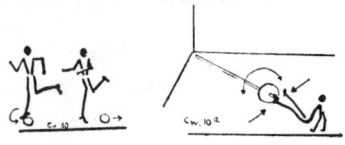

10. Push-kick a heavy medicine ball from side to side, using the inner side of the foot, alternately using one foot and then the other. (10A) While sitting, push (roll) one end of a barbell with the inner side of the foot, alternately using one foot and then the other.

(10B) Two athletes sit on opposite sides of a barbell, hook the feet under the bar, and simultaneously pull on the barbell with the feet.

11. Alternately hopping from one slanted gymnastic box to another, touching the floor between the boxes with one foot as each hop is made.

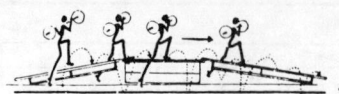

12. With barbell on shoulders, hop from one side of the gymnastic bench(es) to the other, each time alternating the foot which is on the box and on the floor.

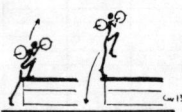

13. Bench stepping. With barbell on shoulders, start with one foot on the high bench and the other on the floor. Step to tip-toe on the high bench, lifting the leg which was touching the floor to a position where the knee is near chest-height. Repeat, alternating the position of the feet with each step.

## MEDICINE BALL EXERCISES

1. From a sitting position, hands supporting the body behind the hips, throw the medicine ball forward with the feet. Repeat.

2. Same as 1, but without hand support.

3. Sitting, with hands supporting body behind hips, using one foot, scoop ball off floor with one foot and throw it forward to a partner. Repeat, alternating the throwing leg.

4. Same as 3, but without hand support.

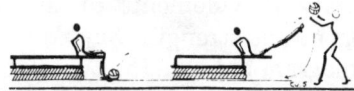

5. Sit on a bench. Support body with hands behind hips. Throw the medicine ball with both feet, forward to a partner. Repeat, alternating feet.

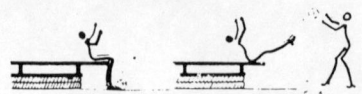

6. Same as 5, but without hand support.

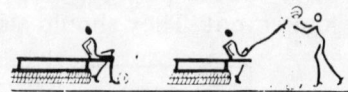

7. Same as 5, but throw medicine ball with one foot. Alternate feet.

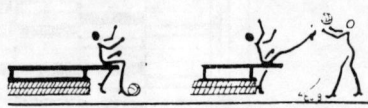

8. Sit on bench. No hand support. Throw medicine ball with one foot, forward to a partner. Repeat, alternating feet.

9. From a stride-position, scoop medicine ball upward-forward with the front foot, throwing it to a partner. Repeat, alternating feet.

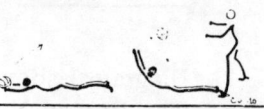

10. While lying on stomach with medicine ball in outstretched arms, throw it backward to a partner.

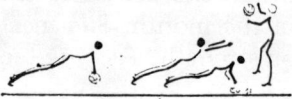

11. With body horizontal, face downward, supported by toes on the floor and arms perpendicular with hands resting on a medicine ball, push the body quickly upward with the arms, and throw the medicine ball to a partner; quickly catch the body weight after the throw with the hands on the floor before the body has a chance to crash to the floor.

## DEPTH-JUMPING EXERCISES WITH GYMNASTIC BOXES

1. Depth jump using left foot. Take off from top of one box, land between boxes on the left foot, take off from the left foot, and land on top of the second box with the left foot. Note boxes are of equal height. Repeat, using the right foot.
2. Repeat 1, but use both feet simultaneously, jumping from a low box to a higher box.
3. Repeat 1, jumping from a high box to a lower box.

4. From a stride-position, with one foot on a low box, take off for the standing long-jump, use a "hang" style mid-air action, and land on both feet. Repeat, alternating the takeoff foot.

5. From a short run-up, step to the high box, take off and long-jump, use a "hang" mid-air action, and land on both feet. Repeat, alternating the takeoff foot.

6. Using three low boxes, starting from a stride-position, with one foot on top of the first box, take off, land astride between boxes with the opposite foot atop the second box, and again take off and land astride with the opposite foot atop the third box. Repeat.

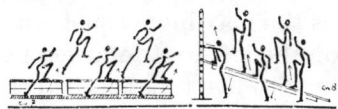

7. Use a long gymnastic bench. Jump along one side only. Stand astride with one foot on top of the bench and the other on the floor. Spring forward, taking off from the foot on top of the bench. Land in the same relative astride position. Cover the full length of the bench(es). Repeat on the opposite side of the bench, alternating the position of the legs.

8. Repeat 7, using an inclined bench proped up on wallbars.

9. Use a long bench. Start from a stride-position, with one foot on the bench and the other on the floor. Progress forward by jumping from one side of the bench to the other. Land with the feet alternating positions each time.

10. Repeat 9, using increasingly higher benches.

11. Repeat 9, using an inclined bench.

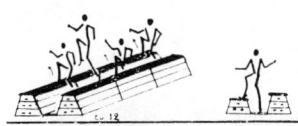

12. Use two parallel benches. Progress forward by hopping from one bench to the other, landing astride with one foot on the floor and the other atop the bench. Alternate the positions of the feet in landing from one box to the other. The height of the benches may be altered.

13. Repeat 12, using inclined benches.

14. Jumping over a series of barriers, one stride apart, which increase in height.

## TRIPLE JUMPING EXERCISES FROM ELEVATION (in depth)

1. From a short run-up, take off from atop a very low box and execute the triple jump.

2. Triple jump from a short run-up, landing at the end of the hop-phase atop a low box, and taking off from this box for the step-phase.

3. Triple jump from a short run-up, landing at the end of the step-phase and taking off for the jump atop a box of varying heights. (3A) One box height. (3B) Two box height. (3C) Three box height.

4. Standing triple jump. Start from standing position atop a high box.

## MULTIPLE-JUMPS

1. Multiple-hops on left foot.
2. Multiple-hops on right foot.
3. Multiple-jumps from one foot to the other; right-left-right-left, etc.
4. Multiple-jumps, using each foot twice before changing; left-left, right-right, left-left, etc.
5. Multiple-jumps in the rhythm of the triple jump; left-left, right, left-left, right, etc.
6. Multiple-jumps in the rhythm of the triple jump; right-right, left, right-right, left, etc.

5. Standing triple jump. Start from a stride position with front foot atop a medium-height box.

6. Standing triple jump. Start from a standing position atop a high box. Land in the step-phase and take off in the jump-phase on a medium-height box.

7. Standing triple jump. Start from a standing position atop a medium-height box. Land in the step-phase and take off in the jump-phase on a high box.

8. Standing triple jump. Start from a standing position atop a medium-height box. During the jump-phase, clear (jump over) a medium-height box before landing.

9. Standing triple jump or triple jump from very short run-up. Land at the end of the jump-phase on one foot and hands grasping high-up on wallbars. (9A) Same as 9, but land on both feet and hands grasping high-up on wallbars.

Multiple jumps may be executed either standing or from a short run-up, and from a variety of surfaces (snow, soft take-off surface, cinder run-up, all-weather surface). These will depend upon the training period.

143

## RECOMMENDATIONS FOR THE EXECUTION OF MULTIPLE-JUMPS

Use an accelerated rhythm. The first two jumps of each triple jumping exercise should be from the athlete's normal take-off foot in executing the competitive triple jump (for example, left-left, or right-right). All multiple-jumps should conclude with a correct landing on both feet. The arms should alternate in their movement, opposite arm moving with opposite leg. It is important that multiple-jumps be executed in a straight line without lateral movement. Execute the multiple-jumps between two parallel lines 50 centimeters/1'1¾" apart (see diagram). The coach must determine the quantity of multiple-jumps to be used in accordance with individual needs of the athletes. Top Polish triple jumpers obtain best results using 10 standing triple jumps and five triple jumps with run-up. An "active landing" is used each time the foot touches the surface in landing prior to takeoff.

## METHODOLOGY OF STRENGTH TRAINING

Before starting the yearly training cycle, it is important to determine the beginning weight to use. Determine this by testing. The starting weight for an advanced athlete is 50% of the maximum weight he lifted or squatted the previous year. For beginners, use 50% of body weight. The most prevalent strength-gauge used in testing Polish triple jumpers is the maximum squat with barbell on shoulders, tested three or four times each year, and five hops on the left foot followed by five hops from the right foot, starting from a standing takeoff, tested three to five times each year. The weight training applied by top Polish triple jumpers includes: (A.) Progressive in series of 3 to 6 repetitions; (B.) Progressive in diminishing series of 3 to 6 repetitions; (C.) Progressive in 2 to 3 series of 3 to 6 repetitions; (D.) Progressive in series of 3 to 6 repetitions, no time limit; (E.) Progressive in series of 3 to 6 repetitions, with time limit; and (F.) Steady (e.g., 30% of maximum) in series of 3 to 6 repetitions.

## REFERENCES

1. Dziedzic, Augustyn, *Weight Training*.
2. Gundlach, Coaches Conference in Warsaw, March 21, 1970.
3. O'Connor, Bob, *Scientific Basis of Weight Training*.
4. Starzynski, Tadeusz, *Triple Jump*.

# TRAINING OF SOVIET TRIPLE JUMPERS

By Z. Chrominski, Poland

*The Soviet Union has always produced excellent triple jumpers and is at the moment leading the world in this event. Their top performers, depth of results, and good training methods indicate that this domination can be expected to continue. In this article Polish coach Chrominski takes a close look at the Soviet training methods, based on the books by W. Kreer and W. Popov. It has been translated from Lehka Atletica, published in Warsaw.*

The development of triple jump technique, as well as the development of specific jumping power, is based on a variety of jumping exercises, including jumps on one leg, jumps from one leg to another and jumps on both legs. These exercises, executed at various knee bends, different speeds and flight angles, are suitable not only for beginners but also for top athletes. They help the learning and improvement of an active take-off, develop balance and relaxation, and form an efficient motor pattern. The fundamental exercises are continuous hops, continuous steps, triple jumps with one to three stride run-ups, jumps down from 2 to 4 ft. heights landing on one leg with an immediate take-off, and jumps with double leg take-off.

All exercises are performed at a flat flight path and it is recommended to have variations in the speed of execution. Occasionally a slightly downhill track is helpful for this purpose. Emphasis is on the stronger leg, which is responsible for two-thirds of the triple jump distance. The jumps either for distance or for speed are done over 30 to 40 meters and are supplemented with a series over 100 meters. A variation of surfaces, including sawdust, snow, sand and track is recommended, as well as jumps uphill up to 30 degrees and downhill up to 5 degrees. To provide a heavier load weighted shoes and weighted jackets are used.

The total jumping and strength training can be performed in two ways: 1. By using artificial loading for the jumping exercises, or 2. By performing jumping exercises after strength training.

(The second method is recommended during the competitive season).

According to the principle that lengthy repetitions are responsible for more permanent biochemical changes in the organism a typical workout would include running, gymnastics, 3 x 100 meters accelerations, 10 x 100 meter hops on the stronger leg, 10 min. gymnastics, 4 x 100 meter hops on the weaker leg, 3 x 100 meter accelerations. While this type of hard work deducts from the quality of jumps, it has a longer lasting influence on improving jumping ability. Of course, it is suitable only for preparation work.

Jumping ability can also be improved by using a variety of exercises with an optimal load. It develops the ability to tolerate great stresses and allows for an extremely high weekly training load. A sample workout would include running, gynmastics, 3 x 100 meters, 6 x 30 meters, crouch starts, 8 x 50 meter hops and steps, repetition jumps with 120 lb. barbell (2 x 6), throwing 16 lb. weight, 2 x 150 meters. Another method employs hops over 150 to 200 meter distances, using 8 to 9 feet long hops and emphasizing the main elements of technique.

Maximum loading and the number of repetitions in jumping exercises must be treated with care to avoid negative results. For this reason jumping until fully fatigued should, during the preparation phase, be included only once in the weekly training program. The distribution of some of the jumping exercises in the yearly schedule is presented in Table 1.

TABLE 1

| Exercise | Nov. Jan. | Feb. Mar. | April May | June July | August | Sept. Oct. |
|---|---|---|---|---|---|---|
| Hops on stronger leg | 5 x 100m 32 sec | 10 x 50m 15 sec | 4 x 40m 10.5 sec | 3 x 40m 10 sec | 8 x 50m 14.5 sec | 2 x 40m 10 sec. |
| Five jumps with 6-8 stride run up | 25 x | 25 x | 10 x | 10 x | 20 x | 8 x |
| Triple jumps | — | 10 x | 25 x | 10 x | 10 x | 8 x |
| Run-up strides | — | 6-8 | 6-8-10 | 12-14 | 6-8-10 | 12-14 |

In analyzing the work for the development of jumping ability it is interesting to note that after the early part of the competitive season another preparation for the end of season competitions takes place in August. In general it is obvious that the working load is very high and the full cycle of the year is responsible for an excellent general conditioning.

## STRENGTH PREPARATION

The basic aim in strength training is to develop the most important muscle group for a triple jumper with the back and leg muscles receiving special attention. An athlete who weighs 154 to 161 lbs. is expected to achieve 245 to 265 lbs. in the clean jerk, throw the shot backwards over the head 49 ft. 2½ in., reach 32 ft. 9¾ in. in the standing triple jump and perform 342 to 364 lb. squats.

Exercises for general strength development are:
1. Trunk bends and twists with the barbell.
2. Medicine ball throws.
3. Clean and jerk with 176 to 265 lb.
4. Shot and stone throwing.
5. Barbell cleans with 198 to 287 lb.
6. Hops with a 132 to 165 lb. partner.
7. Split jumps with 88 to 132 lb. barbell.
8. Exercises for ankle and hip muscles.
9. Exercises for abdominal muscles.

Exercises for specific strength development are:
1. Use of weight jacket for triple jumping (7 to 9 lb.)
2. Running with a 100 to 146 lb. barbell on shoulders.
3. Walking with side splits using 176 to 200 lb. barbell.
4. Pressing the barbell (132 to 165 lb.) on each stride.
5. Repetition jumping from one leg to another over 25 to 30 meters with a 77 to 88 lb. barbell.

Strength training is performed using medium to heavy loads with occasional maximum efforts. Usually four methods are employed:

1. Using 3 to 4 series of 1 to 3 repetitions in the pyramid system, adding weight and reducing the repetitions. For example in clean and jerk 2 x 3 reps with 187 lb., 2 x 3 reps with 198 lb., 2 x 3 reps with 220 lb., 2 x 2 reps with 243 lb., 1 x 2 reps with 265 lb., 1 x 1 rep with 287 lb.

2. Using series with a small number of repetitions and increasing the weight. For example in the clean 5 x 3 reps with 198 lb., 5 x 3 reps with 209 lb., 5 x 3 reps 220 lb., etc.

3. Using a large number of repetitions for exercises with small loads. For example, in split jumps with two series of 30 repetitions, carrying 110 lb.

4. Using medium number of repetitions in a slow rhythm similar to isometric exercises. For example, in squats with 243 to 265 lb., and 10 to 15 repetitions.

These four methods can be used in different ways and are often combined in a workout. If the same muscle groups are involved heavy loads are followed by lighter exercises. For example, after squats the program includes split jumps, or the split jumps are followed by hopping on one leg with a partner on shoulders. On the other hand, it is often advisable to avoid fatigue by changing the muscle groups in action or by including easy acceleration runs and jumping in between the strength exercises.

During the competitive season, when strong demands are made on the neuro-muscular system, the strength exercises should be carried out with great speed and limited number of repetitions. The load is near maximum but administered only in small dosages. Experience has shown that this increases the contraction capacity of the muscles and allows for speed and jumping work to be handled with ease on the following day. It is actually the reason for the inclusion of strength exercises in the competitive warm-up by many jumpers.

Table 2 shows the distribution of some of the strength exercises over a 12 month cycle. It must be kept in mind that strength training should include plenty of variety and made suitable for the individual needs of each athlete. The exercises are dynamic and, besides activating the muscle groups used, often have no other muscle groups used, often have no other direct connection with triple jumping.

TABLE 2

| Exercise | Nov. Jan. | Feb. Mar. | April May | June July | August | Sept. Oct. |
|---|---|---|---|---|---|---|
| Jumps with partners on shoulders | 8 x 19 | 4 x 12 | 4 x 7 | 4 x 8 | 3 x 10 | 2 x 7 |
| Walking with a lounge chair | 4 x 40m 165 lbs. | 3 x 30m 220 lbs. | 2 x 30m 176 lbs. | 40m 176 lbs. | 3 x 30m 198 lbs. | 30m 176 lbs. |
| Clean | 198 lb. | 254 lb. | 220 lb. | 254 lb. | 220 lb. | 254 lb. |

## SPRINTING PREPARATION

This includes sprinting on the run-up track, crouch and flying starts over 60 to 80 meters, runs over 100, 150 and 200 meters, varied speed running over 50 to 70 meters, accelerations and crouch starts uphill, harness runs against resistance, exercises to develop fast movement pattern and hurdling.

To improve running technique runs with emphasis on stride length and drive, runs with high knee lift and varied speed running is employed.

The specific running exercises are continued during the whole preparation phase, starting with medium speeds over 80 to 100 meters at the beginning and gradually changing to fast repetitions over shorter distances (60 to 80 meters) as the competitive season approaches. In addition exercises such as skipping, uphill running, low hurdling, and starts over 30 meters are used to develop speed.

The training load in running depends on speed and not on the distance and the number of repetitions. Recovery should be considered sufficient when the pulse rate has dropped to 100-200 beats a minute but for jumping the run-up should be started only after a complete recovery. Great intensity dominates sprinting over 50 to 100 meters where recoveries are taken by covering the equivalent distance in jogging.

The sprint training includes a variety of distances ranging from 30 meters with a walking start in 2.8 to 3.0 sec. to 150 meters in 19.0 to 20.0 sec. The 150 meter distances are continued through the whole cycle as can be seen from table 3, showing some of the sprinting program.

Our opinion is that Fartlek should be included in the preparation phase and during the competitive season there is not sufficient sprinting over 20 to 30 meter distances.

TABLE 3

|  | Nov. Jan. | Feb. Mar. | April May | June July | August | Sept. Oct. |
|---|---|---|---|---|---|---|
| Longer distances | 8 x 150m 23-21.5 | 6 x 150m 21-20.4 | 3 x 150m 19-18 | 2 x 150m 18.5-17.5 | 5 x 150m 19-18.5 | 2 x 150m 18-17 |
| Shorter distances | 5 x 70m | 5 x 70m | 10 x 50m | 5 x 50m | 10 x 50m | 4 x 50m |
| Run-up repitions | — | 8 | 12-15 | 6-8 | 10 | 6 |

148

# TRAINING A MODERN TOP-CLASS TRIPLE JUMPER

By C.M. Muthiah, Senior Athletics Coach, Patiala, India

In this article we will deal with a jumper who is in his 3rd or 4th year of training and specifically in the 1st or 2nd top training year. To reach a distance over 16m he should also attain the capacity to run 100m in 10.8 sec.-11.0 sec. and long jump between 7m-7.30m. To attain this a triple jumper has to develop three very important factors in that priority given below.
1. Speed; 2. Jumping Force; 3. Technique.

**SPEED:** 50% of our total training is in the development of speed as this is the most important factor. It is not only running speed which is necessary but also jumping speed. He should be able to attain 10.0-10.5 m/second in the last stride and also maintain it as much as possible during the three phases of triple jump. Hence the preparational period of a triple jumper is the same as the sprinter. He will also develop speed-endurance as the sprinters, but to a slightly lower level, as more time is necessary for the development of jumping force and technique.

**JUMPING FORCE:** 30% of our training is done for developing jumping force. This is because the jumper has to take off, land and take off with one leg and requires a special jumping force to be developed. Here we must also develop the jumping endurance so as to be able to stand a great load of jumps. This is developed by a high amount of training during the preparational period. By means of high repetitions the economy of movements are developed. One disadvantage is that explosiveness of the movement is lost after a prolonged time and hence this training should be reduced before competition. We must also differentiate between jumping force and stretching force, its characteristics and development. While developing the jumping force one develops also the elasticity and stretching forces of the muscle. During the development of the stretch force one should also develop the correct direction in which it is used.

**TECHNIQUE:** 20% of the work is concentrated on technique. This is because of the 3 flight phases and co-ordination of the arms with the legs during landing, take off and flight in each of the three phases. Though the 'flat' and 'steep' techniques are widely used it will be helpful for future jumpers to do what we can call the Modern Technique. Here the percentage is 36.5; 30.0; 33.5. Angle is the Hop 16° and Jump 18°. Alternate arm for Hop, double arm for Step and alternate arm for jump. It is also important to work on active landing and take off in each phase.

**WEEKLY TRAINING CYCLE:** Following is the weekly cycle which is advised in the 1st part of pre-competition period or later part of preparational period. The weekly cycle now recommended is of 10 days and not 7 days.

**EXAMPLE: Monday**—Force development. The exercises should be for the development of force in a vertical direction. **Tuesday**—Plenty of loosening exercises and medium pace running. **Wednesday**—Short sprints and some technique work, sub-maximal intensity. **Thursday**—Rest day. **Friday**—Horizontal jump training 50% to 60% intensive work and 40% to 50% sub-maximal. **Saturday**—Long sprints 40% maximal and 60% sub-maximal to maximal speed. **Sunday**—Rhythm exercises, i.e., 5 jump rhythm and 10 jump rhythm with and without load sub-maximal to maximal speed. **Monday**—Exercises to develop agility and mobility loosening exercises. **Tuesday**—Technique work and short sprints with maximum intensity. **Wednesday**—Rest day.

**MONTHLY TRAINING PLAN**

The following plan may be adhered to so as to reach your goal. This is worked out keeping in mind that the Olympics is in the month of August and hence the entire cycle has to change.

## MONTHLY TRAINING CYCLE AND PLAN

| | October | November | December | January | February | March | April | May | June | July |
|---|---|---|---|---|---|---|---|---|---|---|
| 20m. Tempo Runs | 2.9 Sec. | 2.9 Sec. | 2.8 Sec. | 2.8 Sec. | 2.7 Sec. | 2.7 Sec. | 2.6 Sec. | 2.5 Sec. | 2.5 Sec. | 2.5 Sec. |
| 50m. Tempo Runs | — | 5.8 Sec. | 5.8 Sec. | 5.7 Sec. | 5.6 Sec. | 5.6 Sec. | 5.6 Sec. | 5.5 Sec. | 5.5 Sec. | 5.5 Sec. |
| 70m. TR | 8.0-8.5 Sec. | 8.0 Sec. | 7.8-8.0 Sec. | 7.7 Sec. | 7.7 Sec. | 7.6 Sec. | 7.6 Sec. | 7.5 Sec. | 7.5 Sec. | 7.5 Sec. |
| 100m TR | 11.2-11.6 Sec. | 11.0-11.3 Sec. | 11.0-11.1 Sec. | 11.0 Sec. | 11.0 Sec. | 10.8 Sec. | 10.8 Sec. | 10.7 Sec. | 10.7 Sec. | 10.6 Sec. |
| 150 TR | 18.0 Sec. | 17.0-17.5 Sec. | 17.2 Sec. | 17.0 Sec. | 16.8 Sec. | 16.5 Sec. | 16.0 Sec. | 16.0 Sec. | 15.8 Sec. | 15.8 Sec. |
| Three Hop | — | — | — | — | 14.50m | 14.70m | 14.90m | 15.0m | 15.10m | 15.20m |
| Five Hop Step Rhythm | 21.00m | 21.50m | 22.00m | 23.00m | 23.30m | 23.60m | 24.00m | 24.00m | 24.00m | 24.20m |
| Ten Hop Step Rhythm | 38.00m | 38.50m | 39.00m | 39.00m | 39.50m | 40.00m | 40.50m | 41.00m | 42.00m | 43.00m |
| 50m Jumping | | | | | | | | | | |
| Broad Jump Left | — | 6.40m | 6.50m | 6.60m | 6.70m | 6.80m | 6.80m | 7.00m | 7.00m | 7.20m |
| Broad Jump Right | — | 6.30m | 6.40m | 6.50m | 6.60m | 6.70m | 6.70m | 6.80m | 6.80m | 6.90m |
| Full Run up 1 Hop | — | — | 5.80m | 5.80m | 6.00m | 6.00m | 6.20m | 6.20m | 6.40m | 6.40m |
| Stretch Exercise for foot | 100 KP | 100 KP | 120 KP | 130 KP | 140 KP | 140 KP | 160 KP | 160 KP | — | — |
| Concentrated Jump | 76 Cm | 77 Cm | 77 Cm | 79 cm | 80 cm | 78 cm | 82 cm | 82 cm | 83 cm | 84 cm |
| Triple Jump with Short Run up 10 Stride | 14.30m | 14.50m | 14.70m | 14.70m | 14.80m | 15.00m | 15.00m | 15.10m | 15.10m | 15.20m |
| T.J. with Medium Run up 14 Stride | — | — | — | 15.00m | 15.00m | 15.20m | 15.00m | 15.40m | 15.50m | 15.20m |
| T.J. with Long Run up 18 Stride | — | — | — | — | — | — | — | 15.80m | 16.00m | 16.00m |

It is also important to use 2 hours per week exercises to develop agility and mobility. During the pre-competition season the jumper should be able to reach the following standards of rhythm performing from both legs alternatively.

### STAGES TO SHOW THE DIFFERENT TRAINING METHODS AND TOTAL LOAD 6 MONTHS BEFORE OLYMPICS

| Type | 1st Stage | 2nd Stage | 3rd Stage | 4th Stage | 5th Stage | Total |
|---|---|---|---|---|---|---|
| **Running** | | | | | | |
| Sprint up to 100m. | 4 Km. | 8 Km. | 12 Km. | 10 Km. | 10 Km. | 44 Km. |
| Sprint over 100m. | 4 Km. | 3 Km. | 6 Km. | 4 Km. | 3 Km. | 20 Km. |
| Easy Running | 15 Km. | 10 Km. | 15 Km. | 15 Km. | 10 Km. | 65 Km. |
| | | | | | | 129 Km. |
| **Technique Jumps and Check marks Run ups** | | | | | | |
| Jumps with Short Run ups | 200 Jumps | 100 Jumps | 150 Jumps | 100 Jumps | 100 Jumps | 650 Jumps |
| Jumps with Medium Run ups | — | 50 Jumps | 60 Jumps | 40 Jumps | 40 Jumps | 190 Jumps |
| Jumps with Long Run ups | — | — | 10 Jumps | 15 Jumps | 20 Jumps | 45 Jumps |
| Checkmark Run ups | — | — | 50 Runs | 80 Runs | 100 Runs | 230 Runs |
| **Jumps for Rhythm** | | | | | | |
| 3-5-10 Jumps | 40 Jumps | 80 Jumps | 100 Jumps | 80 Jumps | 60 Jumps | 360 Jumps |
| Jumping up to 50-100m. | 20 Jumps | 40 Jumps | 80 Jumps | 20 Jumps | 20 Jumps | 180 Jumps |
| Squats up to 100KP wt. | 100 | 80 | 200 | 80 | 60 | 520 |
| Leg Stretching exercises | 100 | 200 | 200 | 100 | 100 | 700 |
| Isometric | 20 | 20 | 20 | 20 | 20 | 100 |

Analyzing from the world class jumpers a person takes 5-6 years to reach over 16m and should have the ability to run 100m in 11 sec, long jump 7.2m; height 1.80 and weight 73 Kg. To reach 16.55m he should be able to run 100m in 10.8 sec, long jump 7.50m, height 1.85 and weight 75 Kg. To reach 17m he should be able to run 100m in 10.6 sec, long jump 7.85m, height 1.88 and weight 75 Kg.

### 5 Jumps with 6-7 approach strides

| Jumps | Distance | Time |
|---|---|---|
| L-R-L-R-L | 20m — 24m | 2.8 Sec. |
| L-L-R-R-L | 20m — 23m | 2.8 Sec. |
| L-L-L-R-R | 20m — 21m | 2.8 Sec. |
| L-L-R-L-L | 20m — 23m | 2.8 Sec. |

### 10 Jumps with 6-7 approach strides

| Jumps | Distance | Time |
|---|---|---|
| L-R-L-R— | 38m — 42m | 5.5 Sec. |
| L-L-R-R— | 38m — 42m | 5.5 Sec. |
| 5L/5R | 38m — 40m | 5.5 Sec. |
| L-L-R-L-L-R | 38m — 42m | 5.5 Sec. |

# PRACTICAL RATIOS FOR TRIPLE JUMPERS

By Toni Nett, Germany, editor, *Die Lehre der Leichtathletik*

From a number of world class triple jumpers who have jumped over 53' the percentages of each phase of triple jump from the best broad jump performance are as follows:

| Technique | Hop | Step | Jump | Total | Average for each phase |
|---|---|---|---|---|---|
| The long hop type (U.S.S.R.) | 84.81 | 64.89 | 69.05 | 218.75 | 72.91 |
| The "flat" type (Schmidt's technique) | 76.06 | 65.45 | 77.98 | 219.49 | 73.16 |

As most of the triple jumpers probably score a little below their maximum ability in long jump it would be safe to take an average of 75% per phase as reasonable. This means for example that a 20 ft. long jumper should reach 75% from 3 x 20 ft. or 45 ft. in triple jump.

The averages from Schmidt's (30 jumps) and Einarsson (8 jumps) give a following percentage for each phase from the total distance (measured toe-toe-heels):

| | Hop | Step | Jump |
|---|---|---|---|
| Schmidt | 34.7 | 29.8 | 35.5 |
| Einarsson | 34.3 | 30.4 | 35.3 |

From these figures it will be safe to take a 35% hop, 30% step and 35% jump as an average economical distribution for the "flat" technique.

Combining the two tables we could now give a new table with distances that should be reached by triple jumpers according to their long jump abilities and how the distances should be reached on the "flat" technique:

| Best Long Jump | Hop (35%) | Step (30%) | Jump (35%) | Total Distance |
|---|---|---|---|---|
| 18' | 14'2" | 12'12" | 14'2" | 40'6" |
| 19' | 15' | 12'9" | 15' | 42'9" |
| 20' | 15'9" | 13'6" | 15'9" | 45' |
| 21' | 16'6" | 14'2" | 16'6" | 47'3" |
| 22' | 17'4" | 14'10" | 17'4" | 49'6" |
| 23' | 18'2" | 15'5" | 18'2" | 51'9" |
| 24' | 18'10" | 16'4" | 18'10" | 54' |
| 24'6" | 19'3½" | 16'6½" | 19'3½" | 55'1½" |
| 25' | 19'9" | 16'8" | 19'9" | 56'2" |

# DISTRIBUTION OF TRIPLE JUMP PHASES

By Vitold Kreer, U.S.S.R., former world triple jump record holder

Development of a triple jump rhythm, as well as changing it, is based on finding a suitable movement pattern for the individual athlete. For example, from 1963 to 1965 Solotarjev's jumps had a distribution consisting of a 35% hop, 30% step and 35% jump. His 16.51m (54.2) effort was made up of 5.83m (19.1¾) 4.90m (16.1) 5.78m (18.11¾). A 16.22m (53.2½) performance consisted of 5.81m (19.1) 4.61m (15.1½) 5.80m (19.0¼).

In the autumn of 1966 Solotarjev began to change his fundamental jumping rhythm. In two months he performed more hopping and stepping exercises than the combined total of his two previous seasons. This was responsible for considerable improvement in his leg strength as Solotarjev reached in a six-stride approach five hops test 22.50m (73.10), compared with 21.50m (70.6½) in 1965. By using an aggressive acceleration and leg drive at the take off, combined with a further forward reaching action of the lower leg before landing, he increased his hop to 6.15—6.20m (20.2½—20.4) without obvious changes in the height of the flight. The new action also made Solotarjev's take-off into the step more powerful and allowed him to produce three 16.70m (54.9½) performances in 1970. The distribution of his jump changed to a 37% hop, 29½% step, and 33½% jump.

The same development of rhythm is also noticeable in Viktor Sanejev's career. In 1965 his 15.80m (51.10) consisted of a 35% hop, 29% step and 36% jump. In 1967 the percentages had changed to 36, 29 and 35. His 16.59m (54.5½) effort consisted of a 5.99m (19.8) hop, 4.82m (15.9¾) step and 5.83m (19.2) jump. Savejev's world record measured from his take-off spot 20cm (8 in) before the board, further increased the hop percentage in 1968. His 17.59m (57.8¾) consisted of 37% or 6.50m (22.4) hop, 29% or 5.05m (16.7) step and 34% or 6.04m (19.10) jump. The increased load of specific jumping exercises (six-stride five hops improved to 23.50m (77.1¼) and speed (60 meters from 6.8 in 1967 to 6.6 in 1968) assisted Sanejev to a new and more economical distribution of the single phases of his new triple jump rhythm.

The development of rhythm must be based on the physical, optical and acoustical values of the movement pattern. The combination of a fast approach and powerful drive with the distance of the jump and the direction of the drive must be analyzed on film, the actual distances should be measured and the total information fitted into the whole movement pattern. This is the only safe method to avoid mistakes and assure a correct development of the distribution of the three phases, assisted by jumping exercises (hops and steps). The development should aim for a low but ground covering travel of the center of gravity, combined with forward gripping movements.

The triple jump rhythm appears to depend on the particular training phase and form of an athlete. This is explainable by the lack of technical work and the effects of very high training loads. If the same situation exists during the competitive season it usually indicates insufficient power training. In short, the combined hop and step represents a reliable and significant guide—an increase in the hop and step distance is responsible also for an improved overall distance. Based on these analyses and mathematical calculations we believe that the most economical distribution in the triple jump should be 38% hop, 29½% step and 32½% jump. An 18 meters (59 ft.) jump, expected in the near future, would therefore be made up by a 6.85m (22.5¾) hop, 5.30m (17.5) step and 5.85m (19.2¼) jump.

# SHALLOW OR STEEP?

By L. Prihoda, Czechoslovakian National Coach

The majority of the athletes in the triple jump competition at the Olympic Games in Tokyo were experienced and hardened competitors. This is proved by the fact that the highest average age-group of all participants was 26.2 years, and the average age of competitors in the finals was even 27 years! Gold and silver medalists Schmidt and Fedossejew had been figuring in the world top-ranking lists for a number of years; and even the youngest finalist, V. Krawtschenko (23) was no longer "unknown" as a competitor. The techniques and training of these old hands had been repeatedly investigated and discussed in great detail. At first glance therefore—nothing new!

During recent years, two different types of triple-jumping techniques have taken shape quite clearly: the running technique (shallow jump) and the jumping technique (steep jump). Their differences are based on whether it is of greater importance to maintain horizontal speed right into the final jump, at the expense of a slightly-shortened hop, or whether upward lift should be emphasized earlier in the hop and step. As it was very difficult to measure the height of the jumps and their speed in Tokyo, a comparison of the individual distances jumped was used as an indication as to the type of technique. The exponents of the running theory (shallow jump) recommend the proportions 35% : 30% : 35% (Starzynski), while those in favor of the jump theory (steep jump) advise a ratio of 37.8% : 29.7% : 32.5%.

How can these two theories be applied to the finalists in Tokyo? Following a comprehensive survey, the following finalists can be classified as tending mainly to the running (shallow) jump: J.S. Schmidt (Poland), M. Hinze (Germany), and F.J. Alsop (Great Britain). Fedossejew (USSR) and S. Ciochina (Roumania) used a transitional technique, i.e. a mixture of both; and the jumping technique (steep jump) was employed only by V. Krawtschenko (USSR).

During the Olympic competition the judges did not measure the phases jumped in the three separate stages; and the only way in which we could determine individual distances, therefore, was by the cinematographic method. On the basis of our experience it was possible to determine the distance of the separate phases within plus or minus five centimeters (2"), *provided* preparations were made with extreme care and results were accurately evaluated. Such a degree of accuracy was sufficient for our purpose.

When measuring the distances of the separate phases during the finals at the Olympic Games in 1964 we obtained the results shown below in table 1.

In evaluating the distances of the jumps by these finalists, it becomes obvious that, in competition, the phase-proportions approximate each other—somewhat blurring the differences of the two schools of thought! And this can be observed especially when the first two phases are added together, whereby the hop is in each instance close to six meters and the step around five meters, giving approximately 11 meters.

Moreover, when we compare the proportions produced by the athletes, we notice that, in

Tokyo, Fedossejew *shortened* his hop [in his performance of 16.70 meters (54'9½") in 1959, the distances were 6.49 meters (21'3½")—4.81 meters (15'10")—5.40 meters (17'8 5/8")] whereas Schmidt slightly *lengthened* it [in his world record jump of 17.03 meters (55'10½") he had individual distances of 6.01 meters (19'9 5/8")—5.00 meters (16'4 7/8")—6.02 meters (19'9")!].

*(Note by Toni Nett: As the picture-sequence of Fedossejew shows, he hopped about 25 centimeters too early, which has not been taken into account in Prihoda's figures. The actual jump was therefore approximately 16.60 meters. This would alter the figures for this jump as follows: hop 6.30 (20'8")—step 5.00 meters (16'4 7/8") (11.30 meters) 37'0 7/8") = 16.60 meters (54'5½"). Or, in percentages: 38% : 30.1% : 31.9%. Although there is a shortening of the jump here also, it proves, nevertheless, that only the two Russian athletes, Fedossejew and Krawtschenko, had not fully adopted the shallow jumping technique. (Kreer had already done so); both had approximately 38% for the hop, which proves that they employed the steep jumping technique.)*

Of the finalists, Krawtschenko, employing the steep jumping technique, had the longest hop—(see table below); and his jumping behavior was all the more striking when one considers that he used this with the slowest run-up speed!

In order to get exact records as to the technical skill of the individual athletes, we measured the time-lapse of each jump by synchronized photographs of each, and a 1/100 stop watch. Measuring by hand or relying on the running speed of the film camera cannot be sufficiently reliable.

The time was taken over the last five meters (approximately 15') of the run-up, and, for the various phases, at each moment when the center of gravity (pelvis) was above the supporting leg. For the third (jump) phase the time was measured to the instant of first contact with the sand.

The average speed of the separate phases was assessed on the basis of the distance jumped and time interval. The speed of the run-up and of the separate phases by these finalists is given in Table 2.

The approach speed before the board for five of the finalists was fairly equal; in the region of 10.3 to 10.1 m/sec; with Schmidt and Alsop the fastest. The slowest in the run-up was Krawtschenko, whose speed converted to 100 meters (109 yards 1'1") was about 0.4 seconds slower. In assessing the skill of these athletes it is important to note how they utilized their approach speed, and to what extent they lost it in the course of the hop, step and jump. This is the basic question, the answer to which can solve this problem of a better exploitation of jumping technique, shallow or steep, in this event.

The loss of speed during the hop varied from 0.8 to 1.15 m/sec. for the finalists. Schmidt had the smallest loss; Fedossejew the biggest. The size of such a loss is influenced decisively by the take-off; in the first part of this (before the center of gravity or pelvis was vertically over the jumping leg) Schmidt checked less than the others, but pushed himself off more forcefully from there on. For this reason his hop lost less horizontal speed and was of sufficient length.

The speed of the step should most clearly characterize the two different technical conceptions. With the shallow-jump theory the hop and the step should be low and comparatively short in time, enabling the jumper to preserve sufficient speed for the final jump.

How do the measurements support this theory?

The athletes with shallow hops, i.e. Schmidt, Alsop and Hinze, had noticeably higher speeds in the step (8.2 to 8.35 m/sec.) than those with a higher hop, i.e. Krawtschenko, Fedossejew, Ciochina, (7.5 to 7.9 m/sec.). The loss of speed for the first group was 1.95 to 2.00 m/sec.; for the second group, 2.3 to 2.4 m/sec. This would appear to confirm the validity of the shallow jump technique.

However, Schmidt was the only finalist to maintain horizontal speed in his jump. The length of Alsop's and Hinze's jumps, on the other hand, did not differ much from the other athletes.

**Shallow jump technique plus take-off power**

The investigation seemed to indicate that it was not the shallow jumping technique *alone* which enabled Schmidt to carry out his decisive jump, the secret of which was the extraordinary power of his second leg, which enabled him to make proper use of horizontal speed at jumping take-off. The importance of a good take-off for the jump is well known, yet it is frequently forgotten in triple jumping practice! These measurements confirm that importance. Many athletes in this event would do better in training if they paid as much attention to the jump as they give to the hop and step!

The question arises whether athletes who do not have this extraordinary second-leg power can fully exploit the shallow jump technique; whether, without this power, it is advantageous to conform to this theory (as Hinze did). Here it is interesting to observe the results achieved by Krawtschenko who, in spite of the slowest run-up speed and greater speed losses, nevertheless registered the third best performance of the competition.

*(Note by Toni Nett: Probably because he was able to make full use of slower horizontal speed—due to the excellent power of both legs at take-off; whereas, obviously, his opponents could not exploit their faster run-up and better technique, because their power was either inferior, or they did not pay sufficient attention to take-off in all three phases.)*

## Comments by Toni Nett of Germany

*As a result of my observations of the Triple Jumping in the Tokyo Olympic Games, I had come to the conclusion that the shallow jumping technique was gaining in popularity, but, unfortunately, I was unable to give exact figures on the loss in horizontal speed, the speed-loss during the separate phases (hop, step and jump) and the phase-ratios of the individual athletes, for I was occupied with another task (i.e. shooting film).*

*For this reason I welcome all the more the achievement of a team of the Czechoslovak Athletic Association, and in particular that of Prihoda, its national coach. For the first time in the history of athletics we now have exact information relating to the difference between the shallow and the steep-jumping techniques; and, in my opinion, this gives definite proof of the superiority of the shallow jump.*

*Prihoda reaches the same conclusions with regard to the triple jump, as I have: Any technique is effective only when combined with existing strength, for without strength improved technique cannot be utilized! Were this not the case, triple jumpers would need only to apply the trick of a more shallow jumping curve to jump record distances.*

*But it is not as simple as that (and, from a coaching point of view, this is just as well!). Only when the "chocolate leg" (the weaker leg) has been given the same, or very nearly the same, power through well-known special strengthening exercises, and when the athlete in the triple jump directs his attention to a conscious and emphatic FORWARD (not upward!) jump, will he be able to utilize the better shallow jump technique.*

TABLE 1

| Name | Hop | | Step | | Jump | | Result |
|---|---|---|---|---|---|---|---|
| Schmidt | 6.10m (20'0 3/16") | = 36.2% | 5.00m (16'4 7/8") | = 29.7% | 5.75m (18'10 3/8") | = 34.1% | 16.85m (55'3 3/8") |
| *Fedossejew | 6.05m (19'10 3/16") | = 37.0% | 5.00m (16'4 7/8") | = 30.6% | 5.30m (17'4 5/8") | = 32.4% | 16.35m (53'7 3/4")* |
| Krawtshenko | 6.20m (20'4 1/8") | = 37.8% | 4.95m (16'2 7/8") | = 30.2% | 5.23m (17'1 7/8") | = 30.2% | 16.38m (53'8 7/8") |
| Alsop | 6.00m (19'8 1/4") | = 36.4% | 5.05m (16'6 13/16") | = 30.6% | 5.43m (17'9 3/4") | = 33.0% | 16.48m (54'0 7/7") |
| Alsop | 5.80m (19'0 3/8") | = 36.0% | 5.05m (16'6 13/16") | = 31.2% | 5.29m (17'4 1/4") | = 32.8% | 16.14m (53'11 3/8") |
| Ciochina | 5.95m (19'6 1/4") | = 36.6% | 4.95m (16'2 7/8") | = 30.5% | 5.33m (17'5 7/8") | = 32.9% | 16.23m (53'3") |
| Hinze | 5.90m (19'4 5/16") | = 36.5% | 4.90m (16'0 15/16") | = 30.3% | 5.35m (17'6 5/6") | = 33.2% | 16.15m (52'11 7/8") |

TABLE 2

| Name | Performance | Run-up | Hop | Step | Jump | Triple Jump Total |
|---|---|---|---|---|---|---|
| | | (last 5m) | Time in seconds: | | | Time in seconds |
| Schmidt | 16.85m (55'3 3/8") | 0.485 | 0.640 | 0.605 | 0.765 | 2.015 |
| *Fedossejew | 16.35m (53'7 3/4") | 0.490 | 0.670 | 0.635 | 0.780 | 2.085 |
| Krawtschenko | 16.38m (53'8 7/8") | 0.505 | 0.690 | 0.660 | 0.800 | 2.150 |
| Alsop | 16.48m (54'0 7/8") | 0.485 | 0.645 | 0.620 | 0.775 | 2.030 |
| Ciochina | 16.23m (53'3") | 0.490 | 0.660 | 0.640 | 0.790 | 2.115 |
| Hinze | 16.15m (52'11 7/8") | 0.490 | 0.640 | 0.595 | 0.725 | 1.950 |
| | | | | | Speed in meters/seconds: | |
| Schmidt | | 10.30 | 9.50 | 8.30 | 7.00 | 8.40 |
| Fedossejew | | 10.20 | 9.05 | 7.90 | 6.40 | 8.00 |
| Krawtschenko | | 9.90 | 9.00 | 7.50 | 6.20 | 8.12 |
| Alsop | | 10.30 | 9.30 | 8.15 | 6.60 | 8.12 |
| Ciochina | | 10.10 | 9.00 | 7.75 | 6.35 | 7.90 |
| Hinze | | 10.20 | 9.20 | 8.25 | 6.90 | 8.11 |

# DEVIATIONS IN THE TRIPLE JUMP

By Tadeusz Starzynski, Polish National Triple Jump Coach

Well known triple jump coach Tadeusz Starzynski, in analyzing world-class jumpers from films taken above the jumping area, discovered remarkable deviations from the straight line. The drawings below indicate how some of the champions execute their three phases. Only Dudkin (U.S.S.R.) and Neuman (East Germany) travel absolutely straight. Former world record holder Schmidt (Poland) deviates a little left in his jump but the present record holder, Saneyev(U.S.S.R.), takes a noticeably erratic course. Prudencio (Brazil) looses valuable distance by his diagonal path.

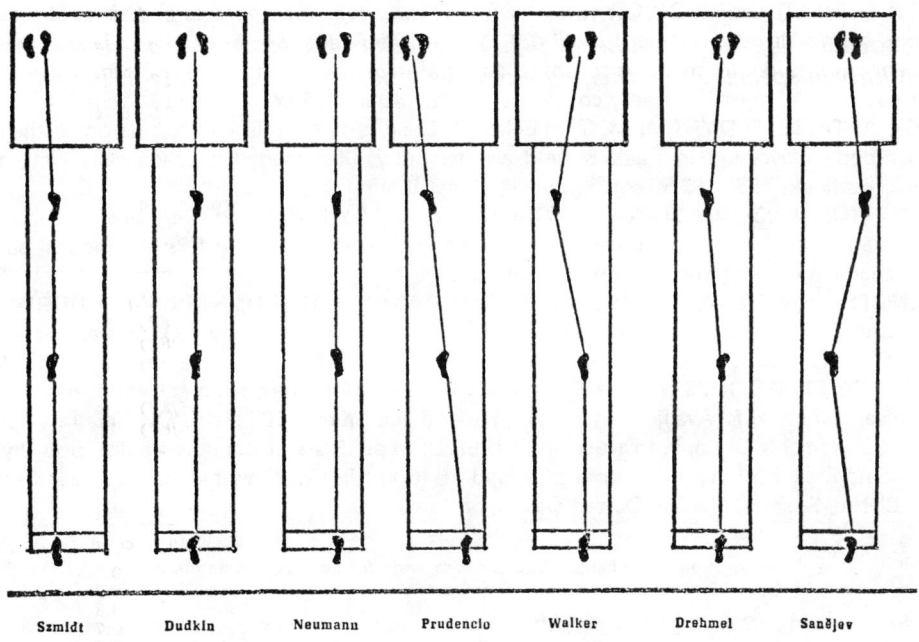

Szmidt   Dudkin   Neumann   Prudencio   Walker   Drehmel   Sanějev

## BOOKS AND FILMS FROM TRACK & FIELD NEWS

**COMPUTERIZED RUNNING TRAINING PROGRAMS,** Gardner and Purdy. The guesswork has been taken out of training by the computer-generated tables and workouts in this useful new work for runner and coach. Speed guidelines are provided for your daily workouts, tailored to your ability and your event. Easy to use and apply. 258pp. $4.50

**GERMAN PHOTOSEQUENCE BOOKS.** Superb photosequence studies of Olympic stars by Toni and Elfriede Nett. German text, but photostrips are unmatched. Book I: Running; Book II: Sprint Starts and Relay Passes; Book III: Hurdling; Book IV: Long Jump; Book V: Triple Jump. Men & women shown, incl. many U.S. aces. $2.50 per book

**RUN RUN RUN,** Fred Wilt. Long considered the most comprehensive and helpful book on running training. All methods, theories, tactics, warm-up, pace—sprints thru marathon. 3rd printing. Paperbound. $3.50

**HURDLERS BIBLE.** Wilbur Ross's fine book on hurdling training, technique, style comparisons, etc. The most complete work o hurdling ever produced. Illustrated. Paperbound. 1969. 2nd edition. $3.95

**MECHANICS OF THE POLE VAULT.** The bible of the event by Dick Ganslen. 7th edition. All you want to know about vaulting. $3.00

**MECHANICS OF ATHLETICS,** Geoffrey Dyson. The most exhaustive, detailed account of the basics of motion in athletics. This is the book for further study of the mechanics of track & field. Hard cover. $5.95

**TRACK TECHNIQUE: The Technical Quarterly of Track & Field.** Edited by Fred Wilt. Articles on technique, training, sports medicine, psychology, theory, etc. $3.00 a year.

**HIGH JUMPING.** Authoritative guide by V. Dyatchkov, USSR, coach of Brumel, Gavrilov, etc. All aspects of HJ analyzed: technique, training, exercises. 34pp. Comprises TT #36. $1.00

**TRACK & FIELD OMNIBOOK.** Ken Doherty's colossal text incorporates all the great sequence drawings from "Movies on Paper" (now out of print) and adds many new ones. Text is the most comprehensive guide to modern coaching and training theories, techniques, etc. available. All events covered. A "must" for every coach and athlete. 498pp. (8½x11") 1971. $9.75

**TRACK AND FIELD DYNAMICS,** Tom Ecker. A clear, easy-to-follow introduction to the dynamics of body movement in track & field events. Fully illustrated. No coach can afford to be without this book. 1971. $3.50 soft cover; $4.95 hardbound

**MOTIVATION AND COACHING PSYCHOLOGY,** by Fred Wilt and Ken Bosen. Part I is a step-by-step guide to the development of motivation in athletes. Part II offers 60 practical pointers for the coach in his relationship with his team. 64pp. $2.00

**STRENGTH, POWER AND MUSCULAR ENDURANCE FOR RUNNERS AND HURDLERS,** John Jesse. Basics of strength development geared to the runner. Many exercises and schedules. 160pp. Well illustrated. $2.95

**FILMS AND FILM LOOPS** show the styles and techniques of the champions and make excellent coaching and study aids. Available in 16mm., Super 8 and 8mm. 1968 Men's Olympic instructional film; 1968 Women's Olympic Instructional; 1968 Olympic Stars of the Pole Vault; 1968 Olympic Champions; Dick Fosbury high jump film, and 46 loop films of Olympic competitors: Beamon, Ryun, Clarke, Seagren, Matson, Oerter, Davenport, etc.

Prices subject to change. Add 25¢ per book for postage and handling.

Write for our complete listing of books, films, stopwatches, and other track merchandise and equipment. Ask for our Track and Field Market Place catalog.

Track & Field News  *  Box 296  *  Los Altos, California 94022 U.S.A.